Olga Lewandowska

POST-TRADE PROCESSING OF OTC DERIVATIVES

IT Solutions under a New Regulatory Paradigm

Bibliografische Information der Deutschen Nationalbibliothek
Die Deutsche Nationalbibliothek verzeichnet diese Publikation in der Deutschen Nationalbibliografie; detaillierte bibliografische Daten sind im Internet über http://dnb.d-nb.de abrufbar.

Bibliographic information published by the Deutsche Nationalbibliothek
Die Deutsche Nationalbibliothek lists this publication in the Deutsche Nationalbibliografie; detailed bibliographic data are available in the Internet at http://dnb.d-nb.de.

Zugl.: Inaugural-Dissertation zur Erlangung des Doktorgrades des Fachbereichs Wirtschaftswissenschaften der Johann Wolfgang Goethe-Universität, 2020.

ISBN-13: 978-3-8382-1444-3
© *ibidem*-Verlag, Stuttgart 2020
Alle Rechte vorbehalten

Das Werk einschließlich aller seiner Teile ist urheberrechtlich geschützt. Jede Verwertung außerhalb der engen Grenzen des Urheberrechtsgesetzes ist ohne Zustimmung des Verlages unzulässig und strafbar. Dies gilt insbesondere für Vervielfältigungen, Übersetzungen, Mikroverfilmungen und elektronische Speicherformen sowie die Einspeicherung und Verarbeitung in elektronischen Systemen.

All rights reserved. No part of this publication may be reproduced, stored in or introduced into a retrieval system, or transmitted, in any form, or by any means (electronic, mechanical, photocopying, recording or otherwise) without the prior written permission of the publisher. Any person who does any unauthorized act in relation to this publication may be liable to criminal prosecution and civil claims for damages.

Printed in the EU

Papers Comprising the Dissertation

Paper 1
Lewandowska, O. (2010). Adoption of a Centralized Post-Trade Processing Market Infrastructure after the Credit Crisis. In: *Proceedings of the 16th Americas Conference on Information Systems (AMCIS 2010), Peru, Lima.*

Paper 2
Lewandowska, O. (2015). OTC Clearing Arrangements for Bank Systemic Risk Regulation: A Simulation Approach. *Journal of Money, Credit and Banking*, 47, 1177–1203.

Paper 3
Lewandowska, O. (2010). Is a Full Scale Straight Through Processing of OTC Derivatives Possible? A Straight Through Processing Potential of a Central Counterparty Clearing Model for Credit Default Swaps: An Exploratory Case. Paper presented at *the FinanceCom, 30 August 2010, Germany, Frankfurt.*

Paper 4
Lewandowska, O. and Glaser, F. (2017). The Recent Crises and Central Counterparty Risk Practices in the Light of Procyclicality: Empirical Evidence. *Journal of Financial Market Infrastructures*, 5, 1–24.

Foreword

This dissertation was written at the Faculty of Economics and Business Administration at Johann Wolfgang Goethe University Frankfurt am Main.

This work is a tribute to all those who made this project possible. First, I thank Dr. Randolf Roth who spurred my enthusiasm for the subject of the OTC clearing. I am grateful for his trust in my person which resulted in his engagement as the supervisor of my thesis at Deutsche Börse.

I would like to express my deep appreciation to my supervisor and committee chair Prof. Dr. Peter Gomber for giving me the opportunity to write this dissertation. His comments and wise guidance are gratefully acknowledged.

Additionally, I would like to acknowledge Prof. Dr. Loriana Pelizzon, who agreed to be the second reviewer of this thesis and serve on my dissertation committee.

Last but not least, I would like to thank my mother for her encouragement and continuous support.

Frankfurt, January 2019

Olga Lewandowska

Table of Contents

Introductory Paper 1
Paper 1 54
Paper 2 73
Paper 3 104
Paper 4 128
Appendix
German Summary/ Deutsche Zusammenfassung............................158
Further Publications..211
Curriculum Vitae 212

Introductory Paper

Post-Trade Processing of OTC Derivatives

- IT Solutions under a New Regulatory Paradigm -

Olga Lewandowska

Table of Contents

1. INTRODUCTION 4
   1.1 The Subject and Objective of This Thesis 4
   1.2 Background 6
   1.3 Research Questions and Structure of the Thesis 9

2 RESEARCH CONTEXT 12
   2.1 OTC Derivative Instruments and Market Structure 12
   2.2 Different Clearing Arrangements 14
   2.3 OTC Derivatives Market Infrastructure 18
   2.4 Regulatory Efforts Addressing Systemic Risk in the OTC Derivatives Market 20
   2.5 Literature Overview 21

3 RESEARCH METHODOLOGIES 27
   3.1 Quantitative Survey 27
   3.2 The Numerical Simulation of the OTC Market 29
   3.3 Case Study Method 31
   3.4 Empirical Quantitative Analysis 32

4 MAIN RESULTS 34
   4.1 Results from Paper 1: Adoption of the OTC CCP 34
   4.2 Results from Paper 2: OTC Clearing Arrangements 35
   4.3 Results from Paper 3: Is a Full STP of OTC Derivatives Possible? 37
   4.4 Results from Paper 4: CCP Risk Practices in the Light of Procyclicality 38

5 CONTRIBUTION TO THEORY AND PRAXIS 39
   5.1. Contribution to Academics 39

5.2. Contribution to Practice 41

6 LIMITATIONS, OUTLOOK AND FUTURE RESEARCH 42
    6.1 Limitations 42
    6.2 Outlook and Future Research 44

1. INTRODUCTION

1.1 The Subject and Objective of This Thesis

The subject of the post-trade processing of off-exchange traded derivatives (OTC, Over-The-Counter derivatives) lies at the intersection of both finance and information systems disciplines. The most important financial topics in this context are the industrial organization of the financial markets, financial market regulation and supervision, as well as risk management in participating institutions such as clearinghouses and banks. The information technology (IT) theme is reflected in the recognition of the new post-trading model for OTC derivatives as an IT-based innovation.

OTC derivatives are financial transactions that are traditionally completed and processed by the counterparties directly involved in a trade, outside of the organized exchanges. Gibson and Murawski (2006) describe OTC markets as typically decentralized, informal, lightly supervised and regulated, and market-discipline driven. They are an informal network of bilateral relationships. Exchanges, in contrast, are centralized, formal, regulated and rule-driven. On exchanges, the risk of loss from default by the counterparty is mutualized through a clearinghouse. Though, default risks were not traditionally shared on OTC derivatives markets. In the absence of information asymmetry and moral hazard, mutualization improves welfare by reducing the expected cost of default by exploiting scale economies. However, private information is more important in OTC transactions because the valuation of OTC derivatives often requires the use of specially designed, proprietary mathematical models. Scale economies were traditionally exploited in OTC markets by the formation of large dealer firms rather than via a clearinghouse (Pirrong 2009). The main microeconomic question regarding the post-trading of the OTC derivatives is about the consequences of the *centralization* of the financial market infrastructure, as, under regulatory pressure, clearing is migrated from bilateral relationships between banks to the central clearinghouses. Both the *centralization* and potential *consolidation* of the market infrastructure involve the concentration of risk in main institutions and implicitly counsel the need for *oversight and regulation* of market service providers in this network industry. The subject of *risk management* plays a crucial role for both clearinghouses and clearing members and concerns not only the mentioned default (counterparty credit) risk, but also liquidity risk, operational risk and market risk.

Because of the complex nature of OTC derivatives, the centralized post-trade model for these financial instruments can be regarded as an IT-based innovation. Mahnke, Overby and Özcan (2006) define an innovation in the IT context as something that "blends hardware and/or software with business functions to generate a new process, new products or new services." Market participants potentially benefit from novel centralized risk management and data processing operations related to OTC derivatives. The valuation of the derivative positions and calculation of required collateral in real time is particularly challenging and, therefore, a clearinghouse for OTC derivatives can be regarded as an IT-enabled innovation.

Research on the post-trade processing of financial transactions is considerably scarcer than the extensive academic research that focuses on trading securities (Campbell 2002; Easley and O'Hara 1987; Madhaven 2000; Ozsoylev and Takayama 2010). In particular, the topic of the post-trade processing of off-exchange traded derivatives has received little attention from academic researchers. The focus of this thesis is the clearing of OTC derivatives. Clearing is understood as the process of calculating market participants' mutual obligations, usually on a net basis, for the exchange of securities and money (Bank for International Settlements 2003). The aim of this dissertation is to analyze the subject of clearing from different risk perspectives like operational, counterparty and systemic risk. The primary research question is "How and to what extent can a clearinghouse improve the post-trade processing in the OTC derivatives market?"

The remainder of this introductory paper is structured as follows. The next sections briefly describe the background of the research and the questions addressed in the dissertation. Chapter 2 details the research context. Chapter 3 provides an overview of the applied research methods, followed by a summary of the main results of the four papers of this cumulative dissertation (Chapter 4). Chapter 5 highlights the contribution of this thesis to theory and practice. Finally, Chapter 6 provides a discussion of the limitations and an outlook on potential future research in the area of the post-trade processing of OTC derivatives.

1.2 Background

The authors of the post-trade processing research published before the 2007-2009 financial crisis primarily described the key features and analyzed the historical evolution of various clearing methods (Moser 1998; Kroszner 1999; Bliss and Steigerwald 2006; Kroszner 2006). They also investigated the economic consequences of those post-trade models (Ripatti 2004; Bergman *et al.* 2004; Bliss and Kaufmann 2005). The credit crisis revealed both the lack of an adequate market infrastructure for OTC derivatives and the risks of the OTC derivatives market. Since then, interest in the subject of OTC clearing has grown among both regulators and academics.

Policymakers and regulators in both the EU and the US believed that OTC transactions were partly to blame for the global financial crisis (Financial Crisis Inquiry Commission 2011; Greenspan 2008), particularly because Lehman Brothers, a US investment bank, was a key player in the OTC derivatives market. When Lehman Brothers defaulted, there was no Central Counterparty (CCP) for the largest part of its portfolio to act as a "circuit-breaker" (Financial Services Authority and HM Treasury 2009). A "chain reaction" of failures in the market was triggered (this domino effect is referred to as "systemic risk").

A CCP interposes itself between the counterparties to a trade, becoming the buyer for every seller and the seller for every buyer. Since the CCP becomes a principal to all trades between its clearing members, it must assume the future performance obligations to which the members initially agreed. In its role as an independent risk manager, the CCP applies different measures to protect itself and the surviving members from a loss in the case of any member's default.

The *novation* process (when a CCP becomes a counterparty to a trade) provides a foundation for centralized risk management (such as the multilateral netting[1] of positions, collateralization, and loss mutualization) and data processing operations (such as trade registration and reporting). Market participants potentially benefit from the reduction of a network of bilateral exposures to a single net exposure to the CCP, allowing for potential reductions in the capital and collateral required to support their trading activity. Nevertheless, the central role of a CCP means that both the counterparty credit risk and the operational risks are concentrated in the CCP. Therefore, the insolvency of a CCP can lead to a greater crisis than the failure of the major banks (Krahnen and Pelizzon 2016). However, CCPs apply strict risk management standards and are supervised by financial market authorities.

CCP clearing service provided by clearinghouses is commonly used for on-exchange traded financial contracts such as, for example, futures. However, in the past, CCP has not been widely applied to OTC derivatives such as, for example, swaps in which two parties agree to exchange one stream of cash flows against another. As the recent financial crisis had a large impact on the bilaterally cleared OTC market, the CCP infrastructure for on-exchange traded derivatives performed well. Notably, no CCP defaulted because of the recent financial crisis. This attracted regulatory attention to the CCP for OTC derivatives.

In the aftermath of the financial crisis, regulators in the EU and the US introduced legislative and regulatory changes aimed at increasing the transparency and stability of the financial markets. The reforms were implemented in the US through the Dodd-Frank Wall Street Reform and Consumer Protection Act ("Dodd-Frank"; US Senate 2010) and in Europe through the European Market Infrastructure Regulation ("EMIR"; Euro-

---

[1] Netting means that offsetting contracts are terminated or similar contracts combined into a single trade.

pean Parliament 2012). Dodd-Frank and the EMIR have created three key clearing-related obligations. The first is a mandatory clearing of relevant OTC contracts through CCPs. The second is the mandatory reporting of the opening, modification, and closure of any OTC contract to approved data repositories. The third is the mandatory trading of OTC contracts on a regulated exchange or at another approved facility. Both legislative regimes anticipate that a limited number of very illiquid, highly bespoke OTC trades will remain unsuitable for CCP clearing, although they still must be reported.

Figure 1. Evolution of the share of the CCP-cleared OTC market 2007-2017 (left side) and the size of the global derivatives market as of December 2017 (right side), adjusted for double counting by CCPs.[2]

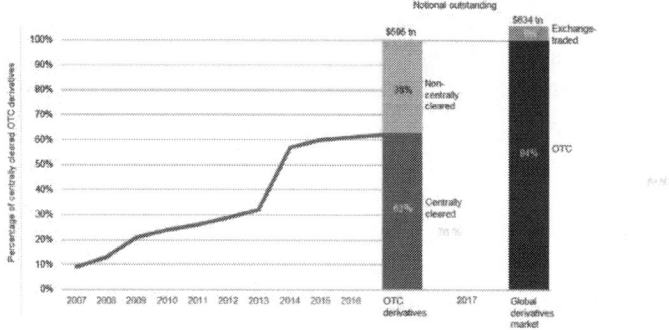

Source: own analysis based on BIS (2018a); ISDA (2013a, 2014, 2016).

Since 2007, increasing OTC volumes in the clearing business became one of the major growth areas in the financial market. Figure 1 shows the size of the global derivatives market as of December 2017 along with the

---

[2] The clearing of OTC derivative transactions by CCPs increases notional amounts by 100% because two trades are generated when the CCP steps in as a counterparty. For this reason, in the underlying statistics, the cleared notionals are correctly reduced by 50% for cleared asset classes.

evolution of the OTC market share that is cleared by CCPs. The OTC derivatives comprise more than 90% of the global derivatives market. By 2017, more than 63% of the OTC market was cleared by CCPs.

After the credit crisis of 2007-2009, interest in the subject of post-trade processing of the OTC derivatives has grown among academic researchers. Recent papers primarily address either the counterparty credit risk implications of CCP clearing becoming mandatory for OTC derivatives under the new market regulation (Duffie and Zhu 2011; Arnsdorf 2012; Cont and Kokholm 2014; Kubitza, Pelizzon and Getmansky 2018), or the resulting changes in collateral demand (Singh 2010; Sidanius and Zikes 2012; Heller and Vause 2012; Duffie, Scheicher and Vuillemey 2015; Vuillemey and Breton 2014). However, the research on OTC clearing primarily focuses on isolated factors. In this thesis, the post-trade processing of the OTC derivatives is investigated from a counterparty risk, operational risk and systemic risk perspective.

1.3 Research Questions and Structure of the Thesis

This cumulative dissertation thesis consists of four papers that address the post-trade processing of OTC derivatives. The remainder of this section details the individual papers and their respective research questions.

Paper 1[3] investigates the factors that influence the adoption of CCP clearing among OTC market participants. The starting point of this research is the idea that a CCP is an IT-enabled innovation. The paper introduces a model based on the diffusion of innovation theory of Rogers (Rogers 1995). Responses from a survey of heads of clearing/operations in banks and asset management companies are analyzed using a partial least squares regression analysis. The main research question is *"Which factors*

---

[3] Lewandowska, O. (2010). Adoption of a Centralized Post-Trade Processing Market Infrastructure after the Credit Crisis. In: *Proceedings of the 16th Americas Conference on Information Systems (AMCIS 2010), Peru, Lima.*

influence the adoption of CCP clearing for OTC derivatives among market participants?"

Paper 2[4] addresses the implication of the recent financial market reforms, particularly the mandatory clearing of all standardized derivatives through CCPs now required by the EMIR and Dodd-Frank. In this research, the numerical simulation provides a basis for the analysis and comparison of the clearing arrangements. Two measures — "netting efficiency"[5] and "loss concentration after default" — allow for the quantification and comparison of the results of various clearing models. The main research question is *"What is the impact of OTC CCP on counterparty risk in the derivatives market?"*

Paper 3[6] evaluates how the *straight through processing* (STP) rate can be improved by a clearinghouse interlinked to existing OTC market infrastructure and which possible enhancements of the existing CCP architecture could further increase the STP rate in the OTC derivative processing workflow. In the financial industry, the term STP is used in the context of achieving the end-to-end processing of financial transactions from trade initiation to settlement through the automation of (sub)processes. Hereby, *external* STP represents the challenge of seamlessly connecting the external partners involved in a financial process, including trading platforms, confirmation platforms, clearinghouses, and other information providers (Vo, Wojciechowski, Weinhardt 2005). The research question is *"How can the existing CCP architecture be enhanced to minimize the operational risks in the OTC processing workflow?"*

---

[4] Lewandowska, O. (2015). OTC Clearing Arrangements for Bank Systemic Risk Regulation: A Simulation Approach. *Journal of Money, Credit and Banking*, 47, 1177–1203.
[5] Netting is "efficient" (or the netting efficiency is high) if it significantly reduces the expected exposures, because exposures of a different sign are compensated.
[6] Lewandowska, O. (2010). Is a Full Scale Straight Through Processing of OTC Derivatives Possible? A Straight Through Processing potential of a Central Counterparty Clearing Model for Credit Default Swaps: An Exploratory Case. Paper presented at *FinanceCom*, Germany, Frankfurt.

Figure 2. The relationship between the papers in this thesis and the chosen research methods.

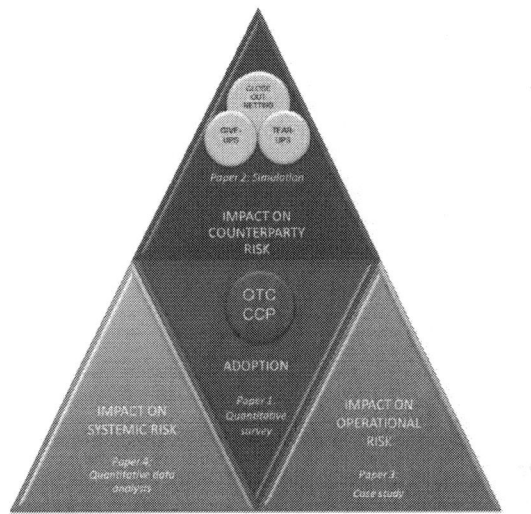

Source: own analysis.

The mandatory central clearing for standardized OTC derivatives introduced by the recent financial market reforms makes CCPs the most systemically important market participants. The literature suggests that CCP risk management practices such as margining and collateral haircuts are potentially procyclical, i.e., they may exacerbate financial cycle fluctuations. Based on empirical data collected over almost ten years from a leading European clearinghouse, **Paper 4**[7] investigates whether and to what extent procyclical effects can be statistically confirmed. The main research question is as follows: *"What is the impact of CCPs' risk management practices on the systemic risk in the financial system?"*

---

[7] Lewandowska, O. and Glaser, F. (2017) The Recent Crises and Central Counterparty Risk Practices in the Light of Procyclicality: Empirical Evidence. *Journal of Financial Market Infrastructures*, 5, 1–24.

Figure 2 illustrates the different sections of this thesis and their applied methods. The core of this dissertation is the study regarding the adoption of a Central Counterparty in the OTC markets (Paper 1). In the single papers, the consequences of the introduction of the OTC CCP are further evaluated: the impact of the OTC CCP on counterparty risk in Paper 2, its impact on the operational risk in Paper 3 and its systemic risk implications via procyclicality in Paper 4. In the context of Paper 2, different clearing arrangements existing in the OTC derivatives market are modelled and serve as a basis for the comparison with the CCP clearing.

The research questions at issue require various research approaches. The investigation of the drivers of the adoption of OTC CCP clearing is approached through both a quantitative survey and a causal model (Paper 1). The analysis of the counterparty risk implications of various clearing arrangements is based on a numerical simulation (Paper 2). The operational risks in the OTC derivatives market infrastructure are analyzed in qualitative research, namely, an exploratory case study of a clearinghouse for OTC derivatives (Paper 3). In Paper 4, an empirical quantitative approach is applied to examine the data of margins and haircuts from a clearinghouse.

2 RESEARCH CONTEXT

This chapter will briefly describe the context of the presented research.

2.1 OTC Derivative Instruments and Market Structure

Derivatives are contracts that derive their value from an underlying asset (e.g., equities or commodities) or reference price (e.g., interest rates, foreign exchange rates or credit indices). They can be used to mitigate the risk of economic loss arising out of changes in the value of the underlying asset (hedging), to speculate on price changes or to profit from price differences between markets (arbitrage). Derivatives can be divided into two groups based on how they are traded. Exchange-traded derivatives are highly standardized contracts traded on regulated exchanges. OTC derivatives are traded bilaterally between counterparties and may have more bespoke terms (Hull 2014).

Notably, clearing derivatives differs from the post-trade processing of cash securities. Compared to cash securities, derivatives may pose greater risks to market participants (see the Bank for International Settlements 1998 for types of risks existing in the OTC markets). Moreover, the significance of counterparty credit risk is much higher for derivatives. The obligations of the buyer and seller of a cash security are settled within a few days, whereas the lifetime of a derivative contract may extend to as long as 30-50 years. Naturally, the creditworthiness of the parties to a derivative transaction can fluctuate between the time of the contract execution and its maturity. With a longer time horizon until transaction completion, the significance of the exposure to the creditworthiness of the counterparty and the greater uncertainty about the value of the ultimate transfer obligations make it far more complex to clear derivative transactions than it is to clear securities (Bliss and Steigerwald 2006).

Among OTC derivative transactions, credit default swaps (CDSs) were the first to be addressed by the financial market reforms because they were publicly blamed for causing the crisis (Stulz 2009). The clearing obligation has been gradually introduced for some types of credit derivatives since February 2017 (Bundesanstalt für Finanzdienstleistungsaufsicht 2017).[8] A CDS is designed to transfer the credit exposure of fixed income products between parties. The buyer of the swap makes payments to the seller of a swap up until the contract's maturity date. In return, the seller agrees to pay off a third-party debt if that third party defaults. However, the largest part of the OTC derivatives market is the interest rate derivatives class, including interest rate swaps and forward rate agreements. Those contracts are based on an underlying asset, the value

---

[8] Globally, approx. 28% of the credit derivatives are centrally cleared (BIS 2018b). Bellia et al. (2017) explain the small market share of the CCP cleared credit derivatives that are clearing eligible but not subject to the clearing obligation (e.g., single name CDSs); compare with Ghamami and Glasserman (2017).

of which is affected by any change in interest rates. In the first quarter of 2018, approx. 60% of the OTC interest rate derivatives were centrally cleared (Bank for International Settlements 2018b).

In contrast to standardized derivatives such as futures, OTC derivatives have traditionally been executed and processed outside of organized exchanges. The on-exchange (order book) and OTC derivatives market architectures differ mostly with respect to the type of order flow interactions, market access, and required intermediation. In the OTC derivatives market, order flow interactions are generally bilateral in nature because transactions are privately negotiated and typically executed over the telephone. Market access is segmented: end-users usually do not trade directly with each other, but utilize intermediaries instead. Trades in OTC markets are typically intermediated by derivatives dealers who maintain a two-sided market, simultaneously buying and selling securities on behalf of investors (Li and Schürhoff 2014). Therefore, they belong to the so-called *sell-side*. The sell-side encompasses financial institutions (primarily large international banks) that offer trading services to institutional investors such as asset managers, hedge funds or commercial hedgers and corporate clients, collectively referred to as the *buy-side* (Harris 2003).

The dominant role of sell-side dealers in their dual capacity as prime brokers (i.e., counterparty risk takers and leverage providers) and market makers (i.e., product structurers and liquidity providers) has been the prominent feature of the OTC derivatives market. Consequently, there is a high degree of concentration of trading liquidity and counterparty risk with a relatively small group of dealers.

2.2 Different Clearing Arrangements

The clearing arrangements that have emerged in the OTC derivatives market differ mostly with respect to the scope of *netting* the exposures across market participants. *Netting* means offsetting an amount due from a market participant on one transaction against an amount owed to that market participant on another transaction to achieve a single, smaller net exposure. It can be differentiated between clearing arrangements based on either bilateral or multilateral netting. Bilateral netting involves offsetting mutual obligations between two parties. Multilateral netting refers to netting among more than two parties, utilizing a central service. *Closeout netting* and *prime brokerage give-ups* represent bilateral netting, whereas *portfolio compression* and *CCP clearing* represent multilateral netting (Bank for International Settlements 2007). These clearing arrangements will be outlined below.

Closeout netting provisions give financial institutions the ability to terminate all of their derivative contracts (across all asset classes) with a counterparty upon its default, reducing their contracts to a single "net" claim (Bergman et al. 2004). *Closeout netting* provisions are included in the master agreements signed between the counterparties before engaging in any OTC transaction (Fuchs 2013).

Another clearing arrangement is a *prime brokerage give-up*. A prime brokerage allows a client to source liquidity from a variety of executing dealers while maintaining a credit relationship, placing collateral, and settling with a single entity: the prime broker (The Federal Reserve Bank of New York 2005). Customer exposures and collateral requirements are netted across all trades handled by the chosen prime broker.

Portfolio compression service *(tear-ups)* is based on a multilateral termination of positions (Figure 3). *Tear-ups* net off bought and sold positions among the participants while maintaining overall market risk neutrality across counterparties. In other words, *tear-ups* cycles aim at replacing trades to reduce bilateral gross position exposures without changing the agent's total net exposure (International Swaps and Derivatives Association 2012).

CCP clearing is based on both the multilateral netting of members' exposures through asset classes and risk mutualization among CCP members. By replacing bilateral agreements between buyers and sellers with contracts between these buyers and sellers and the CCP, the CCP can net out the offsetting transactions. This is shown in Figure 3: bilateral counterparty relationships in OTC derivatives are replaced by the counterparties' exposure to a CCP.

The current market practice is that only the sell-side agents have direct access to a CCP, whereas the buy-side customers utilize the sell-side (clearing members) to enter a CCP.

Under clearing arrangements different from the CCP, the original counterparties risk that the other party will fail to perform its obligations before the maturity of the contract. In contrast, if either the buyer or the seller defaults, the CCP is contractually committed to cover the obligations to the non-defaulting direct clearing members (Pirrong 2011). CCPs manage this counterparty credit risk in several ways, including by taking collateral ("margin") from counterparties. A CCP collects an *initial margin* from its members in the form of cash or highly liquid securities (e.g., government bonds).

The initial margin is intended to cover losses in the value of open positions with a defaulted counterparty that might occur before the position can be replaced at prevailing market prices. It is important to note that a clearinghouse collects the initial margin at the time of the admission of the transaction to the clearinghouse and holds it for the life of the trade to reflect the riskiness of the underlying transaction. In contrast, a *variation margin* is called upon to offset changes in the value of a contract on a mark-to-market basis. In the centrally cleared trades, the CCP acts as an intermediary and passes the *variation margin* between the original counterparties to the transaction.

CCPs allow their members to cover margin requirements through both cash and non-cash collateral. Because non-cash collateral is subject to fluctuations in market variables (such as interest rates, liquidity, etc.), the CCP protects itself through *haircuts* against the envisaged loss in collateral value in the event of counterparty default and before the collateral can be liquidated to provide for losses on the derivatives position. A haircut is a valuation discount on deposited securities (or on cash in foreign currency) that were posted as the initial margin. In other words, the deposited collateral is not taken into account at 100% of its face value. For example, a haircut of 5% means that to satisfy an initial margin of 95 m EUR in cash, the market participant has to post 100 m EUR in non-cash collateral, e.g., in the form of bonds (Sidanius and Zikes 2012).

Figure 3. Netting of bilateral positions (1) through portfolio compression (2) and in CCP (3) in a single asset class.

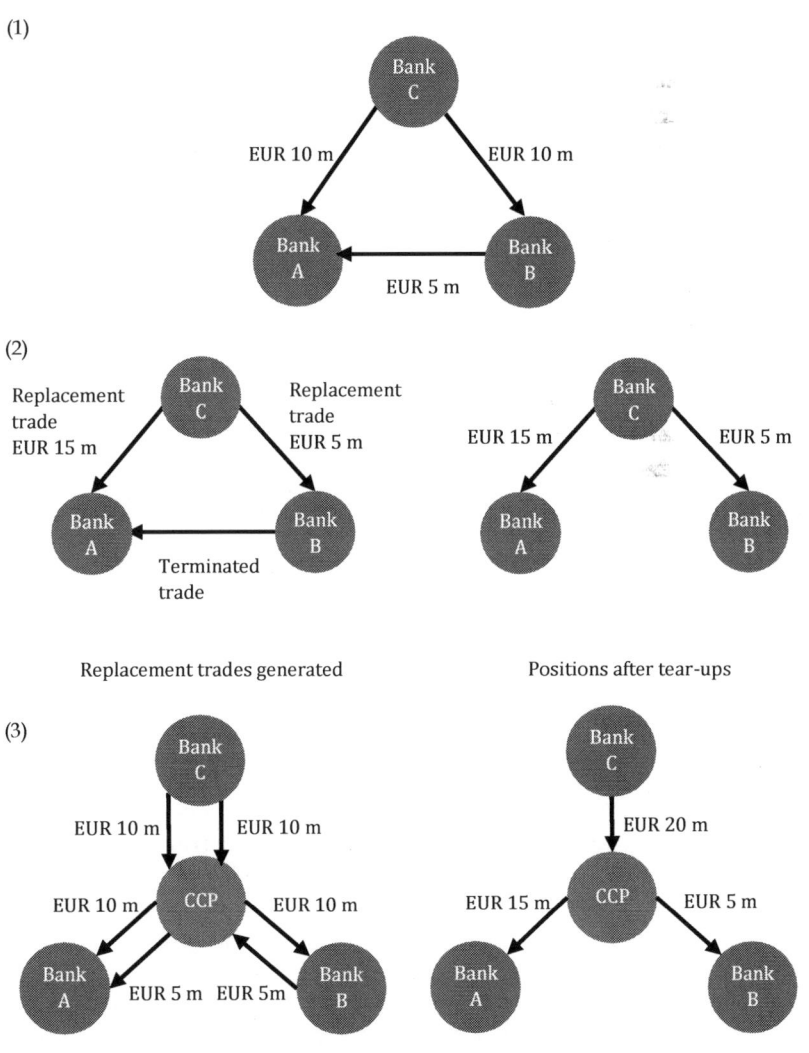

Source: own analysis based on Rehlo and Nixon (2013).

Loss mutualization is a further feature of CCP clearing. Should an individual member's losses exceed the member's resources controlled by the CCP, the non-defaulted members share the losses. Generally, in the event of member default, the CCP subsequently applies so-called "lines of defense." Those measures and resources are as follows (Deutsche Boerse 2014):

1. Position netting of the clearing member in default
2. Collateral of the clearing member in default
3. Clearing fund contribution[9] of the clearing member in default
4. Own capital of a CCP
5. Clearing fund contribution of other clearing members
6. Remaining capital of the CCP[10]

2.3 OTC Derivatives Market Infrastructure

In the previous section, the OTC clearing arrangements were described based on their netting features and systemic risk implications. This section describes the market infrastructure for OTC derivatives, including its main institutions. Figure 4 shows the market infrastructure for CDSs.

Before trading occurs between two counterparties, they usually sign a master agreement, which is a standardized bilateral framework to enter into derivative transactions and negotiate credit lines with each other. The counterparty search and negotiation occur either directly (i.e., between counterparties) or through an interdealer broker. The trades are executed either over the phone or electronically on electronic trading platforms.

Once a trade has been executed, the counterparties must capture the trade details in their internal systems for post-trade processing and risk

---

[9] A clearing fund is a pool of funds contributed by clearing members for use in the event of member default. Its size is established based on a given member's risk exposure and is recalculated by the CCP on a regular basis.

[10] See ISDA (2013) for the CCP loss allocation options after the exhaustion of all these resources.

management. The aim of the next step in the workflow — trade confirmation — is the creation of a final record of the transaction that is agreed upon by both parties. Confirmation can be in paper or electronic form, supported by the electronic confirmation platform.

Figure 4. Market infrastructure for credit default swaps.

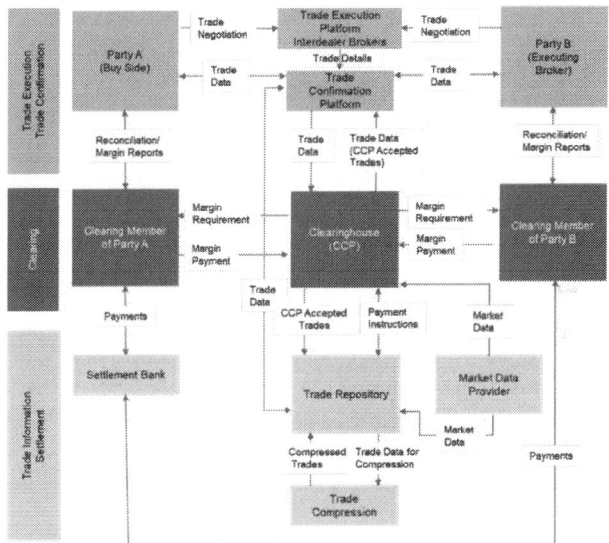

Source: own analysis based on Bank for International Settlements (2007).

If submitted for clearing, trades are loaded from the confirmation platform to the clearinghouse. The CCP calculates the margin requirements for clearing eligible trades, supervises the credit quality of its members and calculates payments from the contracts. The pricing of the open positions is based on input from the market data vendor. The clearing members forward the margin and reconciliation reports to their customers.

Trade repositories are centralized registries that maintain an electronic database of the records of open OTC derivatives transactions. A trade repository may also engage in the management of trade life-cycle events and downstream trade processing services based on the records it maintains (Bank for International Settlements 2010). During the life cycle of an OTC trade, often spanning many years, different trade events occur that either change the contract of the trade or induce additional flows such as cash payments or settlements. Based on the confirmed records and taking into account all trade life-cycle events, the trade repository generates and sends bilaterally netted payment instructions to a central settlement system.

OTC derivatives portfolios may contain many offsetting trades. Market participants may either bilaterally terminate such trades before the transaction maturity date or use the trade compression service. This type of tear-up service enables the systematic, simultaneous cancellation of hundreds of trades by a group of counterparties.

2.4 Regulatory Efforts Addressing Systemic Risk in the OTC Derivatives Market

This section provides a brief overview of the key aspects of the derivatives market regulation after the credit crisis of 2007-2009, along with the current state of its implementation.

The recent financial crisis exposed the weaknesses of the global derivatives market such as limited transparency regarding risk exposures, poor counterparty risk management practices and the risk of contagion arising from interconnectedness in this market. At their 2009 Pittsburgh Summit, the G20 leaders recognized those structural problems in the OTC derivatives market and agreed on regulatory initiatives to reform it (G20 2009).

Following the Pittsburgh agreement, the European Union implemented new rules for derivatives markets primarily through the EMIR. Consistent with the G20 proposal, the EMIR requires that OTC derivatives meeting certain criteria are subject to the clearing obligation; risk mitigation techniques should apply to all OTC derivatives that are not centrally cleared. Moreover, all derivatives transactions must be reported to the trade repositories. Finally, the EMIR establishes the organizational conduct of business and prudential standards for both trade repositories and CCPs (EUR-Lex 2012).

The EMIR came into force on August 16, 2012. However, until now, the clearing obligation has taken effect only for the largest institutions active in the OTC markets and solely for two asset classes, namely, interest rate derivatives and CDSs (Bundesanstalt für Finanzdienstleistungsaufsicht 2017). The reporting of all trades to the trade repository has been in effect since February 12, 2014. Certain risk mitigation techniques for derivatives not cleared through a CCP, such as timely confirmation of trades and daily mark-to-market valuations of trades, have been in effect since 2013. The requirement to exchange collateral for non-cleared OTC derivatives came into force for the largest banks at the beginning of 2017.

In the US, the regulation and governance of the derivatives market are addressed by the Dodd-Frank Wall Street Reform and Consumer Protection Act, which was adopted in July 2010 (US Senate 2010). The Dodd-Frank Act has significant commonalities with the EMIR regarding the implementation of the G-20 commitments, including the objective of achieving a more robust financial infrastructure through the CCP clearing of standardized derivatives, a mandatory reporting requirement for derivatives trades, mandatory margin and capital requirements for non-cleared derivatives transactions and allowing cross-border clearing by recognizing non-domestic CCPs. In the US, the bulk of the legislation entered into force in 2013.

2.5 Literature Overview

One of the most important topics in the clearing-related literature after the crisis of 2007-2009 relates to the implications of the recent financial market reforms on systemic risk in the financial system. Three primary streams of research can be recognized in this context. The first stream concerns the impact of the clearing obligation for OTC derivatives on *netting efficiency and loss distribution* after default (1). The second stream deals with the consequences of the reforms on *collateral demand* in financial markets (2). The third stream focuses on the potential drawbacks of the CCP model resulting from either *consolidation* under CCPs or CCP *risk management practices* (3).

(1) Regarding the first point, the results of the academic research support the thesis that the clearing obligation established by the EMIR and the Dodd-Frank Act may, in a few plausible cases, have an adverse impact on counterparty exposure and increase the replacement cost risk in the OTC derivatives market. This negative influence is primarily driven by distortion of the cross-product netting effects in OTC portfolios if only one part is cleared centrally and the other remains bilateral (Duffie and Zhu 2011; Cont and Kokholm 2014). This concern is attributable to the fact that low standardized OTC derivatives will remain out of scope for central clearing under both the EMIR and the Dodd-Frank Act. In addition, if a clearinghouse clears only a specific asset class and not all OTC derivatives asset classes, one part of the portfolio will remain bilaterally cleared. The coexistence of multiple CCPs has an adverse impact on netting efficiency (Duffie and Zhu 2011; Heath, Kelly and Manning 2013), which can be, however, mitigated by establishing links between the clearinghouses (Cox, Garvin, and Kelly 2013; Anderson, Dion and Perez Saiz 2013). In general, the profile of market participants' trading activities and the degree of fragmentation in CCP clearing venues across jurisdictions and products will influence the overall result of the market reforms for the risks in the financial system as a whole.

Kubitza, Pelizzon and Getmansky (2018) expand the model of Duffie and Zhu (2011) by systematic risk, parameterized as the correlation between S&P 500 index returns and CDS spreads. In the presence of systematic risk, the CCP requires more members to reduce the counterparty risk compared to bilateral clearing. If the margin requirement for centrally cleared derivatives is lower than for non-centrally cleared contracts, this minimum of the clearing members is even higher. For the sufficiently extreme realizations of the market stress scenarios, a CCP does not lead to a reduction of the counterparty risk compared with bilateral clearing. The authors' recommendation for the regulators is to align the margin requirements for central and non-centrally cleared OTC derivatives as this factor may undermine the benefits even of a CCP clearing all asset classes.

In addition, the authors support the revision of market infrastructure reforms including the possibility of suspending the clearing obligation in extreme market stress situations (European Systemic Risk Board 2017b; Financial Stability Board 2017).

Different research methods have been applied to investigate the *netting efficiency* of OTC clearing. Whereas Duffie and Zhu (2011) and Kubitza, Pelizzon and Getmansky (2018) propose a model of average exposure of market participants, Garratt and Zimmerman (2015) extend that proposal by applying a financial network analysis. This method allows them to incorporate agent heterogeneity into the model. The conclusion from Garratt and Zimmerman (2015) is, however, similar to that mentioned above: CCP is unlikely to increase netting efficiency when the network's link structure relies on only a few key nodes, corresponding to a market structure with a few dominant derivatives dealers.

In this thesis, the heterogeneity between the core (large derivatives dealers) and the periphery (buy-side customers) is reflected when modeling different market segments and transforming the position matrices for prime broker give-ups and CCP. In this way, the benefits of applying network dynamics are also achieved in this research. Moreover, the modelling of the OTC market segments and the clearing arrangements like prime brokerage give-ups and portfolio compression allowed the insights that would not be possible if comparing the CCP with only bilateral clearing.

Jackson and Manning (2007) contribute to the discussion on *loss distribution* effects under different clearing arrangements and show that if one asset class is considered, under the CCP, the losses are less concentrated than under a ring agreement (which is similar to compression service).

In the context of *loss distribution* after member default, Pirrong (2009) notes various redistributive effects resulting from CCP clearing in OTC derivatives market, such as, for example, the fact that a CCP guarantees the positions of a clearing member's customers. Thus, a CCP actually insures non-members against default risk.

Kubitza, Pelizzon and Getmansky (2018) point out that the *loss distribution* in CCP can lead to distorted incentives for the market participants with unidirectional portfolios. A CCP is more beneficial for derivatives dealers, whose portfolios are hedged and more balanced than, for example, for asset managers, whose counterparty risk is more correlated to systematic risk. The latter group bears a greater loss after a default, if the CCP allocates the loss to clearing members with gains in times of crisis, for example, by reducing variation margin payments to clearing members whose portfolio values have increased (Elliott 2013).

Paper 2 of this dissertation adds another aspect to this research. It is shown that the buy-side participation in a CCP has an adverse impact on systemic risk. The protection of the customer positions, propagated by regulators, leads to netting-efficiency losses for sell-side and ceteris paribus increases systemic risk. The cost equal to the lost netting efficiency will be passed by sell-side market participants to the buy-side clients, which may, in practice, limit the buy-side participation in the OTC CCPs.

(2) Other recent works on CCP for OTC derivatives investigate the potential change in *collateral demand* caused by mandatory CCP clearing.[11] Most of the models predict an increase in *collateral demand* spurred by recent financial market reforms (Singh 2010; Pirrong 2012; Vuillemey and Breton 2014). Singh (2010) argues first that *collateral demand* driven by mandatory clearing may increase because not all bilateral OTC positions are currently collateralized and, second, that collateral held by banks can be rehypothecated to others (i.e., reused). Under CCP, all positions are collateralized, and no rehypothecation is allowed; therefore, the collateral demand for the banks may increase, possibly requiring them to raise more capital. Pirrong (2012) also argues that margin requirements under CCPs, along with higher collateral requirements under the EMIR and the Dodd-Frank Act on non-cleared OTC derivatives, will drive up overall collateral demand. Margin models tend to be procyclical, and liquidity spirals may

---

[11] In this dissertation, netting efficiency is analyzed as a key driver of expected average collateral cost.

therefore appear (this result agrees with Murphy, Vasios and Vause 2014). Duffie, Scheicher and Vuillemey (2015) also support the thesis that system-wide collateral demand is increased significantly by the application of initial margin requirements for dealers, regardless of whether the CDSs remain bilateral or are centrally cleared. However (and surprisingly, given these dealer-to-dealer initial margin requirements), mandatory central clearing is shown to decrease, not increase, system-wide *collateral demand*, provided there is no significant fragmentation of CCPs.

(3) The recent financial market reforms recognize a CCP as the most systematically important infrastructure, one that is so important that its distress or failure would impose material losses on the real economy. Therefore, both regulators and academics are interested in potential adverse impacts of CCP clearing. On the one hand, the research focuses on the consequences of *consolidation under CCPs* and risk concentration in a CCP (Wendt 2015; Krahnen and Pelizzon 2016). On the other hand, the research analyzes CCP *risk management practices* such as margining, haircut setting or the design of failure resolution regimes for CCPs (Abruzzo and Park 2016; Duffie 2015; Cerezetti *et al.* 2017; Murphy 2017).

Krahnen and Pelizzon (2016) note that because of substantial economies of scale in clearing regarding risk and operations, the consolidation of CCPs emerges. The CCP monopoly represents an ultimate systemic risk in the financial system. A default of a CCP may require a government bailout. The authors point out that as long as no monopoly CCP exists, the CCPs may compete on margin requirements, i.e., reduce the margins to increase market share. Therefore, the authors, as well as Friedrich and Thiemann (2018), recommend a supranational supervision of all CCPs and specific regulation of the resolution framework for CCPs.

In one of few empirical studies on CCPs' margin models, Abruzzo and Park (2016) analyze the margining method used by the US clearinghouse of the Chicago Mercantile Exchange (CME).[12] They provide evidence that the margin setting of the CME Group is indeed sensitive to volatility and that it has a more procyclical impact in times of higher market volatility than in calm times (because the CME does not immediately decrease margins when volatility drops). This implies that the most disruptive effects of increased margins can be observed when a shock appears after an extended period of low volatility markets as margins are increased from a lower level. Acharya and Viswanathan (2011) and Murphy, Vasios and Vause (2014) also support this thesis.

CCP failure resolution procedures should be designed to minimize the total expected distress costs of all market participants, including clearing members and CCP operators, along with unrelated market participants and taxpayers who could suffer from failure spillover costs (Duffie 2015). The literature proposes many models for CCP default management. Elliott (2013) summarizes various strategies in this regard. Cerezetti *et al.* (2017) empirically derive a hedging strategy that minimizes the CCP's risk exposure to a defaulting clearing member. Avellaneda and Cont (2012) and Vicente *et al.* (2015) propose an integrated risk approach that simultaneously addresses market risk and liquidation cost. Heath, Kelly and Manning (2015) analyze the consequences of allocating any uncovered losses to participants through the "haircutting" of the variation margin owed to participants.

Despite the fact that prior studies have contributed significantly to the understanding of the subject of clearing, most research is focused on particular aspects of the clearinghouses and thus does not provide the holistic framework for an assessment of the post-trading of the OTC derivatives. Though, the current dynamics in the clearing industry counsels a need for a holistic approach as it is particularly required for the regulation of the OTC markets. Therefore, like in this thesis, not only the risk

---

[12] The analysis in Paper 4 of this dissertation is based on the history of margins and haircuts for the portfolios of the clearing members, whereas Abruzzo and Park (2016) analyze the margins for few selected financial instruments.

practices of the CCP, but also the operational and IT aspects of the clearinghouses should be investigated.

3 RESEARCH METHODOLOGIES

Paper 3's research questions called for a qualitative research approach (exploratory case study), whereas the other questions called for a quantitative research method. In the following section, the methodologies applied in this thesis are described in detail.

3.1 Quantitative Survey

The research question addressed in Paper 1 (*Which factors influence the adoption of CCP clearing for OTC derivatives among market participants?*) requires a quantitative approach, which allows measurement of the strength of the factors that have an impact on the adoption decision. Therefore, a causal model has been developed and operationalized as a structural equation model (SEM). SEMs allow the modeling of latent variables (i.e., variables that are not directly observable) that are measured by using several manifest (i.e., directly observable) variables.

To evaluate the causal model, a survey was conducted among the heads of clearing/operations at institutions active in the OTC derivatives market. The results of the survey have been analyzed using the partial least squares (PLS) methodology (Chin 1998). Alternative approaches were available to estimate the SEM. However, for various reasons, the component-based approach of PLS has been chosen over covariance-based alternatives such as LISREL. Covariance-based methods focus on how well the available data fit a well-known, accepted causal model. However, PLS aims both to predict behavior and to minimize the residual variance of dependent variables. Therefore, it is more appropriate for new causal models (such as the OTC CCP adoption model) that have not been validated by previous research. Moreover, in contrast to covariance-based methods, PLS does not make any assumption about the distribution of the measured data. Furthermore, it requires smaller sample sizes.

In Paper 1, a PLS regression model was chosen to show the relationships between OTC CCP adoption and the attributes of CCP clearing. The PLS approach was employed to estimate both the measurement and the structural parameters in the structural equation modeling approach. As mentioned above, PLS is considered the most appropriate analytical technique for this study because it supports exploratory research and establishes minimum requirements for sample size (Chin 1998).

CCP clearing for OTC derivatives is understood as IT-enabled innovation (Mahnke, Overby and Özcan 2006). Academic research has developed numerous theories and models to explain the factors that influence the acceptance of technology innovation. Among the most influential of these theories and models is the Rogers' diffusion of innovation model (Rogers 1995), which is based on perceived innovation attributes such as relative advantage, compatibility, complexity, trialability and observability. The underlying model for this research is an extension of the diffusion of innovation theory and utilizes the first three innovation attributes (Tornatzky and Klein's (1982) meta-analysis of 75 studies showed that of several identified innovation attributes, only relative advantage, compatibility, and complexity in most cases showed a significant relationship to innovation adoption). Relative advantage was conceptualized as a multi-dimensional aggregate second-order construct with three subconstructs referring to different aspects of a CCP's potential advantages: processing efficiency, capital efficiency, and counterparty credit risk mitigation.

Although the diffusion of innovation theory has proven to be a viable framework for examining the adoption of innovation (Dwivedi *et al.* 2008), it is necessary to incorporate additional factors that help explain the contextual effects. In the model, two moderating effects were hypothesized. Moreover, product standardization and the economies of scale present in clearing (the latter through the Critical Mass construct) were considered as additional latent variables.

Assessment of the measurement model has been based on an evaluation of item loadings, construct discriminant, convergent validity and composite reliability. The structural model has been evaluated according to R2 and path coefficients, whose significance was tested by applying bootstrapping with 500 samples. Both the discriminant validity of the model and its predictive relevance have been confirmed (Schloderer, Ringle and Sarstedt 2009).

3.2 The Numerical Simulation of the OTC Market

OTC derivatives markets are inherently opaque. Therefore, market data that would reflect the real counterparty exposures and assess the impact of the clearing arrangements are not available. Consequently, the research question addressed in Paper 2 (*What is the impact of OTC CCP on counterparty risk in the derivatives market?*) cannot be answered based on real-world empirical data. Thus, the appropriate method for addressing this research question is a numerical simulation.

Simulation is a commonly used and beneficial method in research on financial markets (Grunenberg, Kunzelmann and Weinhardt 2004). The advantage of a computational simulation is that it may provide deep insight into the highly complex interactions of, e.g., derivatives markets (LeBaron 2006). A computer-based simulation can be regarded as the software implementation of a formal model (Zeigler 1976; Sauerbier 1999). Simulation facilitates the examination of a wider set of scenarios than would be possible using a purely analytical approach.

This method allows a quantitative comparison of distinct clearing arrangements and analysis of some complex interactions, such as the impact of heterogeneity in trading behavior on an agent's exposure under different post-trade arrangements. It provides for the repeatability of the same situation with different parameters, enabling an assessment of the impact of a single factor on the outcome. In this research, the main parameters are the various numbers of asset classes under a given clearing arrangement and the different numbers of participating agents.

The simulation environment presented in Paper 2 is based on the matrix representation of the net trading positions between market participants. In the model, the agents are heterogeneous and differentiated depending on their trading behavior, i.e., sell-side and buy-side agents. In the first step of the analysis, the matrix of trading positions between market participants in each asset class is decomposed into submatrices representing specific market segments such as interdealer trading (sell-side to sell-side), dealer-to-customer markets (sell-side to buy-side) and customer-to-customer markets (buy-side to buy-side). Four OTC clearing arrangements are modeled by transforming the relevant submatrices. The comparison measure for the considered clearing arrangements is their netting efficiency, which measures how far a clearing arrangement may reduce market participants' gross exposure resulting from their trading positions.

For the second part of the analysis, replacement cost losses are modeled based on Bates and Craine (1999). A replacement cost loss will arise only when a counterparty default coincides with an adverse price move in excess of the per-unit margin collected from that counterparty. The loss-concentration ratio is defined as a proportion of a maximal replacement cost loss incurred by a single agent to total replacement losses suffered by all agents.

The inputs for the model are matrices of net bilateral trading positions between different numbers of agents in each of the major asset classes. The positions are drawn from the normal distribution. The parameter for the standard deviation of trading positions is essentially arbitrary. However, the precise values have little effect on the results. Six asset classes are considered in the analysis, corresponding to six major classes reported by the Bank for International Settlements (2018a) on a regular basis. Those are, e.g., equity derivatives or fixed income derivatives. For the second analysis—i.e., the analysis of the replacement cost losses—price changes, margin policy, and agent defaults are modeled.

To compare the netting efficiency of various clearing arrangements, the simulation runs result in a series of netting-efficiency ratios for a particular number of asset classes and agents under each of the analyzed clearing arrangements. The simulation runs for the loss-concentration analysis provide loss-concentration ratios under each clearing arrangement considered and based on the number of agents.

3.3 Case Study Method

For the research questions addressed in Paper 3 (*"How can the existing CCP architecture be enhanced to minimize the operational risks in the OTC processing workflow?"*), a case study approach has been chosen.

The case study method is preferred when "how" and "why" questions (or "what" questions of an explorative character) are the focus of the research (Yin 2003a). The case study approach was chosen for Paper 3 because it enables exploratory insight into a marginally investigated area of the post-trade processing of OTC derivatives. Moreover, Eisenhardt (1989) states, "case studies are particularly well suited to new research areas or research areas for which existing theory seems inadequate." Additionally, the case study research is appropriate when the focus is on a contemporary phenomenon with some real-life context (Yin 2003a), which is the case in the context of the STP processing of OTC derivatives.

Case studies are regarded as the most common qualitative research method in Information Systems (Orlikowski and Baroudi 1991). The single case study method is considered a potentially rich and valuable source of data, suited to exploring relationships between variables in their given context (Benbasat, Goldstein and Mead 1987), and it is appropriate where it represents a critical case (Yin 2003a). Remenyi *et al.* (1998) argue that it is essential to use multiple sources of evidence when conducting a single case study, ensuring validity through, as Denzin (1984) calls it, data source triangulation. To achieve the necessary rigor, it is important to define the research question and the unit of analysis explicitly and properly in the design and preparatory phase. Like field studies, case studies typically utilize questionnaires, coded interviews, and systematic observations as their preferred techniques for data gathering (Yin 2003b).

The subject presented in Paper 3 was chosen as a critical case in relation to improving the STP potential of the OTC derivatives post-trade processing. The data gathering techniques used in this study were semi-structured interviews and document analysis. Semi-structured interviews enhance the overall quality of the data gathered by allowing researchers both to clarify questions and responses and to explore new dimensions.

Yin (2003a) argues that documentation can be utilized to supplement and verify data from other sources. Before designing the case study protocol, all of the relevant documentation on the Eurex Clearing service for CDSs (Eurex Credit Clear) was reviewed. Technical (technical system specification) and functional documents (release notes, credit event handling documents), customer presentations, and field notes were collected in a case study database. Interviews with key members of staff in various roles within the organization/project were conducted. The interviewed persons included the IT and business managers, along with numerous business and IT analysts from the clearinghouse. Interviews were recorded and transcribed. Information was also obtained from secondary sources on the intranet. The accuracy of all data was verified through subsequent meetings and document exchanges over email.

3.4 Empirical Quantitative Analysis

For the research question addressed in Paper 4 (*"What is the impact of CCPs' risk management practices on the systemic risk in the financial system?"*), an empirical quantitative approach has been chosen. In contrast to numerous empirical analyses of the dynamics of trading in financial markets (Biais, Hillion and Spatt 1995; Madhavan, Richardson and Roomans 1997), the empirical approach is only sparsely used in the post-trading area. This can be mostly explained by researchers' limited access to proprietary CCP and clearing members' data. Existing empirical studies on margining practices typically use the margin requirements calculated for single, predefined financial contracts (Abruzzo and Park 2016). Therefore, such analyses do not incorporate the full portfolio effects that occur in the real clearing members' positions or collateral portfolios.

The data used to investigate any procyclical effects should cover the full credit and business cycle; therefore, there is a fundamental question regarding which period is covered by the available data. If only a snapshot in time is revealed by the data, there is no possibility of analyzing and evaluating time-dependent changes over a longer period. Second, the interval length between two data points, i.e., the sampling rate, is crucial.

The closer two data points in the available dataset are (i.e., the shorter the time between two data snapshots), the better the short-term movements and changes in the risk structure are revealed in the data. Because the economy and the financial system are non-stationary systems, both of the components described above are highly relevant for a proper measurement of procyclicality. The dataset used in Paper 4 fulfills both criteria regarding the length of the analyzed period (almost ten years) and the interval between two data points (daily data). Moreover, as noted above, the dataset incorporates portfolio effects that are important when analyzing the overall procyclical effect.

The available data are analyzed based on a statistical model. The exploratory data analysis suggested that the volatility of the margin/haircuts and market stress are clustered and changing in time. Such time-varying volatilities are characteristic of financial markets and often are estimated with Generalized Autoregressive Conditional Heteroscedasticity (GARCH) models (Bollerslev 1986). Engle (2002) proposed a dynamic conditional correlation (DCC-GARCH) model that has the flexibility of univariate GARCH models coupled with parsimonious parametric models for the correlations. The DCC-GARCH is a well-grounded model in the field of financial asset management because correlations are critical inputs for common tasks such as hedging or pricing structured financial instruments. The DCC-GARCH model is estimated in two steps: first, the conditional variance of each univariate time series is estimated; second, the standardized regression residuals obtained in the first step are used to model the conditional correlations that vary through time.

Paper 4 analyzes the dynamic (time-varying) correlations between the total margin requirement/collateral haircuts and market stress index published by the European Central Bank.

4 MAIN RESULTS

4.1 Results from Paper 1: Adoption of the OTC CCP

Based on the diffusion of innovation theory, this empirical study introduces a model aimed at identifying the drivers and inhibitors of the adoption of an IT-enabled innovation in the form of CCP clearing by financial organizations. The PLS SEM technique was applied to analyze the results of the survey of the heads of clearing/operations in various international financial institutions.

The empirical analysis confirmed that the perceived relative advantage of the OTC CCP and compatibility with existing post-trade processes substantially contribute to the adoption of centralized clearing for OTC derivatives, whereas complexity does not appear to be a significant predictor. All three dimensions of the relative advantage, along with the aggregate second-order construct, exhibit a strong influence on OTC CCP adoption.

These findings are in line with the observations on the CCPs' diffusion in the OTC derivatives market (Bank for International Settlements 2007). Because the market participants recently made large investments in post-trade processing solutions and connections to the global infrastructure, it is essential to have operational compatibility between the current processing of OTC derivatives and CCP service. An accelerated OTC CCP adoption has been observed after the turmoil caused by the financial crisis of 2007-2009. This may be explained by an increase in the perceived relative advantage of OTC CCP, mostly at the counterparty credit risk level.

Critical mass was confirmed in the research as having a strong direct influence on OTC CCP adoption. Due to economies of scale in clearing, achieving a critical mass of clearing members and cleared volumes causes OTC CCP adoption to depend on the largest derivatives dealers.

Product standardization was found both to have a strong direct influence on OTC CCP adoption and to moderate the relationship between relative advantage and adoption. Product customization impedes the automation of post-trade processing; the lack of a commonly accepted valuation model makes risk management difficult. Therefore, standardization is a requirement for effective CCP clearing.

The complexity of the OTC CCP was not found to negatively influence willingness to adopt. The explanation for this result may be the perceived relatively low margin requirement within CCP resulting from increasing competition within the clearing sector and/or the increasing use of collateral in bilateral post-trade processing.

In general, the acceptance and adoption of the OTC CCP are growing with the increasing compatibility of this solution with existing market infrastructure, awareness of the counterparty risk among market participants and product standardization.

4.2 Results from Paper 2: OTC Clearing Arrangements

This paper addresses the implications of the regulatory reforms introduced in the OTC derivatives market after the financial crisis of 2007-2009, in particular, mandatory clearing of standardized OTC derivative contracts. In this research, the status quo is compared with the simulated results of the proposed reforms. Therefore, the existing OTC post-trade models are compared with the solution proposed by the regulators: CCP clearing.

The simulation runs for the netting-efficiency analysis deliver results for each market segment. In the sell-side to sell-side market segments, the *CCP* maximizes the netting efficiency. The netting-efficiency ratio increases in both the number of participating agents and the asset classes under CCP arrangement, but with decreasing marginal increments.

CCP and *tear-ups* deliver similar netting-efficiency results in the hypothetical case of a single asset class universe subject to clearing. Moreover, CCP and *closeout netting* lead to a similar netting efficiency in the case in which only two members participate in the post-trade processing arrangements.

When comparing *exclusive* CCP (without buy-side access) with the *prime broker give-ups*, it becomes evident that the shift of the prime broker positions of the sell-side agents to the CCP results in significant netting-efficiency gains. However, allowing buy-side access to a CCP has an adverse effect on the netting efficiency for sell-side because the sell-side agents have the additional burden of maintaining segregated client positions.

In the buy-side to sell-side segment, *prime brokerage give-ups* improve netting efficiency, with the netting ratio increasing both with the number of sell-side agents participating in such multilateral give-up arrangements and with the scope of asset classes covered under such arrangements, but with decreasing marginal increments. The shift of buy-side positions under prime brokerage to a CCP does not provide any efficiency gains. However, the CCP clearing provides other benefits to buy-side clients because their position exposures are mutually assured by all sell-side agents participating in the CCP. In the case of clearing member default, the buy-side agent may transfer its segregated positions to non-defaulting members. However, the segregation of the customer positions places an additional burden on sell-side agents, which decreases the netting efficiency in the sell-side to sell-side market segment.

The results of the loss-concentration analysis show that compared to other clearing arrangements, under a CCP, the losses are at least concentrated. Moreover, losses are more widely distributed with an increasing number of CCP members. In contrast, *prime brokerage give-ups* lead to the highest loss concentration because back-to-back positions generate high exposures and the loss is borne in full by the affected agents.

The results indicate that the mandatory clearing of all standardized OTC derivatives by a CCP propagated by regulators would significantly decrease systemic risk compared to existing clearing arrangements only if the multilateral netting benefits of the CCP and loss mutualization are fully attained.

4.3 Results from Paper 3: Is a Full STP of OTC Derivatives Possible?

In Paper 3, the straight though processing (STP) measure (as defined in Hee, Cheng and Huang 2003) is applied to investigate the impact of the introduction of a clearinghouse in the OTC market. In particular, the external (i.e., industry-wide) STP rate in the CDS market infrastructure is compared before and after the introduction of a clearinghouse.

The results show that the investigated clearinghouse only marginally increased the STP rate in the post-trade processing value chain. The clearinghouse allowed the centralization of position, event and collateral management. However, the former two business functionalities were already highly automated and incorporated in the end-to-end processing workflow before the introduction of the CCP. The STP potential of a clearinghouse lies in further automation of the collateral management function.

As a high non-STP or exception rate of transactions may significantly increase needed headcount, the cost per trade is an implicit STP measure (Best and Weth 2009). The reduction of the cost per trade caused by an introduction of a clearinghouse in the CDS market was estimated in Paper 3 as less than 14% of an absolute trade cost.

Furthermore, in this study, an optimization proposal for the clearinghouse architecture is made. The main shortcoming of the investigated Eurex Credit Clear solution was that it did not fulfill the real-time processing paradigm as it was based on a weekly novation cycle. The critical workflow functions like, for example, trade confirmation, laid beyond the scope of a clearinghouse. This contributed to a delay in trade processing. A direct link between CCP and a confirmation platform would allow the simplification of the processing model and enable a real-time trade submission to a CCP, increasing the STP rate.

4.4 Results from Paper 4: CCP Risk Practices in the Light of Procyclicality

One major policy concern in the centrally cleared derivatives market is that margin requirements and collateral haircuts imposed by CCPs can sharply rise in times of stress, inhibiting trading and causing liquidity problems that exacerbate the crisis. The research in Paper 4 provides the insight into the impact of the risk management practices of CCPs as seen from the systemic risk perspective.

The theory suggests that CCP risk management practices such as margining and collateral haircuts may exacerbate economic cycle fluctuations (Brunnermeier and Pedersen 2009). Based on almost ten years of empirical data from a leading European clearinghouse, Paper 4 investigated whether and to what extent the procyclical effects suggested by the literature could be statistically confirmed. The results for the period encompassing the financial crisis of 2007-2009 and the European sovereign debt crisis do not confirm the hypothesis of the theoretical research that CCP risk practices are procyclical. The results reveal only a low average level of conditional correlation between market stress and the total CCP margin requirement and market stress and haircuts, respectively.

Addressing procyclicality in the financial system is an essential component of strengthening the regulatory framework. Therefore, regulators are considering the introduction of macroprudential tools such as minimum haircuts and margins or countercyclical add-ons. However, it was shown in Paper 4 that the systematic overcollateralization of open positions by clearing members (as observed in the dataset) might already act as a countercyclical break. Moreover, when the markets calm down after a crisis, the CCP risk management model incorporates previous extreme events, leading to a countercyclical margin requirement.

Surprisingly, the CCP's haircut policy was not proven to be prone to fire sales, as suggested by some studies (Brunnermeier and Pedersen 2009). The clearing members did not systematically remove the securities with increased haircuts from their collateral portfolios. Only approximately twenty percent of such dropout events were motivated by the surge in haircuts. However, the collateral portfolios of the clearing members became more diversified in times of market stress than in calm markets. This finding suggests that new types of securities were added to those already present in the collateral portfolio when the clearing members needed to cover the increase in margin requirement under conditions of market stress.

5 CONTRIBUTION TO THEORY AND PRAXIS

In this section, the theoretical and practical contributions and implications of this thesis' results are suggested.

5.1. Contribution to Academics

This dissertation adds to the academic base of knowledge concerning clearing arrangements on different levels.

The thesis positions the OTC CCP as an IT-enabled innovation in the field of information system research. Paper 1 describes the CCP clearing process as a technology innovation in the context of the OTC market (Mahnke, Overby and Özcan 2006). Until now, most authors have regarded CCP clearing as merely a risk mitigation mechanism. This study investigates OTC CCP as a novel service, considering this type of post-trade processing system from multiple perspectives. Further investigation of CCP clearing as IT-enabled innovation is a promising field of research.

The reasons for market participants' adoption of the OTC CCP are also addressed in Paper 1, which makes a threefold contribution to theory. First, the survey extends adoption research in the domain of clearing, which had previously not been covered. Moreover, the survey's underlying research model provides a successful extension of the core of Rogers' diffusion of innovation theory (Rogers 1995), with innovation attributes as factors that facilitate or hinder innovation adoption. This might be a promising suggestion for further research because all but two hypothesized effects proved to be significant. Finally, the results of the survey highlight both the importance of the perceived relative advantage of the

OTC CCP and compatibility with existing post-trade processes because both contribute substantially to CCP acceptance. A critical mass of participants and product standardization were also confirmed as having a strong direct influence on OTC CCP adoption.

Paper 2 adds to the academic research on clearing arrangements by explicitly modeling the tiered market structure within which dealers have the dual capacity of liquidity providers and prime brokers. This allows for an analysis of various clearing mechanisms and a comparison of their impact on netting efficiency as the primary driver of expected average collateral cost and replacement cost risk. The analytical model developed in this paper can serve as the basis for future research analyzing the further implications of the clearing arrangements.

Because the implications of different clearing arrangements cannot be investigated based on the available empirical data, the simulation environment presented in Paper 2 provides an opportunity to assess the impact of those arrangements. The insights gained from the conducted simulations foster an understanding of how the complex interactions between market participants on the micro level and clearing arrangements on the macro level affect systemic risk.

Based on the specific case study research design, Paper 3's contribution to theory is in building concrete, context-dependent knowledge with regard to the identification of new phenomena and trends in the CDS processing workflow. The case study enhances the understanding of researchers concerning the STP potential of a clearinghouse for OTC derivatives, as not enough research had previously been carried out on the subject matter.

The quantitative analysis, conducted in Paper 4, challenges the theory by means of empirical investigation. The unique and sufficiently large dataset was applied for testing the theory of fire sales and the procyclical impact of CCP margins and haircuts.

5.2. Contribution to Practice

This research has practical implications that are of interest to several groups of stakeholders, including market infrastructure providers and their regulators.

The thesis delivers an argument about the OTC market structure in the clearing area, supporting the current regulatory debate (ESMA 2018a; ESRB 2016, 2017a, 2017b; Raykov 2018). In Paper 2, the implications of the EMIR and the Dodd-Frank Act were examined. Based on the results of the numerical simulation of the OTC market, clear policy recommendations could be formulated to minimize systemic risk under the post-trade processing model introduced by the recent reforms. First, to achieve the superior benefits of CCP clearing (compared to other OTC clearing arrangements), policymakers and regulators should strive for an optimum of asset classes under mandatory clearing. For more tailored transactions, other risk mitigation mechanisms (such as *compression service*) should be supported. Second, regulators should also strive for broad market participation in CCP clearing arrangements. The effect of the reduction of average counterparty exposure by introducing a CCP for a limited number of asset classes increases with the number of clearing members. Therefore, access restrictions in the clearinghouses should be mitigated and dealer-dominated CCPs should be opened to further market participants. Third, regulators should allow for less costly client asset segregation solutions, enabling some extent of netting of the buy-side positions by the CCPs. Paper 4 makes recommendations for regulators related to policy measures aimed at limiting the procyclical effects of CCP margin and haircut-setting. Most importantly, the regulators should weigh up the introduction of high-impact countercyclical tools against the implementation issues for such tools, as the CCP risk management is in practice less procyclical than suggested by the theoretical research. Both the effects of the CCP haircut policy on fire sales and the procyclical impact of margins were found weak when analyzing the empirical data. Additionally, it was shown that the burden of reasonably low, non-voluntary collateral floor on the liquidity of clearing members would probably not be high, as the members typically overcollateralize their accounts.

This thesis supports further improvements in the clearinghouse service for the OTC markets. Paper 1 details the factors that influence the adoption of the OTC CCP. Infrastructure providers such as clearinghouses are given clear guidance regarding the design of their service for OTC derivatives to influence their acceptance by the market participants. Furthermore, this thesis makes recommendations about how to improve the STP rate in CDS post-trade processing and lower the operational risk (Paper 3).

6 LIMITATIONS, OUTLOOK AND FUTURE RESEARCH

In this section, the limitations of the research are described and an outlook on potential future research is provided.

6.1 Limitations

The survey conducted in Paper 1 allowed for collecting data that shed light on the internal adoption decision-making process regarding CCP clearing in the OTC markets. However, this research is based on a limited data sample. The sample size of 53 is adequate for an exploratory investigation, as in this study, but larger samples are required for future confirmatory research. Nevertheless, Goodhue, Lewis and Thompson (2006) conclude that there is no evidence that proves that statistically significant results on small sample sizes are invalid. They merely state that, in research with a small sample size, a relationship that did not achieve statistical significance should not be interpreted as evidence that such a relationship does not exist. Instead, it merely means that with the small sample size, it might be impossible to detect relatively weak effects.

The research model used for the survey to investigate the adoption of CCP clearing showed only minor explanatory power regarding complexity. This suggests that there may be additional factors influencing CCP adoption beyond those of the diffusion of innovation model.

The results of numerical simulations and statistical models depend heavily on quantitative assumptions about the model's parameters. The simulation environment presented in Paper 2 is based on several assumptions. It was assumed that the trading positions between market participants are normally distributed. However, the assumption of normality does not apply to the exposures of many individual derivative positions. Empirically, the exposure of many individual derivatives may have heavily skewed and fat-tailed market values. This means that extreme negative values are more likely than would be predicted by a normal distribution (e.g., because of financial market shocks). However, aggregation within a class of all derivatives may result in a net exposure of one entity to another that is substantially less skewed, given diversification across underlying names and the effect of aggregating long and short positions. This is particularly true for the balanced portfolios of large derivatives dealers. However, the applied assumption of normality had little influence on the obtained results because the position matrices were further transformed and comparison measures between clearing arrangements were finally applied.

Moreover, it was assumed that an agent's market risk and counterparty credit risk are independent. Therefore, the default probability was an exogenous variable in relation to position and market price changes. One improvement could be to consider the default probability as an endogenous variable because, in practice, highly concentrated positions and adverse market movements may significantly increase an agent's probability of default.

Because the research study from Paper 3 focused on a single case exploring the CDS market infrastructure, the generalizability and transferability of the findings to other asset classes are somewhat limited. To obtain a more comprehensive and detailed understanding of the processing models, other derivatives classes should also be investigated. Therefore, it is suggested that further empirical studies be conducted to reach a better understanding of the processing models for other off-exchange traded derivatives and their STP potential.

The generalizability of the findings from Paper 3 is also limited. The data used for analyzing the impact of the CCP risk practices on procyclicity in the financial markets came from one clearinghouse. However, different CCPs may apply different risk methodologies, still fulfilling the existing regulatory requirements for margin and haircut settings.

The parameterization and type of the GARCH model used for univariate time series estimation (and the final DCC-GARCH model) from Paper 4 influence the results. Some stylized facts regarding the financial data have already been incorporated and have influenced the parameter and model selection. However, because GARCH modeling evolves over time, application of the newest models may fit the available data even better.

Research on CCP clearing in the OTC derivatives market continues to emerge. Because of the nature of this examination, it lies at the intersection of different disciplines such as finance and information systems and may therefore be addressed by a variety of methodologies in interdisciplinary research.

6.2 Outlook and Future Research

Because one of the objectives of the reforms introduced in the wake of the recent financial crisis is to increase the transparency of the OTC markets, datasets on gross and net exposures between market participants are now becoming available. This represents an opportunity for emerging research on OTC clearing. Several paths of future research will be suggested in this section.

Some assumptions deployed in the simulation from Paper 2 may be challenged in future studies. This concerns mostly the independence of credit and market risks, as mentioned in the previous section. Moreover, because the transparency of the OTC market will be further increasing under regulatory pressure, the underlying simulated data might be replaced with the empirical data at some point.

With multiple CCPs, netting efficiency may decline. However, there is likely to be some consolidation of CCPs over time, and netting agreements between CCPs could be developed. The links between multiple CCPs could improve netting efficiency compared with multiple CCPs that clear only some asset classes. Therefore, it would be worth quantifying netting-efficiency gains and assessing the consolidated impact of interoperable CCPs on systemic risk. The framework from Paper 2 could be reused for this aim.

Because the studies in Papers 1 and 3 were exclusively exploratory in nature, generalizations from their findings could be the work of future research. The OTC CCP adoption model could be extended to cover additional factors influencing the adoption of CCP clearing in the OTC markets, which could increase the explanatory power of the model. The infrastructures for further OTC asset classes could be studied to determine their STP potential.

Finally, because CCPs themselves concentrate systemic risk and their importance to the global OTC derivatives market is growing, it would be valuable to analyze the protection mechanisms that they apply in the event of a member default. In this context, the simulation of the impact of different loss-allocation mechanisms in the CCP would be an interesting subject for future research.

REFERENCES

Abruzzo, N. and Park, Y.-H. (2016). An Empirical Analysis of Futures Margin Changes: Determinants and Policy Implications. *Journal of Financial Services Research*, 49 (1), 65–100.

Acharya, V. V. and Viswanathan, S. (2011). Leverage, Moral Hazard, and Liquidity. *Journal of Finance*, 66, 99-138.

Anderson, S., Dion, J.-P. and Perez Saiz, H. (2013). *To link or not to link? Netting and exposures between central counterparties.* Bank of Canada Working Paper No. 6.

Arnsdorf, M. (2012). Quantification of central counterparty risk. *Journal of Risk Management in Financial Institutions*, 5, 273–287.

Ashcraft, A., Gârleanu, N. and Pedersen, L. H. (2010). Two Monetary Tools: Interest Rates and Haircuts. *NBER Macroeconomic Annual*, 25, 143–180.

Avellaneda, M. and Cont, R. (2013). *Close-Out Risk Evaluation (CORE): A New Risk Management Approach for Central Counterparties.* https://ssrn.com/abstract=2247493 (Accessed 1 Feb. 2019).

Bank for International Settlements. (1998). *OTC Derivatives: Settlement Procedures and Counterparty Risk Management.* Committee on Payment and Settlement Systems Publication, 27, http://www.bis.org/publ/cpss27.pdf (Accessed 5 Feb. 2019).

Bank for International Settlements. (2003). *A Glossary of Terms Used in Payments and Settlement Systems.* http://www.bis.org/publ/cpss00b.pdf (Accessed 5 Feb. 2019).

Bank for International Settlements. (2007). *New developments in clearing and settlement arrangements for OTC derivatives.* CPSS Publication No. 77, http://www.bis.org/publ/cpss77.htm (Accessed 5 Feb. 2019).

Bank of International Settlements. (2010). *Considerations for trade repositories in OTC derivatives markets- consultative report.* http://www.bis.org/cpmi/publ/d90.pdf (Accessed 5 Feb. 2019).

Bank for International Settlements. (2015). *Margin requirements for non-centrally cleared derivatives.* https://www.bis.org/bcbs/publ/d317.pdf (Accessed 5 Feb. 2019).

Bank for International Settlements. (2018a). *Derivatives statistics.* www.bis.org/statistics/derstats.htm (Accessed 5 Feb. 2019).

Bank for International Settlements. (2018b). *Incentives to centrally clear over-the-counter (OTC) derivatives. A post-implementation evaluation of the effects of the G20 financial regulatory reforms.* https://www.bis.org/publ/othp29.pdf (Accessed 5 Feb. 2019).

Bates, D. and Craine, R. (1999). Valuing the Futures Market Clearinghouse's Default Exposure during the 1987 Crash. *Journal of Money, Credit and Banking,* 31, 248–272.

Bellia, M., Panzica R., Pelizzon, L. and Peltonen T. (2017). *The demand for central clearing: to clear or not to clear, that is the question.* ESRB Working Paper No. 62.

Benbasat, I., Goldstein, D. K. and Mead, M. (1987). The Case Research Strategy in Studies of Information Systems. *MIS Quarterly,* 11 (3), 369–385.

Bergman, W. J., Bliss, R. R., Johnson, Ch. A. and Kaufman, G. G. (2004). *Netting, Financial Contracts, and Banks: The Economic Implications.* FRB of Chicago Working Paper No. 2.

Best, E. and Weth, M. (2009) *Geschäftsprozesse optimieren. Der Praxisleitfaden für erfolgreiche Reorganisation,* Wiesbaden: Gabler Verlag/ GWV Fachverlage GmbH, ISBN: 9783834994103.

Biais, B., Hillion, P. and Spatt, Ch. (1995). An Empirical Analysis of the Limit Order Book and the Order Flow in the Paris Bourse. *Journal of Finance*, 50, 1655–1689.

Bliss, R. R. and Kaufman, G. G. (2005). *Derivatives and Systemic Risk: Netting, Collateral, and Closeout*. FRB of Chicago Working Paper No. 3.

Bliss, R. R. and Steigerwald, R. (2006). Derivatives Clearing and Settlement: a Comparison of Central Counterparties and Alternative Structures. *Economic Perspectives*, 30 (4), 22–29.

Bollerslev, T. (1986). Generalized Autoregressive Conditional Heteroskedasticity. *Journal of Econometrics*, 31, 307–327.

Brunnermeier, M. K. and Pedersen, L. H. (2009). Market liquidity and funding liquidity, *Review of Financial Studies*, 22 (6), 2201–2238.

Bundesanstalt für Finanzdienstleistungsaufsicht. (2017). *Clearingpflicht bei Derivaten*. https://www.bafin.de/DE/Aufsicht/BoersenMaerkte/Derivate/EMIR/Clearing/ZentralesClearing/pflichten_zum_zentralen_clearing_node.html (Accessed 5 Feb. 2019).

Campbell, J. Y. (2002). Asset Pricing at the Millenium. *Journal of Finance*, 55, 1515-1567.

Cerezetti, F., Sumawong, A., Shreyas, U. and Karimalis, E. (2017). *Market liquidity, closeout procedures and initial margin for CCPs*. Bank of England Staff Working Paper No. 643.

Chin, W. W. (1998). The Partial Least Squares Approach to Structural Equation Modeling. In: G.A. Marcoulides (ed.) *Modern Methods for Business Research*, Mahwah (N.J.): Lawrence Erlbaum Associates.

Cont, R. and Kokholm, T. (2014). Central Clearing of OTC Derivatives: Bilateral vs Multilateral Netting. *Statistics & Risk Modeling*, 31, 1–20.

Cox, N., Garvin, N. and Kelly, G. (2013). *Central Counterparty Links and Clearing System Exposures*. Reserve Bank of Australia Discussion Paper No. 12.

Denzin, N. K. (1989). *The research act: A theoretical introduction to sociological methods* (3rd. ed.), Englewood Cliffs (NJ): Prentice Hall.

Deutsche Börse. (2014). *How Central Counterparties strengthen the safety and integrity of financial markets*. http://deutsche-boerse.com/dbg-en/about-us/public-affairs/publications/white-papers (Accessed 5 Feb. 2019).

Duffie D. (2015). Resolution of Failing Central Counterparties. In: Scott, K. E., Jackson, T. H. und Taylor, J. B (eds.) *Making Failure Feasible*, Stanford: Hoover Institution Press.

Duffie, D., Scheicher, M. and Vuillemey, G. (2015). Central Clearing and Collateral Demand. *Journal of Financial Economics*, 116 (2), 237–256.

Duffie, D. and Zhu, H. (2011). Does a Central Clearing Counterparty Reduce Counterparty Risk? *Review of Asset Pricing Studies*, 1, 74–95.

Dwivedi, Y., Williams, M.D., Lal B., Schwarz, A. (2008). Profiling Adoption, Acceptance and Diffusion Research in the Information Systems Discipline. In: *Proceedings of European Conference on Information Systems (ECIS 2008), 1204–1215.*

Easley, D. and O'Hara, M. (1987). Price, trade size, and information in securities markets. *Journal of Financial Economics*, 19 (1), 69-90.

Eisenhardt, K. M. (1989). Building Theories From Case Study Research. *Academy of Management Review*, 14, 532–550.

Elliott, D. (2013). *Central counterparty loss-allocation rules*. Bank of England Financial Stability Paper No. 20.

Engle, R. (2002). Dynamic conditional correlation: A simple class of multivariate generalized autoregressive conditional heteroskedasticity models. *Journal of Business and Economic Statistics*, 20 (3), 339–350.

ESMA. (2018a). *Guidelines on EMIR Anti-Procyclicality Margin Measures for Central Counterparties.* https://www.esma.europa.eu/sites/default/files/library/esma70-151-1293_final_report_on_guidelines_on_ccp_apc_margin_measures.pdf (Accessed 5 Feb. 2019).

EUR-Lex. (2012). Commission Delegated Regulation (EU) No 153/2013 December 2012 supplementing Regulation EU No 648/2012 of the European parliament and of Council with regard to regulatory technical standards on requirements for central counterparties. *Official Journal of the European Union*, L 52/41. http://bit.ly/2lMCNmV (Accessed 5 Feb. 2019).

European Parliament. (2012). *Regulation (EU) No 648/2012 of the European Parliament and of the Council of 4 July 2012 on OTC derivatives, central counterparties and trade repositories.* https://eur-lex.europa.eu/homepage.html (Accessed 5 Feb. 2019).

European Systemic Risk Board (ESRB). (2016). *Remarks by Vítor Constâncio, Vice-President of the ECB, at the ESRB international conference on the macroprudential use of margins and haircuts*, Frankfurt am Main, 6. Juni 2016, https://www.ecb.europa.eu/press/key/date/2016/html/sp160606.en.html (Accessed 5 Feb. 2019).

European Systemic Risk Board (ESRB). (2017a). *The macroprudential use of margins and haircuts.* https://www.esrb.europa.eu/pub/reports/html/index.en.html (Accessed 5 Feb. 2019).

European Systemic Risk Board (ESRB). (2017b). *Revision of the European Market Infrastructure Regulation.* https://www.esrb.europa.eu/pub/pdf/other/20170421_esrb_emir.en.pdf (Accessed 5 Feb. 2019).

Financial Crisis Inquiry Commission. (2011). *The financial crisis inquiry report: final report of the National Commission on the Causes of the Financial and Economic Crisis in the United States,* Washington, DC: Financial Crisis Inquiry Commission. ISBN: 9780160879838.

Financial Stability Board (FSB). (2017). *Review of OTC Derivatives Market Reforms: Effectiveness and Broader Effects of the Reforms.* http://www.fsb.org/2017/06/review-of-otc-derivatives-market-reform-effectiveness-and-broader-effects-of-the-reforms (Accessed 5 Feb. 2019).

Financial Services Authority and HM Treasury. (2009). *Reforming OTC Derivative Markets: A UK Perspective.* http://www.fsa.gov.uk/pubs/other/reform_otc_derivatives.pdf (Accessed 5 Feb. 2019).

Friedrich, J. and Thiemann, M. (2018). *A new governance architecture for European financial markets? Towards a European supervision of CCPs.* SAFE White Paper No. 53.

Fuchs, F. (2013). *Close-out Netting, Collateral und systemisches Risiko – Rechtsansätze zur Minderung der Systemgefahr im außerbörslichen Derivatehandel.* Tübingen: Mohr Siebeck, ISBN: 9783161523632.

G20. (2009). *G20 Leaders Statement: The Pittsburgh Summit.* http://www.oecd.org/g20/summits/pittsburgh/G20-Pittsburgh-Leaders-Declaration.pdf (Accessed 5 Feb. 2019).

Garratt, R. J. and Zimmerman, P. (2015). *Does Central Clearing Reduce Counterparty Risk in Realistic Financial Networks?* FRB of New York Staff Report, 717.

Gibson, R. and Murawski, C. (2006). *Default Risk Mitigation in Derivatives Markets and its Effectiveness.* EFA Zürich Meetings Paper.

Ghamami, S. and Glasserman, P. (2017). Does OTC derivatives reform incentivize central clearing? *Journal of Financial Intermediation,* 32, 76–87.

Goodhue, D., Lewis, L.W. and Thompson, R. (2006). Small sample size and statistical power in MIS research. In: *Proceedings of the 39th Annual Hawaii International Conference on System Sciences.*

Greenspan, A. (2008). *Testimony of Dr. Alan Greenspan. Committee of Government Oversight and Reform,* 23. October 2008, http://www.studymode.com/essays/Testimony-Of-Dr-Alan-Greenspan-Committee-596739.html (Accessed 5 Feb. 2019).

Grunenberg, M., Kunzelmann, M. and Weinhardt, Ch. (2004). *Benefits of Computer based Simulations for Financial Markets*. Epistemological Perspectives on Simulation Workshop, Koblenz, Germany.

Harris, L. (2003). *Trading and Exchanges: Market Microstructure for Practitioners*, New York: Oxford University Press, ISBN: 0195144708.

Heath, A., Kelly, G. and Manning, M. (2013). OTC Derivatives Reform: Netting and Networks. In: *Proceedings of Conference Liquidity and Funding Markets*, Reserve Bank of Australia, Sydney, 33–73.

Heath, A., Kelly G. and Manning, M. (2015). *Central Counterparty Loss Allocation and Transmission of Financial Stress*. Reserve Bank of Australia Research Paper.

Hee, J., Chen, Y., and Huang W. (2003). Straight Through Processing Technology in Global Financial Market: Readiness Assessment and Implementation. *Journal of Global Information Management*, 11 (2), 56–66.

Heller, D. and Vause, N. (2012). *Collateral Requirements for Mandatory Clearing of Over-the-counter Derivatives*. BIS Working Paper No. 373.

Hull, J. C. (2014). *Options, Futures and Other Derivatives* (9th ed.), Boston: Pearson, ISBN: 9780133456318.

International Swaps and Derivatives Association (ISDA). (2012). *Interest Rate Swaps Compression: A Progress Report*. https://www.isda.org/a/BeiDE/irs-compression-progress-report-feb-2012.pdf (Accessed 5 Feb. 2019).

International Swaps and Derivatives Association (ISDA). (2013). *CCP Loss Allocation at the End of the Waterfall*. https://www.isda.org/a/jTDDE/ccp-loss-allocation-waterfall-0807.pdf (Accessed 5 Feb. 2019).

International Swaps and Derivatives Association (ISDA). (2013a). *OTC Derivatives Market Analysis Year-End 2012*. https://www.isda.org/a/FeiDE/isda-year-end-2012-market-analysis-final.pdf (Accessed 5 Feb. 2019).

International Swaps and Derivatives Association (ISDA). (2014). *Size and Uses of the Non-Cleared Derivatives Market*. https://www.isda.org/a/zeiDE/final-size-and-uses-of-the-non-cleared-derivatves-market.pdf (Accessed 5 Feb. 2019).

International Swaps and Derivatives Association (ISDA). (2016). *ISDA Research Note: Derivatives Market Analysis: Interest Rate Derivatives*. https://www.isda.org/a/4SiDE/otc-derivatives-market-analysis-dec-2016-v3.pdf (Accessed 5 Feb. 2019).

Jackson, J. and Mark, J. M. (2007). *Comparing the Pre-settlement Risk Implications of Alternative Clearing Arrangements*. Bank of England Working Paper No. 321.

Krahnen, J. P. and Pelizzon, L. (2016). *Predatory Margins and the Regulation and Supervision of Central Counterparty Clearing Houses (CCPs)*. SAFE White Paper No. 41.

Kroszner, R. (1999). Can the Financial Markets Privately Regulate Risk? The Development of Derivatives Clearinghouses and Recent Over-the-Counter Innovations, *Journal of Money, Credit and Banking*, 31, 596–618.

Kroszner, R. (2006). Central Counterparty Clearing: History, Innovation, and Regulation. *Economic Perspectives*, 30 (4), 37-41.

Kubitza, Ch., Pelizzon, L. and Getmansky, M. (2018). *The pitfalls of central clearing in the presence of systematic risk*. ICIR Working Paper No. 31.

LeBaron, B. (2006). Agent-based Computational Finance. In: K. L. Judd and L. Tesfatsion (eds.), *Handbook of Computational Economics*, Amsterdam: Elsevier/ North Holland, 1187–1233.

Li, D. and Schürhoff, N. (2014). *Dealer Networks*. Swiss Finance Institute Research Paper No. 50.

Madhaven, A. (2000). Market microstructure: A survey. *Journal of Financial Markets*, 3, 205–258.

Madhavan, A., Richardson, M. and Roomans, M. (1997). Why Do Security Prices Change? A Transaction-Level Analysis of NYSE Stocks. *The Review of Financial Studies*, 10 (4), 1035–1064.

Mahnke, V., Overby, M. L. and Özcan S. (2006). Outsourcing Innovative Capabilities for IT- Enabled Services. *Industry and Innovation*, 13 (2), 189–207.

Moser, J. T. (1998). *Contracting Innovations and the Evolution of Clearing and Settlement Methods at Futures Exchanges*. Federal Reserve Bank of Chicago, Working Paper No. 26.

Murphy, D. (2017). I've got you under my skin: large central counterparty financial resources and the incentives they create, *Journal of Financial Market Infrastructures*, 5, 57–74.

Murphy, D., Vasios, M. and Vause, N. (2014). *An investigation into the procyclicality of risk-based initial margin models*. Bank of England Financial Stability Paper No. 29.

The Federal Reserve Bank of New York (2005). *Foreign Exchange Prime Brokerage, Product Overview and Best Practice Recommendations*. Foreign Exchange Committee Annual Report. https://www.newyorkfed.org/medialibrary/ microsites/fxc/files/annualreports/ar2005/fxar05PB.pdf (Accessed 5 Feb. 2019).

Orlikowski, W.J. and Baroudi, J.J. (1991). Studying Information Technology in Organizations: Research Approaches and Assumptions. *Information Systems Research*, 2, 1–28.

Ozsoylev, H. N. and Takayama, S. (2010). Price, trade size, and information revelation in multi-period securities markets. *Journal of Financial Markets*, 13 (1), 49–76.

Pirrong, C. (2009). *The Economics of Clearing in Derivatives Markets: Netting, Asymmetric Information, and the Sharing of Default Risks Through a Central Counterparty*. University of Houston Working Paper.

Pirrong, C. (2011). *The Economics of Central Clearing: Theory and Practice*. ISDA Research Paper, https://www.isda.org/a/yiEDE/isdadiscussion-ccp-pirrong.pdf (Accessed 5 Feb. 2019).

Pirrong, C. (2012). Clearing and Collateral Mandates: A New Liquidity Trap? *Journal of Applied Corporate Finance*, 24, 67–73.

Raykov, R. (2018). Reducing margin procyclicality at central counterparties. *Journal of Financial Market Infrastructures*, 7 (2), 43–59.

Rehlo, A. and Nixon, D. (2013). Central Counterparties: What are They, Why Do They Matter, and How Does the Bank Supervise Them? *Bank of England Quarterly Bulletin*.

Remenyi, D., Williams, B., Money, A. and Swartz, E. (1998). *Doing Research in Business and Management*, London: Sage, ISBN: 9780761959502.

Ripatti, K. (2004). *Central Counterparty Clearing: Constructing a Framework for Evaluation of Risks and Benefits*. Bank of Finland Discussion Paper.

Rogers, E. M. (1995). *Diffusion of Innovations* (4th ed.), New York: Free Press, ISBN: 9780029266717.

Sauerbier, T. (1999). *Theorie und Praxis von Simulationssystemen*, Braunschweig: Vieweg Verlagsgesellschaft, ISBN: 9783528038663.

Schloderer, M. P., Ringle Ch. M., Sarstedt, M. (2009). Einführung in die varianzbasierte Strukturgleichungsmodellierung: Grundlagen, Modellevaluation und Interaktionseffekte am Beispiel von SmartPLS. In: *Theorien und Methoden der Betriebswirtschaft: Handbuch für Wissenschaftler und Studierende*. München: Vahlen, ISBN: 9783800636136.

Serifsoy, B. and Weiß, M. (2007). Settling for efficiency - A framework for the European securities transaction industry. *Journal of Banking & Finance*, 31, 3034–3057.

Sidanius, Ch. and Zikes, F. (2012). *OTC derivatives reform and collateral demand impact*. Bank of England Financial Stability Paper No. 18.

Singh, M. (2010). *Collateral, netting and systemic risk in the OTC derivatives market*. IMF Working Paper No. 99.

Stoll, H. R. (2003). Market Microstructure. In: G. M Constantinides, M. Harris and R. Stulz (eds.) *Handbook of Economics of Finance*, Amsterdam: Elsevier Science, 553–604.

Stulz, R. M. (2009). *Credit Default Swaps and the credit crisis*. NBER Working Paper No. 15384.

Tornatzky, L. G. and Klein, K. J. (1982). Innovation Characteristics and Innovation Adoption-Implementation: A Meta-Analysis of Findings. *IEEE Transactions on Engineering Management*, 29, 28–45.

US Senate. (2010). *Dodd-Frank Wall Street Reform and Consumer Protection Act*, http://www.gpo.gov/fdsys/pkg/PLAW-111publ203/pdf/PLAW-111publ203.pdf (Accessed 5 Feb. 2019).

Wendt, F. (2015). *Central Counterparties: Addressing their Too Important to Fail Nature*. IMF Working Paper No. 21.

Vicente, L. A., Cerezetti, F.V. De Faria, S. R., Iwashita, T., Pereira, O. R. (2015). Managing risk in multi-asset class, multimarket central counterparties: The CORE approach. *Journal of Banking & Finance*, 51, 119-130.

Vo, H. T., Wojciechowski, R. and Weinhardt, Ch. (2005). Straight-through processing and Web Services. In: *Wirtschaftsinformatik 2005, eEconomy, eGovernment, eSociety*, O. Ferstl, *et al.* (eds.), Heidelberg: Physika-Verlag.

Vuillemey, G. and Breton, R. (2014). *Endogenous Derivative Networks*. Banque de France Working Paper No. 483.

Yin, R. K. (2003a). *Case Study Research: Design and Methods*, London: Sage, ISBN: 076192552X.

Yin, R. K. (2003b). *Application of Case Study Research*, Thousand Oaks (CA): Sage, ISBN: 0761925511.

Zeigler, B. (1976). *Theory of modelling and simulation*, New York: John Wiley, ISBN: 0471981524.

Adoption of a Centralized Post-Trade Processing Market Infrastructure after the Credit Crisis

Abstract

The recent credit crisis has heightened the awareness of credit risk among financial markets' regulators and participants. However, despite the public discussion on centralized processing systems for the off-exchange traded (Over-The-Counter, OTC) transactions, no research has been conducted on the factors that could explain their adoption among market participants. With this study, an attempt is made to cover this gap, in parallel opening the space for further scientific investigation on centralized clearing for OTC derivatives. Based on the diffusion of innovation theory, this first empirical study in the OTC clearing area introduces a model aimed at identifying the drivers and inhibitors for the adoption of an IT-enabled innovation in the form of centralized clearing by the financial organizations. The partial least squares structural equation modeling technique was applied to analyze the results of the survey with the heads of clearing/operations in various international financial institutions.

Keywords: diffusion of innovation, IS in financial markets, IT-enabled innovation, clearing, OTC derivatives

1 INTRODUCTION

Encouraged by increasing use of electronic trading systems in recent years, centralized clearing has established itself as a standard risk mitigation mechanism in the on-exchange traded financial markets. Clearing is understood as the process of calculating the mutual obligations of market participants, usually on a net basis, for the exchange of securities and money (Bank for International Settlements 2003). In the recent years of its tremendous growth preceding the credit crisis, the OTC market of privately negotiated derivatives has developed a decentralized, bilateral clearing arrangement characterized by low automation and limited transparency (Bliss and Steigerwald 2006). Regulators and policy makers have recognized the potential benefits of centralized clearing for the Over-the-Counter (OTC) derivatives which were blamed for the recent credit crisis and are pushing to clear the privately negotiated transactions through central clearing facilities.

Central Counterparty (CCP) clearing is a service performed by a central clearinghouse. CCP is an entity that interposes itself between counterparties to the financial contracts, becoming the buyer to every seller and seller to every buyer. In this way, the original counterparties to the trade are not exposed to counterparty credit risk of the other party (risk of loss if the counterparty to the trade defaults) but to that of the CCP. Moreover, as the CCP stands between the trading counterparties, multilateral position offsetting is possible (Cecchetti, Gyntelberg and Hollanders 2009).

Central counterparties are structured to manage and mitigate the credit risk of counterparties during the lifetime of the contract (Ripatti 2004). The CCP calculates the change in the value of the positions of its members on a regular basis to determine the collateral the members have to post (margin requirement).

A clearinghouse with its increasing informational and calculative capacity requirement strongly relies on the Information and Communication Technology (Millo *et al.* 2005). In this context, pricing and calculation of margin requirements for relatively complex OTC derivatives is particularly challenging.

The primary focus of this study regards the factors affecting adoption of CCP clearing for OTC derivatives as perceived by sell-side market participants. Sell-side encompasses financial institutions (mostly banks) offering trading services to asset managers, hedge funds, etc. (Harris 2003). The notion that CCP clearing process is indeed an IT-enabled innovation in the context of the OTC market is the starting point of this study. Mahnke, Overby and Özcan (2006) define IT-enabled innovation as something that "blends hardware and/or software assets with business capabilities to generate a novel process, product or service." Up until now, most authors have regarded CCP clearing merely as a risk mitigation mechanism. This study sets out to investigate OTC CCP as an IT-enabled innovation, considering this type of post-trade processing system from multiple perspectives.

The study is broken down into four sections: 1) introduction 2) theory and model development 3) methodology employed to empirically validate the model 4) discussion of the research findings and their implications.

2 THEORY AND MODEL DEVELOPMENT

The conceptual background of the presented model creates the diffusion of innovation (DOI) theory with the innovation attributes as factors that facilitate or hinder innovation adoption (Figure 1). In Rogers' theory (Rogers 1995) innovation is defined as "an idea, practice, or object that is perceived as new by an individual or another unit of adoption." According to Rogers' classification, a CCP is considered as preventive innovation, "a new idea that requires action at one point in time to avoid unwanted consequences at some future time" (Rogers 2002). The role of a CCP clearing arrangement is to minimize the losses to its members after a participant's default using a predefined loss-sharing mechanism (Wendt 2006).

Figure 1. Research model.

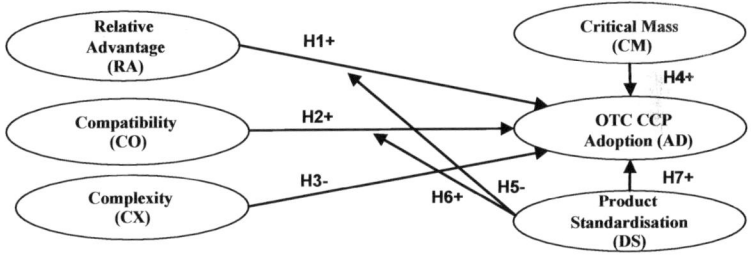

Source: own analysis.

One of the main focuses of DOI are the characteristics of an innovation which may influence its adoption. Whereas in the original work of Rogers five such attributes are identified as to significantly affect the adoption decision, other authors expanded the list by further characteristics (e.g., Benbasat and Moore 1991). Nevertheless, Tornatzky and Klein's (1982) meta-analysis of 75 studies showed that from several identified innovation attributes, only three: relative advantage, compatibility, and complexity had in the most cases the significant relationship to innovation adoption. Therefore, in this study, the set of constructs from DOI related to innovation characteristics will be limited to three.

2.1 Conceptualization of the Innovation Attributes

Relative advantage in the presented model is in agreement with existing DOI literature and refers to the "degree to which an innovation is perceived as being better than the idea it supersedes" (Rogers 2002). In the case of CCP clearing for OTC derivatives, the comparison base is the bilateral clearing process. Relative advantage is conceptualized as multidimensional aggregate second order construct with three sub-constructs referring to different aspects of CCP's potential benefits: processing efficiency, capital efficiency, and counterparty credit risk mitigation.

H1 A higher level of perceived relative advantage (measured by processing-, capital- and risk mitigation efficiency) leads to a stronger adoption of CCP clearing for OTC derivatives.

The conceptualization of compatibility in this study takes into account its operational aspects understood as fit with existing practices, routines and infrastructure rather than individual values. This approach corresponds to the reality of new process implementation within an institution. As the integration of OTC CCP may require substantial changes in the internal processes, operational compatibility may play a significant role in taking adoption decisions.

H2 A higher level of perceived compatibility leads to a stronger adoption of CCP clearing for OTC derivatives.

A productive system is complex if it consists of numerous elements and those elements interact with one another richly (Rivkin 2001). Complexity refers in this study to CCP specific processes spurred by daily margining and their cost (Wendt 2006).

H3 A higher level of perceived complexity leads to a weaker adoption of CCP clearing for OTC derivatives.

2.2 Conceptualization of Context Variables

Although DOI has proven to be a viable framework for examining the adoption of innovation (Dwivedi *et al.* 2008), it is necessary to incorporate additional factors that help in explaining contextual effects.

The critical mass construct is an extension to traditional framework of DOI. Fichmann (1992) recognizes lacking consideration of adopters' interdependencies as a substantial limitation of classic diffusion model. When an innovation is subject to network externalities, like in the case of clearing (Pirrong 2009), achieving the critical mass of market participants who want to adopt the innovation becomes crucial. If critical mass is reached the innovation is likely to be universally adopted; otherwise, it will be probably abandoned (Markus 1987).

H4 Achieving the critical mass of market participant willing to support an implementation of OTC CCP influences positively the adoption of CCP clearing for OTC derivatives.

In the case of CCP, the key moderator is product standardization. According to Chin, Marcolin and Newsted (1996): "The moderator affects the direction and/or strength of the relation between an independent or predictor variable and a dependent or criterion variable." In the case of product standardization, the moderating effect is expected to influence the relation between endogenous variable—CCP adoption—and its predictors, i.e., relative advantage and compatibility.

Due to the recent improvements in automation of the post-trade infrastructure for electronic eligible OTC derivatives, the relative advantage of CCP innovation may be conceived to be higher for highly customized rather than standardized products. Therefore, it is argued that for the standardized products, the influence of the relative advantage on OTC CCP adoption is weakening.

H5 The higher a degree of product standardization, the weaker the influence of relative advantage on adoption of CCP clearing for OTC derivatives.

Conversely, a strengthening effect of product standardization on the relation between compatibility and adoption is hypothesized. Some elements of existing global infrastructure (electronic trade confirmation platforms, trade information warehouse) may still be utilized as complementary to OTC CCP process which may ease the implementation efforts.

H6 The higher a degree of product standardization, the stronger the influence of compatibility on adoption of CCP clearing for OTC derivatives.

The instrument standardization level is defined by three product group features based on existing literature: 1) market commonality of instrument terms and conditions (Bank for International Settlements 2007), 2) existence of a valuation model accepted by majority of market participants (ibidem), 3) level of profit margins on the product group for dealers (Tabb and Iati 2009).

Moreover, the positive direct influence of product standardization on adoption is hypothesized as the standardization is a basic requirement for centralized trade processing within a clearinghouse.

H7 The higher a degree of product standardization, the stronger the adoption of CCP clearing for OTC derivatives (direct influence).

2.3 Adoption Construct

The traditional DOI framework has its limitation. It tends to neglect the realities of implementing technological innovations within organizations, where the decision to adopt the new technology is made at the organization or division level rather than by the individual user. Sullivan (2010) refers to these conditions of non-voluntary adoption as to a "contingent authority adoption decision" meaning that "an authority makes initial decision to adopt and mandates adoption/use of new technology by the targeted users."

The endogenous variable was adjusted to cater for the organizational character of this research. For the purpose of evaluating the construct, both actual usage and intention of the future usage of OTC CCP by organizations have been employed. Adopters may make a binary decision to adopt or reject, or may choose differing levels of CCP usage (Bayer and Melone 1989). Concerning adoption alone, a binary variable is applied based on whether an organization uses/is a member of OTC CCP or not. Moreover, the intensity measure defined as a percentage of eligible trades cleared centrally is used.

3 RESEARCH METHOD

Due to lack of sources on factors affecting adoption of clearing arrangements, the items were developed by the author and tested in interviews with four clearing experts. The objective was to verify the convergent and discriminant validity of the scales by examining how the items were sorted into various construct categories (Davis 1989). The judges were asked to rank how well the items fit the construct definitions and then asked to assign items to specific constructs. Moreover, they were requested to assess the items' wording. Based on the expert assessment of the items' wording and content, in several cases, item formulation was improved, and one item shifted between constructs.

The scale was developed as reflective since it was assumed that for all items a change in the latent variable causes variation in all measures simultaneously; furthermore, all measures in a reflective measurement model are positively intercorrelated (Diamantopoulos, Riefler and Roth 2008).

3.1 Data Collection and Analysis

Survey data was collected using an email questionnaire. To assess and refine the form, the instrument was pre-tested with a mail pilot with 20 heads of clearing/operations from the sell-side institutions. Questions were rearranged to reduce the potential ceiling and floor effect that may induce monotonous responses from participants. Moreover, the scale consists of some items that are worded in opposite directions to alleviate response biases; before statistical data analysis, the reverse-scored items were recoded.

In total, the sample of 256 respondents was approached by phone to participate via email and promised a copy of the results. The sample encompassed the largest international sell-side institutions active in the OTC market and was derived from Capital Market Association database and personal contacts. For the organizational perspective of this research (only) one of the following respondents within each company was invited to take part in the survey: head of (OTC) operations or head of clearing. The respondents who agreed in a phone call to take part in a study received an email questionnaire. Despite the pre-selection, 8 of the contacted persons admitted to having no experience with CCPs and, therefore, were not able to answer the questionnaire. Four weeks after the initial mailing the non-respondents were sent a follow-up email. A resulting sample of 248 respondents was collected, all of which had enough knowledge regarding the specific questions on OTC CCP subject. Overall, 53 completed questionnaires were received, which corresponds to 21% response rate. Addressing the questionnaire to management level professionals with experience in OTC clearing has made it difficult to reach a higher response rate. In most companies only one contact person was available.

However, the sample size fulfilled the requirements imposed by the model specification. Early and late respondent analysis was conducted (Armstrong and Overton 1977). T-test for independent samples of early and late respondents provided evidence that non-response bias does not affect the study results significantly.

The partial least squares (PLS) approach was employed to estimate both the measurement and the structural parameters in the structural equation modeling approach. The PLS is considered to be the most appropriate analysis technique for the current study as it supports exploratory research and places minimum requirements on sample size (Chin 1998).

Missing values represent a challenge if they substantially reduce the number of available cases. According to Schafer and Graham (2002), "if a missing-data problem can be resolved by discarding only a small part of the sample, then the method (case deletion) can be quite effective." In this study, missing data represented only 0.9% of responses and for the reasons outlined above casewise deletion was used to handle them.

The research model (Figure 1) was tested using SmartPLS software Version 2.0 (Ringle, Wende and Will 2005). As this software allows to measure latent multidimensional variables by repeated indicators and maximizes variance explained, it is considered to fit the nature of this study. The indicators presented in Table 1 were used to measure the latent variables. The Lickert type 5 item scale with a neutral middle was employed and adapted for the current context. All indicators and constructs were operationalized using a reflective mode. The dimensions of relative advantage i.e., processing efficiency, counterparty risk mitigation and capital efficiency were aggregated to the second order constructs.

The results will be interpreted in two stages: first, the measurement model and then the structural model. Evaluation of the measurement model is based on an evaluation of the item loadings, the reliability of scales and the constructs' discriminant validity.

Paper 1: Adoption of a Centralized Post-Trade Infrastructure

Table 1. Indicators

Item	Question
AD1	We use CCP clearing for eligible OTC derivatives trades.
AD2	We are members of CCP clearing facility for OTC derivatives.
AD3	What percentage of eligible OTC derivatives trades do you clear centrally by CCP? (1-"100-85%" to 5-"15-0%")
AD4	Given that OTC CCP facility is available I would recommend the executives in our company to use CCP clearing for OTC derivatives we trade.
AD5	I intend to actively support the implementation of CCP facility for OTC derivatives in my organization.
AD6	Assuming that my company can have access to the CCP clearing for OTC derivatives, I think that we should use it.
CX1	The overall collateral requirement of OTC CCP has to be higher than that while clearing on a bilateral basis.
CX2	The margin requirement of OTC CCP is ... in comparison to average collateral paid in the OTC market. (1-"very high" to 5-"very low")
CM1	Our company would support the creation of OTC CCP clearing only if other large market participants support it too.
CM2	Our company would support the creation of OTC CCP clearing only after most active derivatives dealers had expressed their commitment to do it.
CM3	Due to their large trading volume, the dealer support is mandatory to create OTC CCP.
CO1	OTC CCP clearing is not compatible with our work practice (reverse scored).
CO2	I think that it would be easy to integrate CCP process in the internal processes in our company.
CO3	Usage of OTC CCP is consistent with our experience for on-exchange trades.
DS1	The most eligible OTC derivatives products for CCP clearing are a) those for which a broadly accepted valuation models exist.
DS2	The most eligible OTC derivatives products for CCP clearing are b) those with relatively low-profit margins for dealers.
DS3	The most eligible OTC derivatives products for CCP clearing are c) those with relative highly standardized terms and conditions.
DS4	CCP clearing is not applicable for exotic OTC derivatives due to relative low standardization of their terms and conditions.
DS5	Using CCP for clearing standardized OTC trades is more reasonable than for exotic trades.
RC1	CCP clearing will enable us to employ our capital for higher margin products.
RC2	Usage of OTC CCP would enable us to enlarge our business as it frees up credit lines.
RM1	OTC CCP clearing could decrease counterparty credit risk exposure more than other bilateral OTC risk mitigation mechanisms.
RM2	In the case of default of an OTC market participant we trade with a) OTC CCP minimizes the loss for our company.

Item	Question
RM3	In the case of default of an OTC market participant we trade with b) the close out of the position will be faster probably through CCP than bilaterally.
RP1	Compared to bilateral processing, a) CCP clearing for OTC trades has a potential to reduce errors.
RP2	Compared to bilateral processing, b) OTC CCP has a potential to reduce the need for resolving position and valuation discrepancies (portfolio reconciliation).
RP3	Compared to bilateral processing, c) OTC CCP has a potential to improve correctness and completeness of data.

3.2 Measurement Model Evaluation

According to Chin (1998), each factor loading should be greater than 0.707 to share more variance with the component score than with error variance. However, loadings of 0.60 are also acceptable in the early stage of measures development and if additional indicators exist in the block for comparison (Hulland 1999). In this research, only one indicator (CX3) loaded under 0.6 and was dropped. Two items of adoption constructs loaded under 0.707 but still with high and acceptable values of 0.701 and were kept in the model (eliminating these indicators might change the domain of the adoption construct). The individual item loadings for the rest of the constructs exceeded 0.707 (Table 2). In a case of multi-item constructs (which is the case in this study) the composite reliability should be tested (Hulland 1999). All the reflective constructs had a composite reliability above 0.89. Hence, they were above the recommended 0.70 level (Chin, Marcolin and Newsted 1996) suggesting internal consistency. The convergent validity of the reflective constructs was also confirmed, as the average variance extracted (AVE) was above the guideline of 0.5 (Chin 1998). Barclay, Higgins and Thompson (1995) suggest that no manifest variable should load higher on other constructs than on the construct it intends to measure. Results of the cross-loading analysis showed that all items load higher on their respective intended latent variable compared to other latent variables (these results are available upon request). Therefore, discriminant validity at the indicator level is ensured.

Paper 1: Adoption of a Centralized Post-Trade Infrastructure

Table 2. Parameters of the measurement model.

Construct	Indicator	Loading	T-value	AVE	Composite reliability
AD	AD1	0.701	12.026609***	0.733	0.942
	AD2	0.701	12.026609***		
	AD3	0.932	88.455616***		
	AD4	0.938	94.967297***		
	AD5	0.907	57.19231***		
	AD6	0.919	73.818836***		
CX	CX1	0.923	3.638199***	0.712	0.972
	CX2	0.756	3.032265***		
CM	CM1	0.966	70.539003***	0.897	0.963
	CM2	0.963	69.215425***		
	CM3	0.911	34.619182***		
CO	CO1	0.861	21.738284***	0.736	0.893
	CO2	0.824	17.583526***		
	CO3	0.888	53.440538***		
DS	DS1	0.745	3.631701***	0.624	0.892
	DS2	0.747	3.764646***		
	DS3	0.715	3.452306***		
	DS4	0.807	5.76155***		
	DS5	0.919	7.295528***		
RA-CE	RC1	0.972	108.178949***	0.946	0.972
	RC2	0.973	142.851766***		
RA-RM	RM1	0.801	29.288031***	0.863	0.950
	RM2	0.837	102.801703***		
	RM3	0.814	41.115627***		
RA-PE	RP1	0.949	12.554148***	0.853	0.946
	RP2	0.902	10.067567***		
	RP3	0.919	11.46152***		

Significance: *p≤ 0.1; **p ≤ 0.05; *** p≤ 0.01.

3.3 Structural Model Evaluation

Figure 2. Estimated parameters of the structural model.

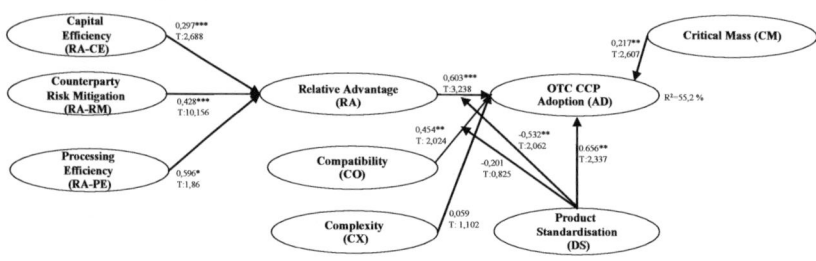

Source: own analysis.

Figure 2 shows all the path coefficients, significance levels and variance explained in the research model. The requirements regarding paths coefficients in the structural model of more than 0.1 (Sellin and Keeves 1994) are fulfilled for all structural relationships except the relationship between complexity and adoption construct. The bootstrap method with 500 samples was used to assess the statistical significance of the path coefficients. The paths between complexity and adoption as well as the moderating effect of product standardization on the relation between compatibility and adoption lack the significance. Further paths were significant. The R-squared value for the dependent variable indicates that the model explained variance accounts for 55.2% which is seen as an average (Chin, Marcolin and Newsted 1996). The Stone-Geisser's Q^2 was calculated using the blindfolding cross-validation method. The test criterion values exceed zero which confirms the predictive relevance of the model (Chin 1998).

The discriminate validity of the model has been confirmed as the diagonal elements (square root of AVE) are significantly higher than off the diagonal values (representing the correlation between constructs) in the corresponding rows and columns (Table 3).

The hypothesis of the influence of complexity on adoption was rejected as well as the moderating effect of product standardization on the relation between compatibility and adoption. The linkages corresponding to rejected hypotheses were dropped, and the PLS model was re-estimated. The analysis revealed that the beta coefficients and t-values of the remaining model were strong and significant. Also the R-squared value changed only slightly (54.5%), which manifests the statistical validity of the remaining linkages.

Table 3. Correlation of the latent variables (square root of AVE on the diagonal).

	AD	CX	DS	RA-PE	RA-RM	RA-CE	CO	CM
AD	0.856							
CX	0.082	0.844						
DS	0.263	-0.025	0.790					
RA-PE	0.251	0.018	0.023	0.923				
RA-RM	0.469	0.046	-0.090	0.198	0.929			
RA-CE	0.594	-0.094	0.212	0.134	0.526	0.973		
CO	0.603	0.029	0.214	0.340	0.444	0.419	0.858	
CM	0.478	0.224	0.234	0.148	0.372	0.256	0.530	0.947

4 DISCUSSION OF RESEARCH FINDINGS AND IMPLICATIONS

Based on DOI framework, this study explored the adoption of Central Counterparty clearing as an innovative IT-enabled system in the OTC market and identified the influential and impeding factors.

The empirical analysis confirmed that perceived relative advantage of the OTC CCP and compatibility with existing post-trade processes contribute substantially to the adoption of centralized clearing for OTC derivatives, whereas complexity does not appear to be an important predictor. All three dimensions of the relative advantage, along with the aggregate second-order construct, exhibit a strong influence on OTC CCP adoption. Critical mass was confirmed as having a strong direct influence on OTC CCP adoption. Product standardization was found to have both strong direct influence on OTC CCP adoption as well as to moderate the relationship between relative advantage and adoption. However, the strengthening effect of the latter on the linkage between compatibility and adoption was not significant.

The findings are in line with the observations on the CCPs' diffusion in the OTC derivatives market. As the market participants had made large investments in the post-trade processing solutions and connections to global infrastructure in the past years, the operational compatibility between current processing of OTC derivatives and CCP service seems essential. An accelerated OTC CCP adoption has been observed after the turmoil caused by the subprime crisis. This may be explained by an increase in perceived relative advantage of OTC CCP, mostly on counterparty credit risk level. The complexity of the OTC CCP was not found in this study to influence the adoption willingness as expected. The explanation may be a perceived relatively low margin requirement within CCP resulting from increasing competition within clearing sector or/and increasing use of collateral in the bilateral post-trade processing. Critical mass was found to influence CCP adoption directly. Due to economies of scale existent in clearing, achieving critical mass of market participants and volumes cleared makes the OTC CCP adoption dependent on the largest derivatives dealers. Product customization impedes automation of post-trade processing; lack of a commonly accepted valuation model makes risk management difficult. Therefore, standardization is a requirement for effective CCP clearing.

This study adds to the base of knowledge concerning clearing arrangements and provides several groups of stakeholders (including clearinghouses and regulatory bodies) with valuable information about the factors influencing adoption of OTC CCPs. Despite the public discussion on CCP clearing for OTC derivatives, no empirical research has been conducted on the factors that might explain CCP adoption among market participants. With this study, an attempt is made to cover this gap, in parallel opening the space for further scientific research on OTC CCPs.

Some limitations of the presented study will be highlighted below to formulate implications for future research. The used sample size of 53 is adequate for an exploratory investigation as in the presented study, but larger sized samples are required for future confirmatory research. The development of a more rigorous model with formative scales (focusing on causes of CCP efficiency) might further improve the variance explained.

This research raises several fields of interest for further investigation. This work is the first that empirically explores the OTC CCP adoption. Up until now, most authors have regarded CCP merely as a risk mitigation mechanism, ignoring the potential impact of this post-trade system on operational risk as well its capital efficiency implications. It is suggested that these factors be considered in future research and their meaning for the effective development of a market infrastructure investigated. As the focus of the study lies at perceptions of sell-side market participants regarding OTC CCP adoption, the public cost/benefit perspective was neglected. However, one possible research direction is to investigate the regulatory pressure as one of the factors influencing OTC CCP adoption if considered in a public context.

REFERENCES

Armstrong, J. S., and Overton, T. S. (1977). Estimating nonresponse bias in mail surveys. *Journal of Marketing Research*, 16, 396–402.

Bayer, J. and Melone, N. (1989). A critique of diffusion theory as a managerial framework for understanding adoption of software engineering innovations. *Journal of Systems and Software*, 9 (2), 161–166.

Barclay, D., Higgins, Ch. and Thompson, R. (1995). The Partial Least Squares (PLS). Approach to Causal Modeling: Personal Computer Adoption and Use as an Illustration. *Technology Studies*, 2 (2), 285–309.

Bank for International Settlements (BIS). (2003). A glossary of terms used in payments and settlement systems. http://www.bis.org/cpmi/glossary_030301.pdf (Accessed 1 Oct. 2008).

Bank for International Settlements. (2007). New developments in clearing and settlement arrangements for OTC derivatives. CPSS Publications, 77, http://www.bis.org/publ/cpss77.htm (Accessed 1 Oct 2009).

Benbasat, I. and Moore, G. C. (1991). Development of an Instrument to Measure the Perceptions of Adopting an Information Technology Innovation. *Information Systems Research*, 2 (3).

Bliss, R. R. and Steigerwald, R.S. (2006). Derivatives clearing and settlement: A comparison of central counterparties and alternative structures. *Economic Perspective*, 30 (4), 22–29.

Cecchetti, S. G., Gyntelberg, J. and Hollanders, M. (2009). Central counterparties for over-the-counter derivatives. Bank for International Settlements. *BIS Quarterly Review*.

Chin, W. W. (1998) The partial least squares approach for structural equation modeling. In: G. A. Marcoulides (ed.), *Methodology for business and management. Modern methods for business research*, 295–336. Mahwah (NJ): Lawrence Erlbaum Associates Publishers.

Chin, W. W., Marcolin, B. L. and Newsted, P. R. (1996). A Partial Least Squares Latent Variable Modeling Approach for Measuring Interaction Effects: Results from a Monte Carlo Simulation Study and Voice Mail Emotion/Adoption Study. *Information Systems Research*, 14 (2).

Davis, F. D. (1989). Perceived usefulness, perceived ease of use, and user acceptance of information technology. *MIS Quarterly*, 13, 319–340.

Diamantopoulos, A., Riefler, P. and Roth, K. (2008). Advancing formative measurement models. *Journal of Business Research*, 61 (12), 1203–1218.

Dwivedi, Y., Williams, M.D., Lal B., Schwarz, A. (2008). Profiling Adoption, Acceptance and Diffusion Research in the Information Systems Discipline. In: *Proceedings of European Conference on Information Systems (ECIS 2008)*, 1204–1215.

Fichman, R. (1992). Information Technology Diffusion: A review of Empirical Research. In: *Proceedings of the International Conference on Information Systems (ICIS 1992)*, 195–206.

Harris, L. (2003) *Trading and Exchanges: Market Microstructure for Practitioners*, New York: Oxford University Press, ISBN: 0195144708.

Hulland, J. S. (1999). Use of Partial Least Squares (PLS) in Strategic Management Research: A Review of Four Recent Studies. *Strategic Management Journal*, 195–204.

Mahnke, V., Overby, M. L. and Özcan, S. (2006). Outsourcing innovative capabilities for IT-enabled services. *Industry and Innovation*, 13, 189–207.

Markus, M. L. (1987). Toward a 'Critical Mass' Theory of Interactive Media: Universal Access, Interdependence and Diffusion. *Communications Research*, 14, 491–511.

Millo, Y., Muniesa, F., Panourgias, N. S., and Scott, S.V. (2005). Organised detachment: Clearinghouse mechanisms in financial markets. *Information and Organization*, 15, 229–246.

Pirrong, C. (2009). *The Economics of Clearing in Derivatives Markets: Netting, Asymmetric Information, and the Sharing of Default Risks Through a Central Counterparty.* University of Houston Working Paper, http://ssrn.com/abstract=1340660 (Accessed 5 Feb. 2010).

Ringle Ch. M., Wende, S. and Will, A. (2005) SmartPLS 2.0 (M3) Beta, http://www.smartpls.de (Accessed 1 Oct. 2009).

Ripatti, K. (2004). *Central Counterparty Clearing: Constructing a Framework for Evaluation of Risks and Benefits.* Bank of Finland Discussion Paper.

Rivkin, J. W. (2001). Reproducing knowledge: replication without imitation at moderate complexity. *Organization Science*, 12, 274–293.

Rogers, E. M. (1995) *Diffusion of Innovations* (4th ed.), New York: Free Press, ISBN: 9780029266717.

Rogers, E. M. (2002). Diffusion of preventive innovations. *Addictive Behaviors*, 27, 989–993.

Schafer, J. and Graham, J. W. (2002). Missing Data: Our View of the State of the Art. *Psychological Methods*, 7.

Sellin, N. and Keeves, J.P. (1994) Path analysis with latent variables. In: T. Husen and T. Neville Postlethwaite (eds.), *International encyclopedia of education* (2nd ed), London: Elsevier Publishers.

Sullivan, Z. Z. (2010) *Adopting Technological Innovations Under Contingent Authority Adoption Decision: An Integration and Extension of Existing Theories*, Stevens Institute of Technology.

Tabb, L. and Iati, R. (2009). *Global Credit Default Swap clearing: Getting the model right.* https://research.tabbgroup.com/report/v07-016-global-credit-default-swap-clearing-getting-model-right (Accessed 1 Oct. 2009).

Tornatzky, L. G., and Klein, K. J. (1982). Innovation Characteristics and Innovation Adoption-Implementation: A Meta-Analysis of Findings. *IEEE Transactions on Engineering Management*, 29, 28–45.

Wendt, F. (2006). *Intraday Margining of Central Counterparties*. Netherlands Central Bank Working Paper.

OTC Clearing Arrangements for Bank Systemic Risk Regulation: A Simulation Approach

Abstract

Based on a simulation approach, this paper compares different over-the-counter (OTC) clearing models regarding their netting efficiency and loss-concentration implications. The results indicate that the mandatory clearing of all standardized OTC derivatives by a Central Counterparty (CCP) propagated by regulators would significantly decrease systemic risk as compared to existing clearing arrangements only if the multilateral netting benefits of the CCP and loss mutualization are fully attained. Therefore, regulators have to ensure that there is a critical mass of asset classes under mandatory clearing, that broad market participation in the CCP is enabled, and that there is an appropriate client asset protection regime.

JEL codes: G01, G14, G18, G28

Keywords: systemic risk, market regulation, derivatives market organization, clearing, over-the-counter derivatives.

1 INTRODUCTION

Although Central Counterparty (CCP) clearing is commonly used for on-exchange traded financial contracts, CCP has so far not been widely applied to over-the-counter (OTC) derivatives. Traditionally, OTC derivatives are completed and processed between counterparties directly involved in the trade, off organized exchanges (Deutsche Boerse Group 2009). With recent financial crisis having a large impact on the bilaterally cleared OTC side, CCP infrastructure performed well. Since then, growing OTC volumes in the clearing business became one of the major growth areas in the financial market receiving major interest from international regulators.

Clearing refers to a process of calculating mutual obligations of market participants, usually on a net basis, for the exchange of securities and money (Bank for International Settlements 2003). Clearing of derivatives differs from clearing of securities. The obligations of the buyer and seller of a security are settled within a few days, whereas the lifetime of a derivative contract may stretch over years. Naturally, the creditworthiness of the parties to a derivative transaction can fluctuate between the time of the contract execution and its maturity. The longer time horizon for transaction completion, the significance of the exposure to creditworthiness of the counterparty, and the greater uncertainty as to the value of the ultimate transfer obligations make clearing of derivative transactions far more complex than clearing of securities.

Among different post-trade arrangements, the CCP clearing can be referred to as "complete clearing." In the sense of Arrow–Debreu's State Preference Theory, this completeness arises from the improved certainty of obtaining a payoff in a given state should that state occur (Debreu 1959, Arrow 1964). As a CCP interposes itself between transaction counterparties, insulating them from each other's default, it improves the overall performance of the contract terms (Cecchetti, Gyntelberg and Hollanders 2009). In this sense, a CCP acting as a guarantor provides "complete" clearing. Under traditional clearing arrangements for OTC transactions, the original counterparties risk that the other party will fail to perform its obligations until the maturity of the contract. On the contrary, if either the buyer or the seller defaults, the CCP is contractually committed to cover the obligations to the nondefaulting direct clearing members (but not the customers of those direct clearing members) (Pirrong 2011).

Policymakers in the EU and the US believe that OTC transactions were partly to blame for the global financial crisis of 2007-2009, particularly because Lehman Brothers was a key player in the OTC derivatives market. When Lehman Brothers defaulted there was no CCP to act as a "circuit breaker" between itself and its counterparties and clients, triggering a "chain reaction" of further defaults in the market (this domino effect is referred to as "systemic risk"). Furthermore, regulators generally lacked reliable information as to the amount of OTC positions held by the financial institutions. This lack of transparency made it difficult for regulators to accurately assess risk. Fundamental weaknesses in managing a key area of systemic risk in the global financial system had been exposed.

In the aftermath of financial crisis, regulators in the EU and US have introduced legislative and regulatory changes aimed at increasing transparency and stability of the financial markets. The Dodd–Frank Bill, an act of the US Congress, was signed into law in July 2010. In Europe, the European Market Infrastructure Regulation (EMIR) sets out to increase stability within derivative markets. Dodd–Frank and EMIR will create three key clearing-related obligations. The first one is a mandatory central clearing of relevant OTC contracts through CCPs. The second obligation from EMIR and Dodd–Frank is a mandatory reporting of opening, modification, and closure of any OTC contract to approved data repositories. The third obligation is mandatory trading of OTC contracts on a regulated exchange or other approved facility. Generally, both legislative regimes anticipate that a limited number of very illiquid, highly bespoke OTC trades will remain unsuitable for CCP clearing, although these will still have to be reported.

This study addresses the first clearing obligation, that is, mandatory central clearing of the standardized OTC derivative contracts through CCPs. The main question considered in this research paper is whether the

CCP model envisioned by upcoming regulation will increase the netting efficiency and reduce the loss concentration after default, as both measures implicitly mitigate systemic risk in the OTC derivatives market. Systemic risk is understood as the likelihood that the failure of one market participant will cause the failure of others. Netting efficiency is defined as the potential of a clearing arrangement to reduce the gross exposure of the market participants resulting from their trading positions. Maximizing netting efficiency reduces replacement-cost risk, which reflects the cost for the market participants if they are forced to replace the contract with a defaulting party at the current market value. Therefore, increasing netting efficiency reduces losses that surviving agents suffer as a result of the default. Moreover, a loss-sharing agreement between the members of a clearing arrangement may prevent the replacement-cost loss from falling disproportionately on a single counterparty, leading to its default. How the replacement-cost losses are distributed among surviving counterparties under a given clearing arrangement is referred to in this paper as "loss concentration."

So far and to the best knowledge of the authors, there has been no research aimed at a comprehensive assessment of the risk implications of diverse clearing arrangements considered in the specific OTC market context. Already existing literature addresses mostly the clearing of on-exchange traded derivatives. This paper aims at covering this research gap by using a simulation of distinct clearing arrangements existing in the OTC market.

The structure of the paper is as follows. The next section provides an overview of relevant literature on clearing arrangements. Section 3 introduces the simulation model. In Section 4, the simulation results are presented. Section 5 discusses the results and ends with a conclusion and outlook.

2 REVIEW OF THE RELEVANT ACADEMIC CONTRIBUTIONS

Prior to the recent credit crisis, only a few authors focused on the subject of clearing arrangements. Moser (1998) and Kroszner (1999) analyze the historical evolution of clearing methods and their implications on the counterparty credit risk (risk of loss in case of counterparty default). Hills et al. (1999) describe different models of loss allocation in the financial markets and focus on the clearinghouses providing CCP services. Bergman et al. (2004) discuss the economic consequences of close-out netting provisions in the derivatives agreements. Close-out netting gives financial institutions the ability to terminate all of their derivative contracts with a counterparty upon its default and reduce the contracts to a single "net" claim. As a result, close-out netting may reduce the counterparty credit risk exposures of derivatives market participants. However, Bergman et al. (2004) as well as Bliss and Kaufmann (2004) suggest that close-out netting may have adverse effects on systemic risk. If the financially troubled firm is not able to meet collateral calls, the counterparty will immediately trigger the close-out process. Thus, close-out could prove a source of systemic risk by making it more difficult to avoid the failure of a distressed but still viable large financial institution.

Despite the above-mentioned descriptive analyses, only a few academic contributions have addressed the quantitative assessment of alternative post-trade arrangements. Jackson and Manning (2007) use a simulation approach to quantify the benefits of moving from bilateral to multilateral clearing arrangements. Bilateral netting means offsetting of mutual obligations between two parties. Multilateral netting involves netting among more than two parties, possibly utilizing a central service. Jackson and Manning show for the case of homogenous agents and for onexchange traded markets that the benefit of multilateral position netting increases with an increase in number of agents but at a decreasing rate. The results speak for increasing benefits of the CCP clearing with broad market participation. Jackson and Manning also show that despite the same netting efficiency, if one asset class is considered, CCP clearing leads to lower systemic risk. Default losses are less concentrated than in the case of other multilateral clearing arrangements. However, Jackson and Manning do not take into account the specifics of the OTC market structure. They consider only complete agent positions matrices, ignoring such eminent features of the OTC markets as market segmentation, high market concentration, or the coexistence of various post-trade arrangements. In this paper, diverse segments of the OTC markets are explicitly modeled and the coexistence of different clearing arrangements has been taken into account.

As the solution to the financial crisis is sought, recent academic publications indicate a growing interest in the subject of OTC clearing arrangements. Duffie and Zhu (2011) show that the netting efficiency of CCP clearing depends on the ratio of all OTC derivatives centrally cleared and the number of CCPs. One global CCP processing all OTC derivatives would provide the most efficient allocation of capital compared to a CCP processing only specific products. Central clearing of one class of derivatives may reduce netting efficiency, leading to higher than expected counterparty exposures and collateral demands. Nevertheless, Duffie and Zhu ignore in their model the implications of a tiered OTC market structure and do not address loss distribution effects under considered clearing arrangements. The analysis of loss concentration under different clearing arrangement is a part of the presented research.

Pirrong (2009) focuses on the redistribution effects of a CCP with a customer access. The CCPs have usually a tiered membership structure due to heterogeneity in credit quality of the market participants (see Jackson and Manning 2007 for evidence that tiered membership structure will emerge if it is costly to tailor the margin requirement to different credit quality of the members). The direct members of a CCP are large trading firms, including banks and brokerages. The CCP guarantee extends only to its direct members; the customers have to clear through clearing members, who guarantee their contracts. If a customer defaults, his clearing member assumes the defaulter's obligation to the CCP. As CCPs insure customers against losses arising from a member default, they effectively transfer the burden of these losses from customers to the financial institutions that are direct members of CCPs. According to Pirrong, these effects can more than offset the benefits of multilateral netting in a CCP. Moreover, if the direct clearing members are systematically more important than the customers, the redistribution of default losses may, in some situations, increase systemic risk.

So far, no academic research has performed a quantitative analysis of the structural dynamics and the distribution effects of different clearing arrangements in the OTC market. The analysis below aims at closing this gap in the research on default risk-mitigation mechanisms and presents a comprehensive picture of the risk implications of distinct post-trade arrangements.

3 SIMULATION MODEL

Computational simulation has become a widely accepted method of economic research as it may provide a deep insight into the highly complex interactions of, for example, financial markets (see LeBaron 2006 for an overview of the agent-based simulation models of financial markets). A computer-based simulation can be regarded as a software implementation of a formal model (Zeigler 1976). Nevertheless, simulation facilitates the examination of a wider set of scenarios than would be possible with a purely analytical approach. This method allows a quantitative comparison of distinct clearing arrangements and examination of some complex interactions, such as the impact of the heterogeneity in the trading behavior on agent's exposure under different post-trade arrangements.

One should, however, keep in mind that simulation methods have their limitations. Their results heavily depend on specific quantitative assumptions made about model's parameters. The simulation environment presented below is based on the matrix representation of the normally distributed trading positions between market participants. The assumption of normality does not apply well to the exposures of many individual derivatives positions. Empirically, the exposure of many individual derivatives may have heavily skewed and fat-tailed market values. This means that the extreme negative values are more likely than would be predicted by the normal distribution (e.g., due to financial market shocks). However, aggregating within a class of all derivatives may result in net exposure of one entity to another that is substantially less skewed given the diversification across underlying names and the effect of aggregating long and short positions. This is especially true for the balanced portfolios of large derivatives dealers. Nondealer portfolios may be less balanced as they may be composed of single positions, which are by definition unhedged long-only or short-only portfolios. However, data limitations prevent us from constructing representative portfolios. Furthermore, in our model the basic matrix of the normally distributed positions is transformed to incomplete position matrix when more complex clearing arrangements are modeled. It reflects the fact that traders are tied to a particular counterparty. In this way, the assumption of the normal distribution of the trading positions is mitigated.

In the model, the agents are heterogeneous and differentiated depending on their trading behavior, that is, sell-side and buy-side agents. Sell-side encompasses financial institutions offering trading services to institutional investors like asset managers, hedge funds, or commercial hedgers and corporate clients referred to as buy side (Harris 2003). To the sell side belong, in particular, the OTC derivatives dealers- the firms that enter into transactions as counterparty on both sides of the market. It is recognized that OTC derivatives dealers are primarily large international banks. The term "sell side" refers to a dealer's elemental function of "selling liquidity" to the buy side. In our model, the buy-side-to-buy-side matrix contains the trading positions between buy-side participants on both sides of the contracts. OTC markets have evolved over time as highly intermediated. If an asset manager or industry company wanted to buy a derivative contract, he would be inclined to execute a trade with a dealer (executing broker), rather than with another buy-side participant, that is, another asset manager. Empirically observed trading volumes between buy-side participants have so far not been significant (Depository Trust and Clearing Corporation 2012; Bank for International Settlements 2013).

Taking into consideration this fact, which simplifies the analysis, our model sets buy-side-to-buy-side-matrix to zero.

The asset class refers in this model to one of the major derivatives classes reported on a regular basis by the Bank for International Settlements (Bank for International Settlements 2013), for example, credit derivatives class, OTC interest rate derivatives, or OTC equity derivatives.

In the first step of our analysis, the matrix of trading positions between market participants in a given asset class is decomposed in four submatrices representing specific market segments such as interdealer trading (sell-side-to-sell-side), dealer-to-customer markets (sell-side-to-buy-side), and customer-to-customer markets (buy-side-to-buy-side). Five different OTC clearing arrangements are modeled by transforming relevant submatrices. The netting results under different clearing arrangements are set in relation to the initial measure and then compared with each other. The analyzed clearing arrangements (close-out netting, prime brokerage give-ups, tear-ups, *exclusive* CCP, and CCP with buy-side participation) will be outlined below.

The close-out netting is the primary means of mitigating credit risks associated with OTC derivatives (International Swaps and Derivatives Association 2010a). Close-out netting provisions in master agreements governing the OTC derivative transactions give financial institutions an ability to terminate all of their derivative contracts (across all asset classes) with a counterparty upon its default and reduce the contracts to a single "net" claim (Bergman *et al.* 2004).

The second analyzed clearing arrangement is a prime brokerage give-up. Prime brokerage is a business branch of sell-side agents that offers services to buy-side customers. A buy-side customer can trade with several sell-side agents (called executing brokers) while still having all trades given up to their chosen prime broker for clearing. Prime brokers provide a centralized clearing facility to the buy-side agent so that customer exposures and collateral requirements are netted across all trades handled by the chosen prime broker.

The portfolio compression service (tear-ups) is based on a multilateral termination of positions. Since 2003, tear-ups have contributed to an estimated 30% reduction in the interest rate swap market (International Swaps and Derivatives Association 2012), and even a larger part of the credit default swap market has been terminated (Trioptima 2012).

Tear-ups net off bought and sold positions among the participants while maintaining overall market risk neutrality across counterparties. In other words, tear-up cycles aim at replacing portfolio positions to reduce bilateral gross position exposures without changing the agent's total net exposure.

CCP clearing is based on the multilateral netting of exposures of its members through asset classes. By replacing bilateral agreements between buyers and sellers with contracts between these buyers and sellers and the CCP, the CCP can net out the offsetting transactions. The current market practice is that only the sell-side agents have direct access to CCP, whereas the buy-side customers utilize sell-side (clearing members) to access a CCP. In our initial setup, only sell-side agents participate in the CCP clearing (*exclusive* CCP); further, we keep the tiered CCP membership structure but allow indirect buy-side participation in a CCP.

After the analysis of the netting efficiency under the above-mentioned clearing arrangements, we add to our analysis the following additional dimensions: margin requirement, price changes, and finally the loss concentration. This process allows for an analysis of loss distribution after the agent's default under diverse clearing arrangements.

3.1 Netting-Efficiency Ratio for Distinct Clearing Arrangements

Distinct clearing arrangements are modeled by drawing on the analytical framework introduced by Lewandowska and Mack (2010). The model is based on the matrices of net bilateral trading positions between agents. The initial matrix is defined as follows:

$$X_{n \times n \times k} = \left(X_{i,j,l}\right)_{i=1\ldots n; j=1\ldots n; l=1\ldots k}, \tag{1}$$

where $X_{i,j,l}$ is net market value of the bilateral positions between any agent i and any agent j in any asset class l. The matrix $X_{n \times n \times k}$ is negatively

Paper 2: OTC Clearing Arrangements

symmetric against the diagonal with $X_{i,j,l} = -X_{i,j,l}$ for all $i \neq j$ and $X_{i,j,l} = 0$ for all $i = j$. Table 1 shows an example of two initial matrices for three agents in two different asset classes. In the first asset class, the first agent has a net long exposure of 3 to the second agent and the second agent has a net short exposure of 3 to the first agent.

To reflect different market segments with s sell-side agents and b buy-side agents in k asset classes, the matrix $X_{n \times n \times k}$ is decomposed to:

$$X_{n \times n \times k} = \begin{pmatrix} X_{s \times s \times k} & X_{s \times b \times k} \\ X_{b \times s \times k} & X_{b \times b \times k} \end{pmatrix}_{n=s+b} \quad (2)$$

As a result, we get four submatrices in each asset class, one for each market segment: sell-side-to-sell-side, buy-side-to-buy-side, sell-side-to-buy-side, and buy-side-to-sell-side. As mentioned above, in the OTC markets, direct trading between customers alike, that is, two asset managers, is rare. Thus, the buy-side-to-buy-side submatrix is a zero matrix, that is, $X_{b \times b \times k} = 0_{b \times b \times k}$. Due to symmetry property, the buy-side-to-sell-side submatrix results from a transformation of the respective sell-side-to-buy-side submatrix, that is, $X_{b \times s \times k} = (-1)(X_{s \times b \times k})^T$.

Table 1. An example of initial matrices of the net bilateral trading positions in two different asset classes.

	Asset class 1				Asset class 2		
	Agent 1	Agent 2	Agent 3		Agent 1	Agent 2	Agent 3
Agent 1	0	3	-5	Agent 1	0	-3	5
Agent 2	-3	0	-1	Agent 2	3	0	2
Agent 3	5	1	0	Agent 3	-5	-2	0

Source: own analysis.

The benchmark α, used as a basis of comparison for different clearing arrangements, is the average absolute market value of contract positions per agent in all asset classes in the initial matrix segments (without any clearing arrangement applied). We calculate α for each relevant market segment:

- for the sell-side-to-sell-side market segment:

$$\alpha_{sxs} = \frac{1}{s}\left(\sum_{i=1}^{s}\sum_{\substack{j=1\\j\neq i}}^{s}\sum_{l=1}^{k}(|X_{i,j,l}|)\right) \qquad (3)$$

- for the sell-side-to-buy-side market segment:

$$\alpha_{sxb} = \frac{1}{s}\left(\sum_{i=1}^{s}\sum_{j=s+1}^{s+b}\sum_{l=1}^{k}(|X_{i,j,l}|)\right) \qquad (4)$$

- for the buy-side-to-sell-side market segment:

$$\alpha_{bxs} = \frac{1}{b}\left(\sum_{i=s+1}^{s+b}\sum_{j=1}^{s}\sum_{l=1}^{k}(|X_{i,j,l}|)\right) \qquad (5)$$

An absolute market value of the positions of a given agent in the initial matrix is a sum of the absolute values of each position that an agent holds to all other agents. There is no netting across agents or asset classes. Based on the example shown in Table 1, the first agent has a net exposure of +3 to the second agent and a net exposure of −5 to the third agent, resulting in an overall exposure of the first agent in this asset class of +8. In the second asset class the first agent has a net exposure of −3 to the second agent and a position of +5 to the third agent, resulting in an overall exposure of the first agent in this asset class of 8 and across both considered asset classes of 16.

To compare different clearing arrangements, the average absolute market value of the contracts of an agent in relevant market segments under given post-trade agreement is calculated and set in relation to the relevant benchmark measure. Five major clearing arrangements are analyzed: close-out netting, prime brokerage give-ups, tear-ups, *exclusive* CCP, and CCP with buy-side participation. The netting-efficiency measure φ^β is a ratio of the average agent exposure in the initial matrix α to the absolute market value of net position exposures of an agent under close-out netting:

- for the sell-side-to-sell-side market segment:

$$\phi^\beta_{sxs} = \frac{\alpha_{sxs}}{\frac{1}{s}\left(\sum_{i=1}^{s}\sum_{\substack{j=1\\j\neq i}}^{s}(|\sum_{l=1}^{k} X_{i,j,l}|)\right)}, \qquad (6)$$

- for the sell-side-to-buy-side market segment:

$$\phi_{s\times b}^{\beta} = \frac{\alpha_{sxb}}{\frac{1}{s}\left(\sum_{i=1}^{s}\sum_{j=s+1}^{s+b}\left(\left|\sum_{l=1}^{k}X_{i,j,l}\right|\right)\right)}, \qquad (7)$$

- for the buy-side-to-sell-side market segment:

$$\phi_{b\times s}^{\beta} = \frac{\alpha_{bxs}}{\frac{1}{b}\left(\sum_{i=s+1}^{s+b}\sum_{j=1}^{s}\left(\left|\sum_{l=1}^{k}X_{i,j,l}\right|\right)\right)}. \qquad (8)$$

Under close-out netting, the positions in all asset classes are netted between the pairs of agents. Based on the values from Table 1, the positions between the first agent and the second agent across both asset classes (+3 and −3) will fully offset each other so that for this pair of agents the exposure will be reduced to zero.

The second analyzed clearing arrangement is a prime brokerage give-up. A give-up arrangement allows a buy-side agent j to trade with several sell-side agents other than its prime broker (called executing brokers h) while still having all trades given up to their chosen prime broker i. A prime broker give-up results in the decomposition of the original trade in any asset class l between executing broker h and buy-side *agent j* into two coextensive contracts between buy-side agent j and prime broker i and between prime broker i and executing broker h so that the resulting change in the net contract position of i is $\sum_{j=1}^{n}\Delta X_{i,j,l} = 0$, but the net contract positions of j and h with prime broker i changes so that $-\Delta X_{j,i,l} = \Delta X_{h,i,l}$. As a result, a prime broker plays the role of the middle man (Figure 1).

Figure 1. Decomposition of a trade A in two trades B and C under a prime brokerage agreement (example).

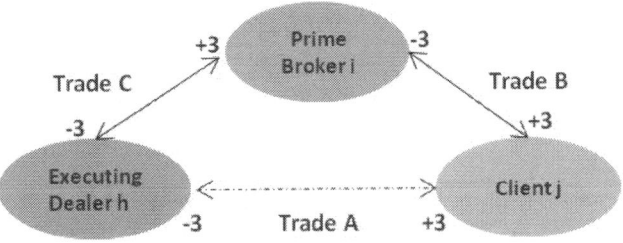

Source: own analysis.

According to the above, the original matrix $X_{n \times n \times k}$ is transformed into the prime brokerage matrix $X'_{n \times n \times k}$. In the first step, the respective buy-side positions are consolidated across all sell-side agents and assigned to particular prime broker. Therefore, we reset the new sell-side-to-buy-side submatrix so that $X'_{s \times b \times k} = 0_{s \times b \times k}$ and then consolidate all initial bilateral positions of each buy-side agent j = s + 1,..., s + b across all his sell-side counterparties to a single sell-side prime broker agent p, p ∈ 1...s, each so that $X'_{p,j,l} = \sum_{i=1}^{s} \sum_{l=1}^{k} X_{i,j,l}$.

Subsequently, we generate the respective buy-side-to-sell-side matrix by applying the symmetry property so that $X'_{b \times s \times k} = (-1) \cdot (X'_{s \times b \times k})^T$ (Figure 2). In the next step, we will modify the sell-side positions in order to reflect the relationship prime broker–executing broker. Thus, we copy the positions from the initial sell-side-to-sell-side submatrix to the new one, that is $X'_{s \times s \times k} = X_{s \times s \times k}$. Then we modify the positions above the diagonal (the matrix $X_{s \times s \times k}$ is negatively symmetric against the diagonal). Marking the prime broker as p, we adjust the new sell-side-to-sell-side submatrix, $X'_{p,i,l} = X'_{p,i,l} - X_{i,s+p,l}$ for $i > p$ and $X'_{p,i,l} = X'_{p,i,l} + X_{i,s+p,l}$ for $i < p$ (Figure 3).

Figure 2. Step one: consolidation of the buy-side positions from the initial matrix to a given prime broker.

	Sell-side agent 1	Sell-side agent 2	Sell-side agent 3	Buy-side agent 1	Buy-side agent 2	Buy-side agent 3		Sell-side agent 1	Sell-side agent 2	Sell-side agent 3	Buy-side agent 1	Buy-side agent 2	Buy-side agent 3
Sell-side agent 1	0	3	-5	1	-2	4	Sell-side agent 1	0	6	-2	5	0	0
Sell-side agent 2	-3	0	-1	3	1	1	Sell-side agent 2	-6	0	-1	0	1	0
Sell-side agent 3	5	1	0	1	2	1	Sell-side agent 3	2	1	0	0	0	4
Buy-side agent 1	-1	-3	-1	0	0	0	Buy-side agent 1	-5	0	0	0	0	0
Buy-side agent 2	2	-1	-2	0	0	0	Buy-side agent 2	0	-1	0	0	0	0
Buy-side agent 3	-4	1	-1	0	0	0	Buy-side agent 3	0	0	-4	0	0	0

Figure 3. Step two: transformation of the initial sell-side-to-sell-side sub-matrix to the final prime brokerage matrix.

	Sell-side agent 1	Sell-side agent 2	Sell-side agent 3	Buy-side agent 1	Buy-side agent 2	Buy-side agent 3		Sell-side agent 1	Sell-side agent 2	Sell-side agent 3	Buy-side agent 1	Buy-side agent 2	Buy-side agent 3
Sell-side agent 1	0	3	-5	1	-2	4	Sell-side agent 1	0	-2+3-2	-2+-5+1+4	5	0	0
Sell-side agent 2	-3	0	-1	3	1	1	Sell-side agent 2	2	0	-4+-1-2-1	0	1	0
Sell-side agent 3	5	1	0	1	2	1	Sell-side agent 3	2	4	0	0	0	4
Buy-side agent 1	-1	-3	-1	0	0	0	Buy-side agent 1	-5	0	0	0	0	0
Buy-side agent 2	2	-1	-2	0	0	0	Buy-side agent 2	0	-1	0	0	0	0
Buy-side agent 3	-4	1	-1	0	0	0	Buy-side agent 3	0	0	-4	0	0	0

In the example, the first sell-side agent is a prime broker of the first buy-side agent, the second sell-side agent is a prime broker of the second buy-side client, and the third sell-side agent is a prime broker of the third buy-side client. As shown in Figure 3, the new exposure of -2 of the first sell-side agent (being a prime broker of the first client) to the second sell-side agent results from a consolidation of the following three positions: original proprietary trading position of 3, taking over the buy-side position of 3 from the second sell-side agent, and losing the exposure to the second buy-side client (his prime broker is now the second sell-side agent).

For prime broker give-ups, the netting-efficiency ratio $\phi^Y_{s \times s}$ in each market segment is calculated as a ratio of the average agent exposure in the initial matrix a to the absolute market value of net position exposures of an agent under prime brokerage agreement:

- for sell-side-to-sell-side market segment:

$$\phi^Y_{s \times s} = \frac{\alpha_{sxs}}{\frac{1}{s}\left(\sum_{i=1}^{s}\sum_{\substack{j=1 \\ j \neq i}}^{s}\left(\left|\sum_{l=1}^{k} x'_{i,j,l}\right|\right)\right)} \qquad (9)$$

- for sell-side-to-buy-side market segment:

$$\phi^Y_{s \times b} = \frac{\alpha_{sxb}}{\frac{1}{s}\left(\sum_{i=1}^{s}\sum_{j=s+1}^{s+b}\left(\left|\sum_{l=1}^{k} x'_{i,j,l}\right|\right)\right)} \qquad (10)$$

- for buy-side-to-sell-side market segment:

$$\phi^Y_{b \times s} = \frac{\alpha_{bxs}}{\frac{1}{b}\left(\sum_{i=s+1}^{s+b}\sum_{j=1}^{s}\left(\left|\sum_{l=1}^{k} x'_{i,j,l}\right|\right)\right)}. \qquad (11)$$

The scope of netting under prime brokerage is the same as in the case of close-out netting. However, the transformed prime brokerage (and not the initial) matrices are subject to the netting agreement.

The next clearing arrangement, the so-called tear-ups, are based on a multilateral termination of trading positions. A simplification of tear-ups is the algorithm introduced by Jackson and Manning (2007). The algorithm starts with creating agents' net positions in a given asset class and ends with generating a new bilateral matrix with the smallest possible number of new trades. More precisely, the algorithm looks up the largest net long position and matches it with the largest net short position; subsequently, it adjusts the net positions accordingly (the difference in absolute values). This process is repeated iteratively until all positions have been reallocated. It is assumed that the contracts are fungible, that is, identical regarding their terms and creditworthiness of the counterparty, and therefore, compressed at original prices.

For example, in the first asset class, the agents from Table 1 have net exposures across all other agents of −2, −4, and +6, respectively. In the first iteration, 6 will be matched with −4, and in the second iteration the remaining 2 with −2. As a result, two new bilateral exposures will be generated under the compression agreement. The second agent will have a long exposure of 4 to the third agent, and the first agent will have a short exposure of 2 to the third agent.

In the current market practice, the buy-side agents are not participating in the large-scale tear-up cycles. If the buy-side was included in compression cycles, the allocation algorithm could result in sell-side-to-buy-side or buy-side-to-buy-side positions. Due to different credit quality of the agents and a specific business model of client clearing, sell-side would not back such a reallocation.

The new sell-side-to-sell-side submatrix after applying the tear-ups per asset class is marked as $X''_{s \times s \times k}$. For each asset class l, $l \in 1 \ldots k$ the submatrix $X_{s \times s \times k}$ is transformed into submatrix $X''_{s \times s \times k}$ by setting $X''_{s \times s \times k} = 0_{s \times s \times k}$ and subsequently filling it in with the new positions created by the tear-up algorithm based on the initial submatrix $X_{s \times s \times k}$. As mentioned above, only sell-side agents are allowed to participate in the tear-up cycles; the average agent exposure will be calculated only for the sell-side-to-sell-side matrix. Other segments remain unaffected.

The netting-efficiency ratio after tear-ups $\phi^{\delta}_{s \times s}$ is calculated as a ratio of the average sell-side agent exposure in the initial matrix $a_{s \times s}$ to the absolute market value of net position exposures of an agent after tear-ups, for the sell-side agents:

$$\phi^{\delta}_{s \times s} = \frac{a_{s \times s}}{\frac{1}{s}\left(\sum_{i=1}^{s}\left(\sum_{l=1}^{k}\left|\sum_{\substack{j=1 \\ j \neq i}}^{s} X''_{i,j,l}\right|\right)\right)}. \qquad (12)$$

Assuming that, for example, after the termination cycle, the given agent has an exposure of 5 across all counterparties in OTC interest rate derivatives and a short position of 2 in credit derivatives, the total absolute exposure of this agent in both asset classes and across all counterparties will be 7.

CCP clearing is based on the multilateral netting of exposures of its members through asset classes. Importantly, only the sell-side agents have direct access to CCP, whereas the buy-side customers utilize sell-side (clearing members) to access a CCP. Therefore, CCP clearing is represented by further submatrices that are filled in with the market values of net positions the CCP has with sell-side agents acting as clearing members ($X_{c \times s \times k}^{m}$) and vice versa ($X_{s \times c \times k}^{m}$). Hence, the expanded matrix is defined as the third instance of the original representation:

$$X_{(n+1)\times(n+1)\times k}^{m} = \begin{pmatrix} X_{s \times s \times k}^{m} & X_{s \times b \times k}^{m} & X_{s \times c \times k}^{m} \\ X_{b \times s \times k}^{m} & X_{b \times b \times k}^{m} & X_{b \times c \times k}^{m} \\ X_{c \times s \times k}^{m} & X_{c \times b \times k}^{m} & X_{c \times c \times k}^{m} \end{pmatrix}_{n=s+b}. \quad (13)$$

The new matrix inherits all properties of the prior matrices and is filled by simply copying the initial submatrices, appropriately: $X_{s \times s \times k}$, $X_{s \times b \times k}$, $X_{b \times s \times k}$, and $X_{b \times b \times k}$ to the proper parts of $X_{(n+1)\times(n+1)\times k}^{m}$. The CCP-to-CCP ($X_{c \times c \times k}^{m}$) and buy-side-to-CCP ($X_{b \times c \times k}^{m}$) and the CCP-to-buy-side ($X_{c \times b \times k}^{m}$) sub-matrices are set to zero as no direct buy-side participation in CCP is allowed.

In the exclusive CCP, all asset classes are subject to CCP clearing arrangements, and only sell-side agents participate in the CCP clearing. The sell-side-to-CCP matrix $X_{s \times c \times k}^{m}$ is populated so that for all sell-side agents, the positions are netted across sell-side counterparties and moved to the the proprietary accounts held with the CCP, i.e., $X_{i,n+1,l}^{m} = \sum_{j=1}^{s} X_{i,j,l}^{m}$ for all $i = 1,\ldots,s$. The matrix $X_{s \times s \times k}^{m}$ is set to zero, and the corresponding CCP-to-sell-side sub-matrix is set to $X_{c \times s \times k}^{m} = (-1) \cdot (X_{s \times c \times k}^{m})^{T}$.

For mandatory CCP clearing of all asset classes in a single *exclusive* CCP, the netting-efficiency ratio $\varphi_{s \times (s+c)}^{K}$ is a ratio of the average exposure of a sell-side agent in the initial sub-matrix $a_{s\times s}$ to the average sell-side agent exposure to a CCP:

$$\phi_{s\times(s+c)}^{\kappa} = \frac{a_{sxs}}{\frac{1}{s}\left(\sum_{i=1}^{s}\left(\left|\sum_{l=1}^{k} x_{i,n+1,l}^{m}\right|\right)\right)}. \tag{14}$$

For example, the net positions of three agents from Table 1 across all counterparties in the first asset class of −2, −4, 6, and in the second asset class of 2, 5, −7, will be moved to a CCP, so that the net absolute exposure of the agents to a CCP would be, respectively, 0, 1, −1.

Maintaining the tiered CCP membership structure but allowing indirect buy-side participation leads to a netting-efficiency ratio of the sell-side agents $\varphi^{\tau}_{s\times(s+c)}$ (assuming s = b).

$$\phi_{s\times(s+c)}^{\tau} = \frac{a_{sxs}}{\frac{1}{s}\left(\sum_{i=1}^{s}\left(\left|\sum_{l=1}^{k} x_{i,n+1,l}^{m}\right|\right)\right) + \frac{1}{b}\left(\sum_{i=s+1}^{s+b}\left(\left|\sum_{j=1}^{s}\sum_{l=1}^{k} x_{i,j,l}'\right|\right)\right)} \tag{15}$$

$\phi_{s\times(s+c)}^{\tau}$ is a ratio of the average exposure of a sell-side agent in the initial matrix $a_{s\times s}$ to the average sell-side agent exposure to a CCP taking into account the average exposure of the sell-side agents to their clients. Allowing indirect buy-side participation in a CCP puts an additional burden on the sell-side agents, which is exposed in the second summand in the denominator in (15). Clearing members for buy-side customers are not allowed to net their agent and proprietary positions but have additional exposure to the CCP in maintaining customer positions (see Pirrong 2011 for different client asset protection regimes and their implications on cost and default loss distribution between clients, clearing members, and CCP). The beneficiaries are the buy-side customers, as they gain additional protection: the segregated positions may be transferred to another clearing member should their clearing member default. The netting-efficiency ratio in the buy-side segment remains the same as after the prime broker give-ups ($\varphi^{\gamma}_{b\times s}$). In the client-clearing model, only the back-to-back transactions are reflected in the CCP (prime broker-CCP, executing broker-CCP).

3.2 Margin Setting and Loss-Concentration Ratio

In the previous section, distinct clearing arrangements were modeled to serve as a basis for the netting-efficiency analysis. In this section, a model for replacement-cost losses is introduced. Therefore, the additional dimensions will be added: margin policy and default probability of the agents. The aim of the analysis is to simulate and compare the loss distribution under different clearing arrangements.

Collateralizing the exposure (also called margining) is a popular way of addressing credit risk arising from derivatives transactions (International Swaps and Derivative Association 2014). Margin is the collateral the agents have to post to mitigate potential loss in case of counterparty default, that is, counterparty credit risk. The per unit collected margin is set in this model based on the optimization approach introduced by Baer, France and Moser (2004). The optimal margin level for asset class k minimizes the expected joint pre-settlement cost (PC) with respect to margin m_i^k ; that is, it minimizes the joint opportunity cost of posting collateral and the expected replacement-cost loss. In the case of OTC derivatives, replacement-cost risk is the main type of credit risk (Bank for International Settlements 1998). Replacement-cost risk arises during the period between opening the contract and its settlement. It reflects the cost for the market participants if they are forced to replace the contract with a defaulting party at the current market value. A condition is set that the agents cannot profit from counterparty default and have to return the excess margin after closing out the position to the defaulting agent, $m_i^k > 0$. The requirement to post collateral imposes a cost on agents as the opportunity cost of margin $c > 0$. Under decentralized clearing arrangements, two agents will set the margin to minimize the expected PC defined below:

$$E(\sum_{i=1}^{2} PC_i) = |X_{1,2,k}| \cdot (c_1 m_1^k + c_2 m_2^k) + |X_{1,2,k}|$$
$$\left(\delta_2^a \int_{m_2^j}^{\infty} (\Delta p^k - m_2^k) f(\Delta p^k) d\Delta p^k + \delta_1^a \int_{m_1^j}^{\infty} (\Delta p^k - m_1^k) f(\Delta p^k) d\Delta p^k \right), \quad (16)$$

where c is the per-unit opportunity cost of collateral, δ_i^a is the ex-ante default probability of the agent i, and Δp^k is the change in contract price of asset k. A CCP owned by its members sets a margin level so as to minimize the joint expected pre-settlement costs of all participants.

An agent's ex-post default probability δ_i^e is defined by a default vector. For each agent i and asset class k, the default vector D_i is a binary variable, taking the value $D_i = 1$ if agent i has suffered a default and taking the value $D_i = 0$ if the agent has not defaulted:

$$D_i \begin{cases} 1 \text{ with probability } \delta_i^e \\ 0 \text{ with probability } 1 - \delta_i^e \end{cases} \quad (17)$$

The second measure for the comparison of distinct clearing arrangements is the loss-concentration ratio, which is defined as a proportion of a maximal replacement-cost loss incurred by a single agent i to total replacement losses suffered by all agents. Replacement-cost loss L_i will only arise when a counterparty default coincides with an adverse price move in excess of the per unit margin collected from that counterparty (Bates and Crain 1999), for the agent i and initial matrix:

$$L_i = \sum_{j=1}^{s} D_j \max\left[0, \left(X_{i,j,l}\Delta p^l - |X_{i,j,l}|m_j^l\right)\right] \quad (18)$$

The calculation of the agent's replacement-cost losses for decentralized clearing arrangements is analogous. For a CCP, the concentration is calculated based on the net position vectors sell-side-CCP, as they are a basis for risk sharing. The replacement-cost losses are calculated for all scenarios where losses occur, and the mean is taken. The following approach is applied to reflect the loss mutualization scheme for a CCP: the losses are shared between CCP members proportional to the agent's total position with the CCP. Under a decentralized clearing arrangement, the loss is borne to the full extent by counterparties involved in a trade.

4 SIMULATION RESULTS

4.1 Parameterization

The first step of the netting-efficiency analysis is to generate 2,500 matrices of net bilateral trading positions in each major asset class k ($k = 1 \ldots 6$), assuming that they are drawn from the normal distribution $N(0,\sqrt{20})$. The number of asset classes corresponds to six major classes reported by the Bank for International Settlements (Bank of International Settlements 2013) on a regular basis. The parameter for the standard deviation of trading positions is essentially arbitrary. However, the precise values have little effect on the results. Distinct clearing arrangements will be compared based on their netting efficiency.

Replacement-cost losses are a function of price changes, margin policy, and agent defaults. Therefore, for the loss distribution analysis, 25,000 different scenarios for price changes in asset k, drawn from a normal distribution $N(0,\sqrt{2})$, and 25,000 default vectors will be generated assuming the *ex post* default probability of 1%. The chosen parameter for default probability reflects that defaults are rare events. The number of position matrices used in this analysis is 25,000 as they have to be appropriately high to obtain stable results. Again, the parameter for the standard deviation of price changes is arbitrary, but it has little impact on the results. A collateral cost of 15 basis points is set, which is assumed to be the difference between secured and unsecured borrowing rates. To reflect the differences between a conservative CCP margin policy and collateralization practice under decentralized clearing arrangements, the CCP margin is calculated based on the *ex ante* probability of default being set to 5% (and to 1% for the other arrangements). The resulting margin level applied by CCP corresponds to a 97% confidence level in a value-at-risk analysis and is higher than the average margin levels observed under decentralized OTC clearing (International Swaps and Derivatives Association 2010b, 2011).

The loss-concentration ratio for each clearing arrangement is calculated, and the results compared across different clearing arrangements.

4.2 Results

Figure 4. Netting efficiency of close-out netting, tear-ups and exclusive CCP (based on the initial matrix) in the sell-side-to-sell-side segment.

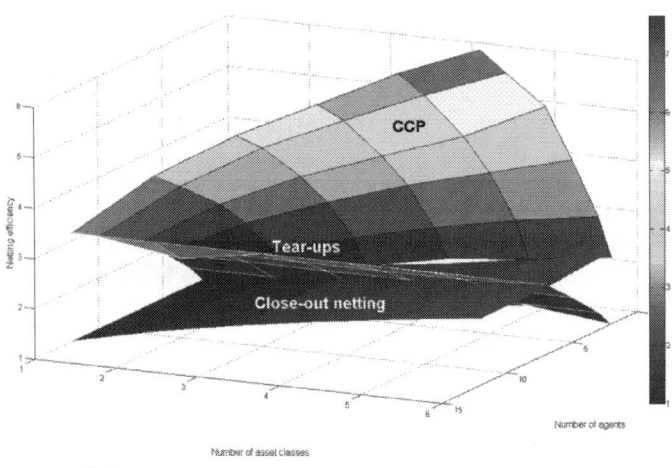

Source: own analysis.

Figure 4 shows the netting efficiency of close-out netting, tear-ups, and *exclusive* CCP. It is evident that in the sell-side-to-sell-side segment, the *exclusive* CCP clearing (with sell-side participation only) maximizes the netting efficiency. The netting-efficiency ratio increases in both the number of participating agents and the asset classes under CCP arrangement but with decreasing marginal increments. The netting efficiency after close-out netting increases in the number of asset classes included but with decreasing marginal increments and is independent of the number of agents participating in this clearing arrangement. The netting efficiency of the tear-ups increases with the number of participating sell-side agents (but with decreasing marginal increments) and is independent of the number of asset classes, as the tear- up cycles are always performed per asset class.

Interestingly, for relatively small number of agents, close-out netting delivers higher netting efficiency than tear-ups. Broad participation of the sell-side agents in the tear-up cycle is a prerequisite for achieving netting-efficiency gains.

Figure 5. Netting efficiency of prime broker give-ups, an exclusive CCP and a CCP with buy-side participation (based on the prime brokerage matrix) in the sell-side-to-sell-side segment.

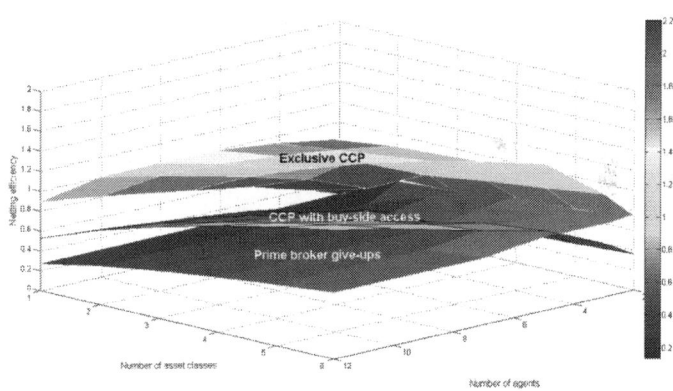

Source: own analysis.

Figure 5 shows a comparison of a netting efficiency of prime broker give-ups and a CCP in the sell-side-to-sell-side market segment. The creation of back-to-back positions under prime brokerage changes the market structure significantly. The resulting high market concentration minimizes the netting-efficiency ratios based on the initial position matrix. However, it becomes evident that the shift of the prime broker positions of the sell-side agents to the CCP results in significant netting-efficiency gains. Allowing buy-side access to a CCP has an adverse effect on the netting efficiency, as the sell-side agents have an additional burden in maintaining segregated client positions.

Figure 6. Netting efficiency of close-out netting, prime broker give-ups and a CCP (based on prime brokerage matrix) in the buy-side-to-sell-side segment.

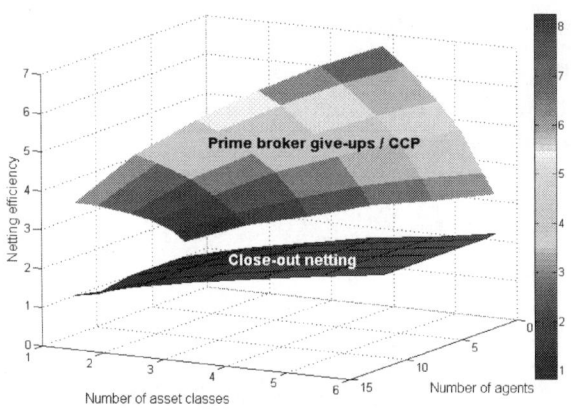

Source: own analysis.

Figure 6 shows the netting efficiency of close-out netting, prime broker give-ups, and a CCP in the buy-side-to-sell-side segment. Prime broker give-ups improve netting efficiency in the buy-side segment, with the netting ratio increasing with the number of sell-side agents participating in such multilateral give-up arrangements and with the scope of asset classes covered under such arrangements but with decreasing marginal increments. The shift of buy-side positions under prime brokerage to a CCP does not provide any efficiency gains. However, the CCP clearing brings other benefits to buy-side clients, as their position exposures are mutually assured by all sell-side agents participating in the CCP. In case of clearing member default, the buy-side agent may transfer its segregated positions to nondefaulting members. However, the segregation of the customer positions places an additional burden on sell-side agents, which decreases the netting efficiency in the sell-side-to-sell-side market segment. As tear-ups are performed for sell-side agents only, the buy-side segment is not affected.

Figure 7 shows the comparison of netting efficiency of close-out netting, prime broker give-ups, and a CCP in the sell-side-to-buy-side segment. Prime broker give-ups improve netting efficiency compared with close-out netting, with the netting ratio increasing with the number of sell-side agents participating in give-up agreements and with the scope of asset classes covered under such arrangements but with decreasing marginal increments. The CCP clearing delivers the same netting-efficiency results as give-ups.

Figure 7. Netting efficiency of close-out netting, prime brokerage give-ups, and a CCP (based on the prime brokerage matrix) in the sell-side-to-buy-side segment.

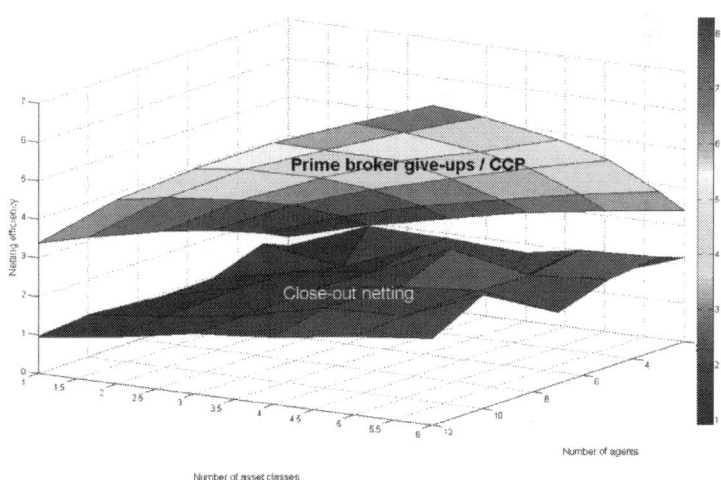

Source: own analysis.

Table 2 summarizes the results of the analysis of loss distribution in asset k under different clearing arrangements. Owing to the loss mutualization scheme under the CCP agreement, the losses are at least concentrated under a CCP and are more widely distributed with the increasing number of participating members. However, prime brokerage give-ups lead to the highest loss concentration, as the back-to-back positions generate high exposures and the loss is borne in full by the affected agents.

Table 2. Loss concentration under different clearing arrangements.

	Number of agents		
	5 agents	7 agents	10 agents
Clearing arrangements			
No netting arrangement	36.84%	52.63%	67.74%
Prime broker give-ups	37.74%	64.73%	87.20%
Tear-ups	23.09%	26.54%	25.10%
CCP	10.81%	8.29%	6.18%

5 CONCLUSION AND OUTLOOK

The presented research paper focuses on the upcoming financial market regulation regarding the mandatory clearing of the standardized OTC derivatives through a CCP. The main question considered in this paper was whether the CCP model envisioned by upcoming regulation would increase the netting efficiency and reduce the loss concentration after default, both implicitly reducing systemic risk in the OTC derivatives market. The results of the presented simulation indicate that the mandatory clearing of the OTC derivatives by a CCP would significantly decrease systemic risk as compared to existing OTC clearing arrangements but only if the multilateral netting benefits of the CCP and loss mutualization are fully attained. To achieve this goal, the policymakers have to ensure that a few prerequisites are fulfilled: first, the critical mass of asset classes should be included in mandatory clearing; second, the critical mass of members should participate in CCPs; and third, the client assets should not be fully excluded from the multilateral netting. Those policy recommendations will be detailed below.

(i) The policymakers and regulators should strive for an optimum of asset classes under mandatory clearing and support other risk mitigation mechanisms for more tailored transactions. It is shown in this paper that excluding some derivatives asset classes from mandatory clearing reduces the netting efficiency and, in the same way, the effectiveness of the financial market reform. This result is consistent with that of Duffie and Zhu (2011) who find that adding a new CCP dedicated to only a limited number of asset classes, for example, only to credit default swaps, actually reduces the netting efficiency of an agent, thereby increasing the average exposure to counterparty default. Against this background, the regulators should avoid any clearing exemptions for any particular asset class (like planned for foreign exchange derivatives). The standardization of the OTC derivatives should be further supported, as it enables the inclusion of additional financial products under CCP clearing. Nevertheless, one should keep in mind the high degree of customization of the OTC instruments and that a part of them will always remain not eligible for CCP clearing (inter alia due to liquidity and price transparency limitations).

(ii) The regulators and policymakers should strive for a broad market participation in the CCP clearing arrangements. The effect of the reduction of average counterparty exposure by introducing a CCP for a particular set of asset classes increases with the number of clearing members. Therefore, the access restrictions in the clearinghouses should be mitigated; in particular, the dealer-dominated CCPs should open to further market participants.

(iii) The regulators should allow also less costly client asset segregation solutions, enabling some extent of netting of the buy-side positions by the CCPs. The protection of the customer positions, propagated by regulators, may lead to increase of systemic risk. The default of Lehman Brothers revealed a need for a buy-side protection mechanism. The segregation of customer positions provides an additional protection to the buy-side clients but has an adverse effect on the sell-side. This segregation leads to netting-efficiency losses for sell-side and ceteris paribus increases systemic risk. The cost equal to the lost netting efficiency will be passed by sell-side market participants to the buy-side clients, which may, in practice, limit the buy-side participation in the CCPs or the OTC market. Pirrong (2009) also concludes that the additional burden, the sell-side has in maintaining customer positions, may have an adverse effect on systemic risk.

The presented simulation provides a more comprehensive picture of the risk implications of distinct OTC post-trade arrangements than existing literature. Jackson and Manning (2007) show that CCP and decentralized arrangements based on multilateral netting provide the same netting efficiency if one asset class is considered. In the presented research, it was shown that, taking into account the OTC market segmentation, for a plausible number of participants and in the multiasset setup, the CCP maximizes the netting efficiency in the OTC market. Moreover, it was shown that a threshold of number of asset classes included in CCP clearing has to be achieved to significantly improve the netting efficiency in the OTC market. Duffie and Zhu (2011) also prove that when moving asset classes from bilateral to central clearing, a critical mass of asset classes is required to achieve superior netting efficiency gains. However, their model does not reflect the risk implication of loss distribution under bilateral and CCP clearing. In this paper it was shown that CCP clearing may significantly decrease the systemic risk in the OTC market as the loss sharing under CCP effectively limits the risk of financial contagion.

The simulation environment developed in this paper aimed at comparing the netting efficiency and loss distribution under distinct clearing arrangements. It was assumed that an agent's market risk and credit risk are independent. Therefore, the default probability was an exogenous variable in relation to position and market price changes. One improvement could be to consider the default probability as an endogenous variable, as in practice, highly concentrated positions and the adverse market movements may significantly increase an agent's probability of default. In addition, different loss-sharing schemes under CCP clearing could be analyzed in future studies. With multiple CCPs, the netting efficiency may decline. However, there is likely to be some consolidation of CCPs over time, and netting agreements between CCPs could be developed. As the links between multiple CCPs (interoperability) could improve the netting efficiency compared to multiple CCPs clearing only some asset classes, it would be worth identifying which netting-efficiency gains could be possible and determining the consolidated impact of interoperable CCPs on systemic risk.

REFERENCES

Arrow, K. J. (1964). The Role of Securities in the Optimal Allocation of Risk-Bearing. *Quarterly Journal of Economics*, 31, 91–6.

Baer, H. L., France, V. G., and Moser, J.T. (2004). Opportunity Cost and Prudentiality: An Analysis of Collateral Decisions in Bilateral and Multilateral Settings." *Research in Finance*, 21, 201–227.

Bank for International Settlements. (1998). *OTC Derivatives: Settlement Procedures and Counterparty Risk Management.* Committee on Payment and Settlement Systems Publications, 27.

Bank for International Settlements. (2003.). *A Glossary of Terms Used in Payments and Settlement Systems.* http://www.bis.org/publ/cpss00b.pdf (Accessed 1 Oct. 2012).

Bank for International Settlements. (2013). OTC Derivatives Statistics at End-June 2013, November 2013. https://www.bis.org/publ/otc_hy1311.htm (Accessed 1 Oct. 2014).

Bates, D. and Craine, R. (1999). Valuing the Futures Market Clearinghouse's Default Exposure during the 1987 Crash. *Journal of Money, Credit and Banking*, 31, 248–272.

Bergman, W. J., Bliss, R., Johnson, Ch. A. and Kaufman G. (2004). *Netting, Financial Contracts, and Banks: The Economic Implications.* FRB of Chicago Working Paper No. 2.

Bliss, R. R and Kaufman G. G. (2005). *Derivatives and Systemic Risk: Netting, Collateral, and Closeout.* FRB of Chicago Working Paper No. 3.

Cecchetti, S. G., Gyntelberg, J. and Hollanders, M. (2009). Central counterparties for over-the-counter derivatives. Bank for International Settlements. *BIS Quarterly Review.*

Paper 2: OTC Clearing Arrangements

Debreu, G. (1959). *Theory of Value: An Axiomatic Analysis of Economic Equilibrium.* New Haven: Yale University Press.

Deutsche Boerse Group. (2009). *The Global Derivatives Market. A Blueprint for Market Safety and Integrity.* Deutsche Börse White Paper, http://deutsche-boerse.com (Accessed 1 Oct. 2012).

DTCC Deriv/SERV LLC. (2012). *Trade Information Warehouse, CDS data.* http://www.dtcc.com/en/market-data/section-1/table-1.aspx (Accessed 1 Oct 2013).

Duffie, D. and Zhu, H. (2011). Does a Central Clearing Counterparty Reduce Counterparty Risk? *Review of Asset Pricing Studies*, 1, 74–95.

Harris, L. (2003). *Trading and Exchanges: Market Microstructure for Practitioners,* New York: Oxford University Press, ISBN: 0195144708.

Hills, B., Rule, D., Parkinson S., and Young, Ch. (1999). Central Counterparty Clearing Houses and Financial Stability. *Financial Stability Review*, 122–134.

International Swaps and Derivatives Association (2010a). *The Importance of Close-Out Netting.* ISDA Research Note, 1.

International Swaps and Derivatives Association (2010b). *Market Review of OTC Derivative Bilateral Collateralization Practices.* http://www.isda.org/c_and_a/pdf/Collateral-Market-Review.pdf (Accessed 1 Oct. 2012).

International Swaps and Derivatives Association (2011). *Margin Survey 2011.* http://www2.isda.org/functional-areas/research/surveys/margin-surveys (Accessed 1 Oct. 2012).

International Swaps and Derivatives Association (2012). *Interest Rate Swaps Compression: A Progress Report.* http://www2.isda.org/functional-areas/research/studies (Accessed 1 Oct. 2012).

International Swaps and Derivatives Association (2014). *Margin Survey 2014.* http://www2.isda.org/functional-areas/research/surveys/margin-surveys (Accessed 1 Oct. 2012).

Jackson, J. and Manning, M. J. (2007). *Comparing the Pre-settlement Risk Implications of Alternative Clearing Arrangements.* Bank of England Working Paper No. 321.

Kroszner, R. (1999). Can the Financial Markets Privately Regulate Risk? The Development of Derivatives Clearinghouses and Recent Over-the-Counter Innovations. *Journal of Money, Credit and Banking*, 31, 596–618.

LeBaron, B. (2006). Agent-based Computational Finance. In: K. L. Judd and L. Tesfatsion (eds.), *Handbook of Computational Economics,* Amsterdam: Elsevier/ North Holland. 1187–1233.

Lewandowska, O. and Mack, B. (2010). Squaring the Circle: Clearing Arrangements in Over-the-Counter Derivatives Markets. Paper presented at the 2nd International Conference: *The Industrial Organization of Securities Markets: Competition, Liquidity and Network Externalities*, June 28-29, Germany, Frankfurt.

Moser, J. T. (1998). *Contracting Innovations and the Evolution of Clearing and Settlement Methods at Futures Exchanges*. Federal Reserve Bank of Chicago Working Paper No. 26.

Pirrong, C. (2009). *The Economics of Clearing in Derivatives Markets: Netting, Asymmetric Information, and the Sharing of Default Risks Through a Central Counterparty*. University of Houston Working Paper, http://ssrn.com/abstract=1340660 (Accessed 5 Feb. 2012).

Pirrong, C. (2011). *The Economics of Central Clearing: Theory and Practice*. ISDA Discussion Paper, https://www.isda.org/a/yiEDE/isdadiscussion-ccp-pirrong.pdf (Accessed 1 Oct. 2012).

TriOptima (2012). *www.trioptima.com* (Accessed 1 Oct. 2012).

Zeigler, B. (1976). *Theory of modelling and simulation*, New York: John Wiley, ISBN: 0471981524.

Is a Full Scale Straight Through Processing of OTC Derivatives Possible?

Straight Through Processing Potential of a Central Counterparty Clearing Model for Credit Default Swaps: An Exploratory Case.

Abstract

The recent credit crisis revealed the lack of adequate infrastructure for OTC derivatives processing resulting in weakness of operational and counterparty risk management. This research uses a case-based approach to develop an improved understanding of the straight through processing (STP) potential of a Central Counterparty model for OTC derivatives. In an exploratory case study, the Eurex Clearing's service for credit derivatives—Eurex Credit Clear—is analyzed on the background of the traditional transaction processing venues and the established industrial organization. The paper analyses the change in the STP level caused by the introduction of a clearinghouse, identifies challenges in STP approach implementation and finally makes proposals for future enhancements of the OTC transactions processing infrastructure.

Keywords: IT-enabled innovation, electronic market innovation, financial market infrastructure, post-trade processing, CCP, clearing, OTC derivatives

1 INTRODUCTION

Clearing is understood as "the process of calculating the mutual obligations of market participants, usually on a net basis, for the exchange of securities and money" (Bank for International Settlements 2003).

Over-The-Counter (OTC) derivatives trading, clearing and settlement have historically evolved as bilateral processes, characterized by low level of automation and prone to error as it is to a large extent based on mail, faxes or phone communications between the involved parties.

For several years, the major OTC derivatives market participants grouped in the International Swaps and Derivatives Association (ISDA) have committed themselves to standardize and improve the operational efficiency of the privately negotiated derivatives industry (Federal Reserve Bank 2009). As the recent market turmoil revealed the absence of adequate trade processing infrastructure and the resulting weakness of operational and counterparty risk management, the regulators on both sides of the Atlantic undertook efforts to strengthen the financial market backbone. In Europe, the European Commission envisaged in the communication from October 2009 that the future policy actions will mandate Central Counterparty (CCP) clearing for all standardized contracts (European Commission 2009).

Central Counterparty clearing is a service performed by a clearinghouse. The Central Counterparty (CCP) clearing model has demonstrated itself to be effective for the on-exchange traded derivatives market and is believed to serve as a solution to improve operational efficiency in the OTC derivatives market. A CCP interposes itself between original counterparties to the trade, becoming seller to every buyer and buyer to every seller (the so-called novation process). As a result, not only the counterparty credit risk may decrease (the risk of counterparty not fulfilling its payment obligations), but also the information becomes centralized (Cecchetti, Gyntelberg, and Hollanders 2009). Central counterparties are structured to ensure performance of the contractual obligations embedded in the derivatives positions and to manage and mitigate the credit risk of counterparties during the lifetime of the contract (Ripatti 2004). The CCP calculates the change in value of the positions of its members on a regular basis to determine the collateral the members have to post (margin requirement).

Due to the complex nature of the OTC derivatives, in the context of the off-exchange traded markets, CCPs are seen as IT-enabled innovations (Lewandowska 2010). Mahnke, Overby and Özcan (2006) define an IT-enabled innovation as something that "blends hardware and/or software assets with business capabilities to generate a novel process, product or service." In this context, pricing and calculation of margin requirements for relatively complex OTC derivatives is particularly challenging.

In 2009, under regulatory demands, four clearinghouses had successfully extended their service to OTC credit derivatives. One of them — Eurex Clearing, a clearinghouse of Eurex derivatives exchange — started clearing Credit Default Swaps (CDS) contracts at the end of July 2009.

CDSs are highly standardized privately negotiated transactions giving the protection buyer a right to compensation from a protection seller in case of an occurrence of a credit event on the entity the contract refers to (like failure to pay, bankruptcy, debt restructuring). In exchange, a protection buyer pays a premium (upfront payment) at the contract interception. Due to the recent industry initiatives, the CDS contract terms like coupon payment have been further standardized so that centralized processing became more feasible.

This paper presents a case study of the Eurex Credit Clear`s trade processing model for CDS transactions and focuses on its end-to-end automation potential and interoperability with the established trade processing practice and infrastructure.

The structure of the paper is as follows. First, straight through processing (STP) will be defined and the literature on financial process automation reviewed. Research method and data collection are described in Chapter 3. In Chapter 4, the case study of Eurex Credit Clear on the background of existing OTC derivatives trade processing infrastructure is presented. Chapter 5 presents the case findings. Finally, Chapter 6 discusses research contribution and limitations.

2 STRAIGHT THROUGH PROCESSING DEFINITION AND LITERATURE OVERVIEW

Hee, Chen and Huang (2003) define straight through processing as "an end-to-end automation of security trading process from order to settlement." It involves a seamless, automated electronic transfer of trade information to all parties in as close to real time as possible. STP involves the workflow from trade execution to settlement without manual intervention. According to Chen et al. (2004) the aims of STP are:

- no need for re-keying once the transaction has entered the workflow,
- automatic linkages and paperless processing from front-end to back-end, regardless of parties involved or their geographic location,
- workflow automation to facilitate transaction monitoring and exception alerts,
- manual intervention or data processing only on an exceptional basis.

Chen et al. (2004) underline that STP may be implemented on several levels: intra-organization, industry-wide, or globally (covering worldwide boundaries). The intra-organizational context of STP is covered in the literature under the Enterprise Application Integration approach (EAI) (Linthicum 2000; Ruh, Maginnis and Brown 2001). Enterprise Application Integration seeks for methods and tools enabling to connect application and share data within a company. Weitzel and Martin (2003) describe initiatives aiming at establishing international communication standards with a goal of a global STP for the financial industry. The paper at hand analyses the external i.e., industry-wide straight through processing potential for privately negotiated derivatives. External STP addresses a challenge to connect seamlessly external partners involved in a financial process: trading platforms, clearinghouses, confirmation platforms and other information providers. In the literature, external STP is discussed in the context of Business-to-Business Integration (B2Bi) (Samtani and Sadhwani 2002).

The advantages of seamless, automated trade processing are diverse. STP may reduce operational risk, enhancing control and minimizing transaction costs, all of which may deliver added value to the client and ensure a competitive advantage for a company. As increasing commoditization of financial products decreases profit margins. Maintaining the profit level will depend on cost reduction which can be achieved by increasing the STP rate. Soaring trading volumes and regulatory pressure are further drivers for STP solutions in the financial markets (Khanna 2007).

Samtani and Sadhwani (2002) identify critical success parameters of external STP. Those are: speed (in order to achieve STP, the trade information has to be passed between the buying entity, selling entity, and any other entity involved in the trade processing on a real-time basis at fast speeds), the accuracy of trade information, stability, extensibility, the standardization of business processes and security.

The topic of OTC derivatives processing has not received much of attention of academic researchers yet. Few industry studies deal with the subject of OTC processing automation (McPartland 2008; Ding, Easthope and Farha 2008; McClymont 2007) including the annual ISDA Operations Benchmarking study measuring automation of the trade workflow functions (International Swaps and Derivatives Association 2009). The Bank of International Settlement (2007) analyses new developments in clearing and settlement of OTC derivatives and the recent changes in the post-trade processing infrastructure and clearing practice. Ledrut and Upper (2007) focus on the increasing multilateralism of the existing trade processing solutions. The results suggest that trade processing infrastructure for credit derivatives is the most automated compared to other OTC asset classes. However, none of the studies focuses on the STP potential of a clearinghouse and its position when interlinked to the current infrastructure. This paper aims at closing this gap.

3 RESEARCH METHOD AND DATA COLLECTION

The case study approach was chosen for this research as it enables an exploratory insight into an as yet only marginally investigated area of post-trade processing of OTC derivatives. Eisenhardt (1989) states that "case studies are particularly well suited to new research areas or research areas for which existing theory seems inadequate." Corbitt (2000) advocates the need for interpretative methods in studying Information Systems (IS) issues, especially in inter-organizational electronic business environments. Case studies are regarded as the most common qualitative research method used in the IS domain (Orlikowski and Baroudi 1991). The single case study method is a potentially rich and valuable source of data, suited to exploring relationships between variables in their given context (Benbasat, Goldstein and Mead 1987), and is appropriate where it represents a critical case (Yin 2003). Remenyi et al. (1998) argue that it is essential to use multiple sources of evidence when conducting a single case study as it helps ensure validity through, as Denzin (1984) calls it, data source triangulation.

The data gathering techniques used in this study were semi-structured interviews and document analysis. Semi-structured interviews enhance the overall quality of the data gathered by allowing researchers to clarify questions and responses, and to explore new dimensions. Yin (2003) argues that documentation can be utilized to supplement and verify data from other sources. The subject of the case was chosen as it represents a critical case in relation to improving the STP potential of the OTC derivatives post-trade processing. Data was gathered in the period from October 2008 to October 2009 covering a whole timeframe of the service implementation. The researcher began by reviewing all relevant documentation on the Eurex Credit Clear before designing a case study protocol. Technical (technical system specification) and functional documents (release notes, credit event handling documents), customer presentations, as well as field notes of the researcher were collected in a case study database.

Interviews with the principal members of staff in various roles within the organization/project were conducted. The interviewed persons included the IT and business managers as well as numerous business and IT analysts. Interviews were recorded and transcribed. Information was also obtained from secondary sources from the intranet. The accuracy of all data was verified through subsequent meetings and document exchange via email. Against the background of the regulatory demands to improve the operational efficiency in the OTC markets through the introduction of a clearinghouse, the following research questions have been formulated: 1) How can a clearinghouse improve the operational efficiency and STP potential when applied to the CDSs? 2) How should the market infrastructure model with a clearinghouse be set up to establish the most efficient STP infrastructure?

4 CASE STUDY DESCRIPTION

4.1 Credit Default Swap Processing Workflow

To answer the research questions stipulated above, first, the functions within the CDS processing chain will be presented. Figure 1 shows the main functions involved in the trading, clearing and settlement workflow of a CDS transaction. Functions are defined as groupings of required business functionality. The figure also shows the main relationships between the functions. A growing number of outsourced and in-house systems enable the automation and streamlining of specific functionalities; however, to some extent, the workflow remained manual and based on phone, email or fax communication.

Before trading takes place between two counterparties, they usually sign a master agreement, which is a standardized bilateral framework to enter into derivative transactions, as well as negotiate credit lines with each other. The first steps in the trade workflow — the counterparty search and negotiation — take place directly between counterparties or through an inter-dealer broker. The trades are executed over the phone or electronically. It is estimated that in Europe only 45% of the CDS inter-dealer market is traded on electronic trading platforms corresponding to an even smaller percentage in the USA (Creditex 2010).

Figure 1. The simplified functions within CDS trade processing.

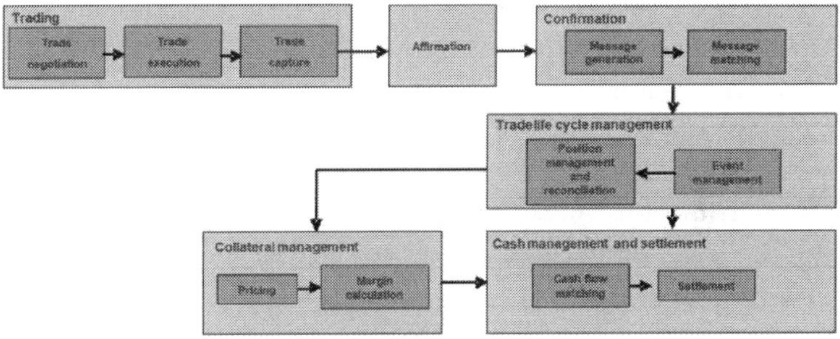

Source: Bank of International Settlements (2007); own analysis.

The post-trading processing phase begins with trade capture, goes through affirmation and confirmation of contract terms, trade life-cycle management and usually ends with settlement. Trade capture is a process of inputting trade information to the firm's internal systems, and according to the STP paradigm ideally the only manual process in a chain. According to ISDA Operations Benchmarking Survey (2009) still 12% of CDS trade records must be amended in front or back office systems because of errors. False record of reference entity or obligation represents the most common error for CDSs, followed by errors in upfront payment recording.

The next step in the CDS workflow is to reconcile the trade details with the counterparty. Most market participants have an affirmation process in place by which they agree on the key economic terms of a trade - in approx. 64% of the cases by electronic message, in approx. 35% over phone (ISDA 2009). As in the affirmation process, only the main details of the trade are matched with a counterparty, only the trade confirmation ensures a legally binding trade copy (as all trade details are reconciled with the counterparty).

Approximately 92% of the CDS transactions are electronically confirmed and 5% are still being confirmed on paper (whereas only 3% are not eligible for electronic processing) (ISDA 2009; Markit 2009). Electronic confirmation of trades established itself as standard in CDS processing. In this context, the past few years have seen many significant industry efforts to automate the confirmation matching processes. More than 90% of CDSs are sent for electronic confirmation one day after a trade date, awaiting a finalization of the confirmation on an average 3.8 days after trade execution (ISDA 2009). The delays in dispatch are caused mostly by nonstandard elements of the contract or high volumes for processing. Timely confirmation is essential for the overall effectiveness of the post-trading process. Confirmation delays weaken the enforceability of a trade and increase the risk that incorrect book-keeping will go undetected for some time, which leads to an incorrect measure of the market or counter-party credit risk (European Central Bank 2009).

A high rate of electronic confirmations corresponds to a high level of usage (approx. 90% of the market) of the Trade Information Warehouse (TIW), an electronic trade data hub performing a position and event management function (DTCC 2010). In TIW each transaction receives a unique identifier and the life time events may be aligned between counterparties to the trade. During the life cycle of an OTC trade, often spanning many years, different trade events occur which change either the contract of the trade or induce additional flows like cash payments or settlements. The counterparties agree that the trade copy in repository represents the legally binding and most current trade version. Trade Information Warehouse supports CDS credit event processing for events like bankruptcy or failure to pay. However, the fully automated process for restructuring events is still under development.

Based on the confirmed records and taken into account all trade life cycle events, TIW generates and sends bilaterally netted payment instructions to a central settlement system (TIW performs the function of cash flow matching and facilitates the payment exchange between market participants).

Currently, all major market participants are connected to TIW and settle coupon payments and payments resulting from credit events through the central settlement system. Moreover, major market participants have committed themselves to settle 90% of settlement volume on electronically matched transactions via TIW and the central settlement system (Federal Reserve Bank 2009). Due to netting (offsetting) of payment obligations central settlement enables significant reductions in the number of settlement instructions decreasing bilateral effort employed to effect those payments. Moreover, central settlement matching may eliminate cash breaks and resulting compensation claims.

TIW has the STP links to various third-party providers. They offer value added services for OTC derivatives like portfolio reconciliation, portfolio compression, and exposure management. OTC derivatives portfolios may contain many offsetting trades. Trade compression services reduce the number of outstanding credit derivative trades and, in consequence, counterparty credit exposures, capital charges, and operational burden. Portfolio reconciliation service is based on verification of the existence of all outstanding trades and comparison of their principal economic terms. Portfolio reconciliation is also a prerequisite for collateral management function as it allows detecting and removing of the discrepancies on a trade level; further exposure matching highlights discrepancies in calculating mark-to-market values for recognized trades. Matched exposures are netted which potentially reduces the collateral requirement. Finally, the collateral has to be exchanged and cash reconciled by both counterparties.

4.2 Eurex Credit Clear Case Study

Eurex's Central Counterparty solution for credit default swaps, Eurex Credit Clear, was launched on July 27, 2009 and started clearing on July 30, 2009. The new clearing service is accessible for participants domiciled in the EU, Switzerland or the US and licensed by a local authority. For Eurex Credit Clear, Eurex Clearing has developed a CDS-specific risk management model; implementation has been supported by deploying modules from Calypso back office processing system. The initial product scope covers European benchmark iTraxx indices and 17 single name CDSs from the utility sector.

Figure 2 presents an STP CDS processing infrastructure with a clearinghouse. In a processing chain with a clearinghouse, the trade execution remains bilateral. Once the trade is confirmed and registered in TIW it is novated to a CCP substituting the original bilateral trades. The clearinghouse guarantees financial performance, especially if the party to the offsetting trade defaults.

Eurex Credit Clear is interlinked with the Trade Information Warehouse and receives from it trade information for positions flagged by the counterparties for clearing. Eurex Credit Clear reconciles with TIW and updates there the positions accepted for clearing (in order to keep both the warehouse and CCP in synchronization), however the "golden copy" of the novated trade (primary record of the trade over and above any records held by the parties to a trade) is held by Eurex Credit Clear. To use the CDS clearing service, the clearing members do not require technical adjustments to the existing Eurex Clearing infrastructure established for the listed derivatives. Clearing members automatically receive the CDS margin requirements and position reports.

The daily CDS evaluation prices are distributed via a third-party price provider infrastructure (Markit). The price provider delivers the raw market prices which are then verified and enriched so that the daily evaluation prices may be derived by Eurex Credit Clear. Settlement price, also called daily evaluation price, is the official daily quotation for each CDS contract as determined by the clearinghouse for the purpose of margining. It is envisaged that in the near future the daily evaluation prices will be based on the direct input from the clearing members. To ensure the price quality, the members can be forced to trade at the provided prices.

Paper 3: Is a Full STP of OTC Derivatives Possible?

Figure 2. Automated CDS processing infrastructure with a CCP.

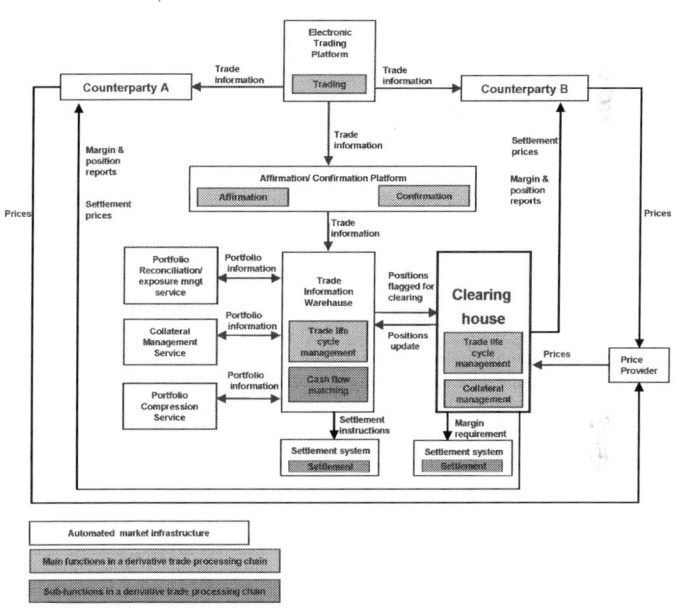

Source: own analysis based on Eurex Credit Clear (2009a, 2009b).

Payments regarding the trade (coupon and credit event payments) are settled centrally via TIW in the settlement system, whereas all other payments (margins) are settled via a separate settlement infrastructure (TARGET2 i.e., Trans-European Automated Real-time Gross Settlement Express Transfer System – a unified technical settlement infrastructure of the central banks of the European Union).

Figure 3 shows in detail the functions carried out by Eurex Credit Clear and its interaction with external systems. The communication channels between external systems are defined based on the topology of IT-enabled inter-firm relationships from Legner (2009).

115

Figure 3. Functions of a clearinghouse and its interaction with the external systems (names of the service providers in brackets).

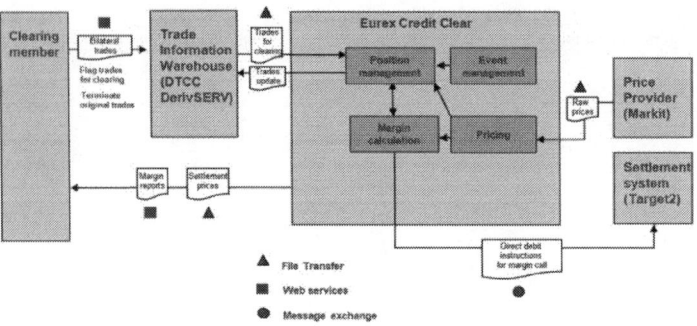

Source: Eurex Credit Clear (2009a); own analysis.

Eurex Credit Clear concentrates the functions of position, event, and collateral management. Positions accepted for clearing are maintained by Eurex Credit Clear and adjusted regarding the post-trade events e.g., succession events. Collateral management encompasses calculation of the margin requirement for the cleared positions. The margin requirement is reported to the clearing members at the end of the day. The pricing of the cleared positions is based on the input from the market data vendor. The calculation of position value is a prerequisite for margin calculation. The reckoned daily evaluation CDS prices for the cleared trades are distributed to the clearing members at the end of the day.

4.3 Weekly Novation Cycle

The straight through processing paradigm assumes processing as close to real time as possible. Currently, the operating CCPs for CDSs have, however, implemented a similar T+5 clearing mode.

Eurex Credit Clear offers a weekly clearing cycle with trades accepted for clearing on Thursday and clearing finality on Friday. Figure 4 shows the Eurex Credit Clear timeline for a weekly clearing cycle. Clearing members continuously submit CDS trades to TIW for bilateral trade confirmation. Trades with trade date up to the previous Friday and confirmed up to and including the previous Tuesday are eligible for the weekly clearing cycle. The timeline to accept the trades for clearing ensures the bilateral upfront payment has been settled bilaterally before Eurex Credit Clear performs clearing. The participants mark trades which they want to clear in TIW.

On Wednesday and Thursday morning, Eurex Credit Clear distributes clearing forecast files for participants to perform a final reconciliation with their internal systems. Participants must then report via email any exclusions of individual trades to Eurex Credit Clear. If no email or other notification is received by this time, Eurex Credit Clear will include all trades into the clearing cycle. Otherwise, Eurex Credit Clear excludes trades as indicated, re-runs and distributes the forecast for approval files (OTC Trade Daily Summary and Netting Forecast reports).

The participants should immediately reconcile and respond to Eurex Credit Clear via email with approval for clearing. Eurex Credit Clear performs clearing and netting and distributes the report with trades accepted for clearing. Concurrently, Eurex Credit Clear sends termination messages to TIW to terminate the original bilateral trades and create new trade messages. If no netting has occurred, a new trade message with Eurex Credit Clear as the counterparty will be sent for all original bilateral trades. For those trades that have been netted, only the new net trade message will be sent. Trades will be accepted for clearing with clearing finality (contingent on the availability of collateral) on the following morning. At approximately 22:00 GMT, Eurex Credit Clear commences the end of day processing. This includes a full portfolio valuation using a given day's final valuation prices, publication of end of day reports with settlement prices and end of day reconciliation. Clearing finality is created with the OTC Trade Event Report.

The above-described novation cycle represents a T+5 processing, as it takes at least five business days from the trade being executed to the trade being cleared.

Paper 3: Is a Full STP of OTC Derivatives Possible?

Figure 4. Weekly novation cycle. T is trade execution day; C is trade confirmation day.

	T+0 –	T+2	T+3	T+4				T+5
	C-4	C-2	C-1	C-0				C+1
	Friday	Tuesday	Wednesday	Thursday				Friday
Business Day	Trade execution	Upfront payment settlement / Mark trades for clearing	Reconcile preliminary clearing forecast files.	Trade confirmation	Reconcile final clearing files.	Clearing approval	Initiate internal rebookings.	Verify margin forecast. / End of day processing	Fund overnight margin
Clearing Member		Transfer files from TIW.	Send preliminary clearing and netting forecast report. Upload trades marked for clearing from DTCC.	Send margin forecast.	Send final netting forecast report.	Mark trades accepted for clearing. Perform netting. Distribute Trade Daily Summary Report.			End of day processing; full portfolio evaluation, publication of the end-of-day reports and end-of-day reconciliation.
Eurex Credit Clear									Process overnight margin. Create clearing finality and distribute OTC Trade Event Report.

118

4.4 Case Study Findings

Two research questions have been investigated in this study. The first relates to how STP of CDS trade processing has been improved with a clearinghouse interlinked to existing infrastructure. An appropriate measure is necessary to assess the impact of the introduction of a clearinghouse on the end-to-end automation of a CDS processing chain.

Figure 5. Change in the external STP volume due to an introduction of a CCP in the CDS market.

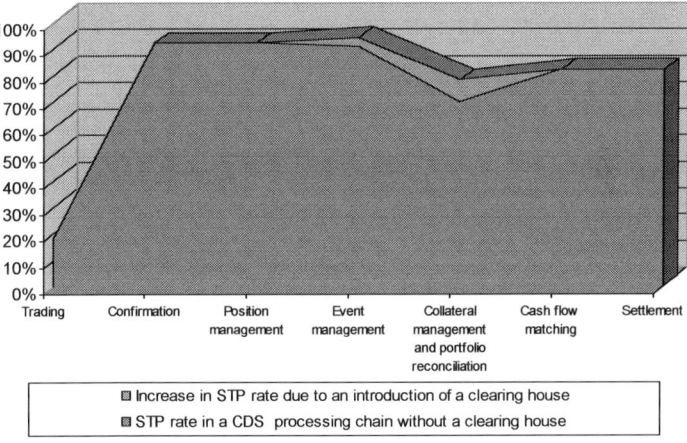

Source: own analysis based on British Banker Association (2006); Creditex (2010); DTCC (2010); Eurex Clearing (2010); Intercontinental Exchange (2010); ISDA (2009); Trioptima (2010).

Previous research has primarily used the adoption of Electronic Data Interchange (EDI) as a surrogate measure for Electronic Integration (EI), understood as the integration of business processes of two or more independent organizations through the exploitation of the capabilities of computer and communication technologies. While researchers have called for the assessment of the degree of EI instead of presence/absence of EDI between two firms, a conceptually grounded measure has still not been developed (Kim and Umanath 2005). In the context of financial markets, the widely used but not thoroughly researched measure is the STP rate. The STP rate is defined as the ratio of the automatically processed transactions (that did not require manual handling or correction) to the whole transactions universe (Smith 2008). The change in the external STP rate due to the introduction of a clearinghouse is shown on the background of already achieved STP levels in Figure 5. In the current workflow system architecture, a clearinghouse for the credit default swaps centralizes the functions of collateral, event, and position management.

However, the two last mentioned business functionalities are already highly automated and incorporated in the end-to-end processing workflow of a TIW.Therefore, there is no substantial increase in the STP rate. The STP potential of a clearinghouse lies in further automation of the collateral management function. With a growing volume processed centrally by the CCPs, the STP rate may be further increased.

As a high non-STP or exception rate of transactions may significantly increase needed headcount, the cost per trade is an implicit STP measure (Best and Weth 2009). Before introduction of clearinghouses for CDS transactions, high share in the trade cost structure had the functions of trade capture and confirmations/affirmations. They constituted over 50% of OTC post-trade processing costs. Collateral management cost-share lies at 14% (Ding, Easthope and Farha 2008). Therefore, a potential reduction of a cost per trade caused by an introduction of a clearinghouse (interlinked to TIW and central settlement system) can be estimated as less than 14% of an absolute trade cost. Therefore, the findings of this study are that an introduction of a clearinghouse service for CDS trades like Eurex Credit Clear has only marginally increased the market-wide STP. The introduction of the CDS clearinghouse has increased the automation level for a previously relatively low automated function of collateral management. However, the automation of the other operational processing steps has not been significantly improved. Still, a workflow critical function like trade confirmation lies beyond the scope of a clearinghouse. On the other hand, a clearinghouse has enabled information centralization. The functions of position, event, and collateral management as well as trade reconciliation have been concentrated allowing for business application integration within one institution. The quantification of the STP potential of a clearinghouse requires further research. It is inappropriate to generalize from a single case, but the analysis of a single case can provide important insights that may be used in the further investigation. The next step is to quantify the incremental change in external STP rate in the OTC derivatives processing chain caused by the introduction of a clearinghouse and the operational cost savings. In a simulation approach, the sample transaction data will be processed by the institutions bound in the clearing and settlement to calculate the STP rate as described above. The focus will be on collateral, position and event management functions automation and integration as found in this study. Moreover, additional critical success parameters of external STP mentioned in chapter 2 like information accuracy, security and stability will be assessed.

The second research question applies to the possible enhancements of the existing CDS trade processing architecture to design an optimal STP infrastructure. To increase the STP potential of a clearinghouse in the CDS processing chain, a few drawbacks of the existing solutions must be removed, as listed below. The main shortcoming of current solutions is that they do not fulfill the real-time processing paradigm as it is based on a weekly novation cycle. As mentioned above, the workflow critical functions like, for example, confirmation lie beyond the scope of a clearinghouse, which contributes to the delay in trade processing. The CDS contract event management, like the credit or succession events processing, remains the major challenge for the full scale automation in the CDS life cycle. An adequate infrastructure for credit event processing enables market participants to quickly identify and assess the counterparties, the affected trade population, and risk positions. It also enables the market to determine a settlement price and carry out efficient cash settlement in an orderly manner. The recent credit event of French electronics producer Thomson engaged back office staff for many weeks (Pengelly 2009). An automated solution with the seamless involvement of a clearinghouse may improve the time and operational burden if such an event occurs.

Figure 6 presents the proposed CDS processing architecture with a clearinghouse. A direct link between CCP and confirmation platform allows simplification of the processing model and enables a real time trade submission to a CCP. The financial industry aims to shrink latency for processing trade records end-to-end with the ultimate goal of T+0. The term T+0, in the context of OTC derivatives, represents an idea of trade confirmation and novation on the day of its execution. To achieve T+0, a CCP must shift from a weekly to a daily novation cycle and develop a way to centrally process the upfront payment.

Figure 6. Optimal trade processing architecture with a clearinghouse.

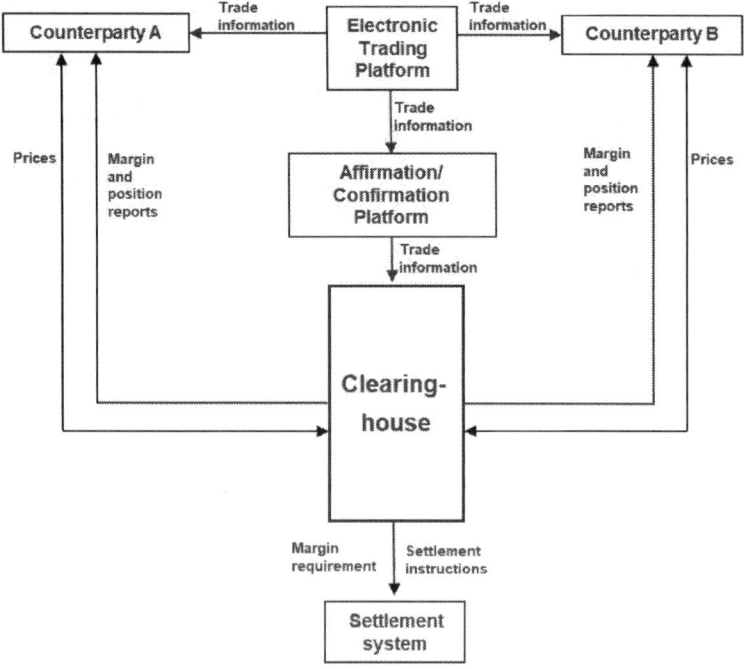

Source: own analysis.

Maintaining the "golden copy" of a trade record in the clearinghouse instead of in TIW already allows for on-line and incremental novation which would fulfill the real-time processing paradigm. As electronic trading platforms for CDS are already in place, their increased use instead of phone trading would further speed up the process of trade capture and allow to avoid errors in trade record details up front. The high degree of standardization of CDS transactions already enables their electronic trading (Mengle 2007). Moreover, the usage of one infrastructure for all payments (margin requirement, coupon, credit event payments) would further simplify and streamline the post-trade process. Currently, only approx. 17% of CDS market volume is processed by CCPs (Vause 2010). However, the major market participants have committed to clear over 90% of eligible CDSs centrally (FED 2009). The implementation of the proposed STP-oriented enhancements would certainly support the fulfillment of the industry commitment.

The future research will focus on the comparison of the STP rate achieved within the existing and proposed models.

5 RESEARCH CONTRIBUTION AND LIMITATIONS

5.1 Research Contribution

The contributions of this research are twofold. First, this study offers an insight into the positioning and influence of the CCP clearing on the OTC derivatives processing and existing infrastructure landscape. So far, there has been no study on the operational aspects of the clearinghouse model in the context of OTC derivatives processing. Contrary to common opinion, it was shown that a clearinghouse with its current architecture might only marginally improve the external STP rate. This hypothesis will be further tested based on the simulation for presented CDS processing chain. Second, the study helps regulators and service providers to identify points in the global trade processing infrastructure which need to be strengthened to further improve the STP rate in off-exchange traded derivatives clearing.

5.2 Limitations and Future Research

In this study, no specific architecture for buy-side customers with indirect access to a clearinghouse is considered. As customer solutions represent a further challenge for automation of derivatives processing, the subject will be treated in a separate work.

Moreover, since this research focused only on a single case exploring the CDS market infrastructure, the generalizability and transferability of the findings to other asset classes are somewhat limited. To gain more comprehensive and detailed understanding of the processing model, also other derivatives classes should be investigated. Therefore, it is suggested that further empirical studies be conducted to reach a better understanding of the processing models for other off-exchange traded derivatives and their STP potential. Nevertheless, the paper at hand defines the functions and market participants' roles in CDS workflow and establishes a framework for the external STP measurement in the OTC derivatives market which may also be useful for other than CDS derivatives studies. A continuation of the framework presented in this paper will be a simulation based on sample transaction data aimed at quantifying the incremental STP rate.

REFERENCES

Bank for International Settlements. (2003). *A Glossary of Terms Used in Payments and Settlement Systems*. http://www.bis.org/publ/cpss00b.pdf (Accessed 1 Oct. 2012).

Bank for International Settlements. (2007). *New developments in clearing and settlement arrangements for OTC derivatives*. CPSS Publication No. 77, http://www.bis.org/publ/cpss77.htm (Accessed 1 Oct. 2009).

Benbasat, I. D. Goldstein, K. and Mead, M. (1987). The Case Research Strategy in Studies of Information Systems. *MIS Quarterly*, 11 (3), 369–385.

Best, E. and Weth, M. (2009) *Geschäftsprozesse optimieren. Der Praxisleitfaden für erfolgreiche Reorganisation*, Wiesbaden: Gabler Verlag/ GWV Fachverlage GmbH, ISBN: 9783834994103.

British Banker Association. (2006). *Credit Derivatives Report*. www.bba.org.uk (Accessed 1 Oct. 2009).

Paper 3: Is a Full STP of OTC Derivatives Possible?

Cecchetti, S. G., Gyntelberg, J. and Hollanders, M. (2009). Central counterparties for over-the-counter derivatives. *Bank for International Settlements Quarterly Review*.

Chen, Y., Hee, J. Huang, W. (2004). STP Technology and Global Financial Market: An Assessment Framework and A Case Study. In: *Advanced Topics of Global Information Management*, G. Hunter and F. Tan (eds.), volume 3, Hershey: Idea Group Publishing.

Corbitt, B. J. (2000). Developing intraorganizational electronic commerce strategy: an ethnographic study. *Journal of Information Technology*, 15 (2), 119–130.

Creditex. (2010). *https://www.theice.com/creditex.jhtml* (Accessed 1 Feb. 2010).

Denzin, N. K. (1984). *The research act*. Englewood Cliffs, NJ: Prentice Hall.

Depository Trust and Clearing Corporation. (DTCC). (2010). *Deriv/SERV Trade Information Warehouse Reports*, www.dtcc.com (Accessed 1 Feb. 2010).

Ding, C., Easthope, D., Farha, R. (2008). *OTC Derivatives Operations: The Path to STP*. Celent Report, https://www.celent.com/insights/514589105 (Accessed 1 Dec. 2009).

Eisenhardt, K. M. (1989). Building Theories From Case Study Research. *Academy of Management Review*, 14, 532–550.

Eurex Clearing. (2010). *Eurex Credit Clear - Cleared Volume*. http://www.eurexclearing.com/markets/creditclear/credit_clear_volume_en.html (Accessed 1 Oct. 2010).

Eurex Credit Clear. (2009a). *Functional Release Notes*. Eurex Clearing internal documentation. Unpublished.

Eurex Credit Clear. (2009b). *Customer Presentation*. Eurex Clearing internal documentation. Unpublished.

European Central Bank. (2009). *OTC derivatives and post-trading infrastructures*. http://www.ecb.int/pub/pdf/other/overthecounterderivatives200909en.pdf (Accessed 1 Dec. 2009).

European Commission. (2009). *Commission Communication from 20.10.2009*. http://ec.europa.eu/internal_market/ financial-markets/derivatives/index_en.htm (Accessed 1 Feb. 2010).

Federal Reserve Bank. (2009). *Summary of Industry Commitments and Commitment Letter*. http://nyfed.org/2hJvHwk (Accessed 1 Oct. 2009).

Hee, J., Chen, Y., and Huang W. (2003). Straight Through Processing Technology in Global Financial Market: Readiness Assessment and Implementation. *Journal of Global Information Management*, 11 (2), 56–66.

Intercontinental Exchange. (2010). *ICE Report Center*. https://www.theice.com (Accessed 1 Feb. 2010).

International Swaps and Derivatives Association (ISDA). (2009). *Operations Benchmarking Survey.* www.isda.org (Accessed 1 Oct. 2009).

Kim, K. K. and Umanath, N. S. (2005). Information transfer in B2B Procurement: An Empirical Analysis and Measurement. *Information & Management*, 42 (6), 813–828.

Khanna, A. (2007). *Straight Through Processing for Financial Services. The Complete Guide*, USA: Elsevier, ISBN: 9780124664708.

Ledrut, E. and Upper, Ch. (2007). Changing post-trading arrangements for OTC derivatives. *BIS Quarterly*.

Legner, Ch. (2009). Understanding the Manifold Forms of B2B Integration - A Transaction Cost Perspective. In: *Proceedings of the 17th European Conference on Information Systems*, 1–13.

Lewandowska O. (2010). Adoption of a Centralised Post-Trade Processing Market Infrastructure after the Credit Crisis. In: M. L. Nelson, M. J. Shaw and T. J. Strader (eds.), *Sustainable e-Business Management. AMCIS 2010. Lecture Notes in Business Information Processing*, Berlin, Heidelberg: Springer.

Linthicum, D. S. (2000). *B2B Application Integration*, Massachusetts: Addison-Wesley.

Mahnke, V., Overby, M. L. and Özcan S. (2006). Outsourcing Innovative Capabilities for IT- Enabled Services. *Industry and Innovation*, 13, 189–207.

Markit. (2009). *Q3 Metrics Trend Report*, www.markit.com (Accessed 1 Feb. 2010).

McClymont, S. (2007). Achieving Operational Efficiency in the OTC Derivatives Market. Paper presented at *ECB Global Operations Managers Conference*, 23rd April, Frankfurt, http://www.ecb.int/events/pdf/conferences/omg_conf/McClymont.pdf (Accessed 1 Feb. 2009)

McPartland, K. (2008). *OTC Derivatives Processing: Blazing a Trail to Automation*, Tabb Group Report. https://www.tabbgroup.com (Accessed 1 Feb. 2009).

Mengle, D. (2007). Credit Derivatives: An Overview. Paper presented at the *Financial Markets Conference, Federal Reserve Bank of Atlanta, May 15, Sea Island, Georgia*.

Orlikowski, W. J., and Baroudi, J.J. (1991). Studying Information Technology in Organizations: Research Approaches and Assumptions. *Information Systems Research*, 2, 1–28.

Pengelly, Mark. (2009). CDS changes considered in the wake of Thomson restructuring. *Risk Magazine*, 26.11.2009.

Remenyi, D., Williams, B., Money, A. and Swartz, E. (1998). *Doing Research in Business and Management*, London: Sage, ISBN: 9780761959502.

Ripatti, K. (2004). *Central Counterparty Clearing: Constructing a Framework for Evaluation of Risks and Benefits.* Bank of Finland Discussion Paper.

Ruh, W. A., Maginnis, F. X. and Brown, W.J. (2001). *Enterprise Application Integration: a Wiley tech brief,* New York: John Wiley and Sons Inc.

Smith, J. (2008). *Cost per trade and STP benchmarking.* McLagan Report, http://www.wallstreetsystems.com (Accessed 1 Oct. 2009).

Samtani G. and Sadhwani D. (2002). Web Services and Straight Through Processing (STP). In *Web Services Business Strategies and Architectures.* Berkeley (CA): Apress.

TriOptima. (2010). *www.trioptima.com* (Accessed 1 Feb. 2010).

Vause, N. (2010). BIS Quarterly Review, December 2010. BIS *Quarterly Review.* https://www.bis.org/publ/qtrpdf/r_qt1012g.pdf (Accessed 30 Dec, 2010).

Weitzel, T. and Martin, S. V. (2003). XML-Standards für ein Straight Through Processing im Wertpapiergeschäft. *Wirtschaftsinformatik,* 45, 409–420.

Yin, R. K. (2003). *Case Study Research: Design and Methods,* London: Sage, ISBN: 076192552X.

The Recent Crises and CCP Risk Practices in the Light of Procyclicality: Empirical Evidence

Abstract

The mandatory central clearing for standardized over-the-counter derivatives introduced by the recent financial market reforms makes central counterparties (CCPs) the most systemically important market participants. However, the theory suggests that, aside from their potential to reduce systemic risk, the CCP risk management practices like margining and collateral haircuts may exacerbate financial cycle fluctuations. Based on almost ten years of empirical data from a leading clearinghouse, we investigate if and to what extent the procyclical effects suggested by the literature can be statistically confirmed. Our results for the period encompassing credit crisis and European sovereign debt crisis do not confirm the hypothesis from theoretical research that CCP risk practices are procyclical. Instead, they reveal only a low average level of conditional correlation between market stress and the margin/haircut requirement in the investigated period. Moreover, increases in the CCP haircuts did not make clearing members (CMs) systematically drop the bonds with increased haircuts from their portfolios. Our results indicate that the effectiveness of the regulatory action in the form of macroprudential haircut add-ons is doubtful as systematic overcollateralization of open positions by clearing members, as observed in our data set, may already act as a countercyclical break.

Keywords: central counterparty (CCP), clearing, procyclicality, systematically important institutions, margins, haircuts.

1 INTRODUCTION

The 2007-2009 financial crisis exposed the weakness in the risk management of the global financial markets. As a result, policymakers have undertaken a number of initiatives intended to increase the stability of the financial system. One of the main reforms is the obligation to clear all standardized off-exchange traded (over-the-counter, or OTC) derivatives via Central Counterparties (CCPs). Traditionally, OTC derivatives, like swaps, were negotiated and processed between the counterparties directly involved in a trade. Now, the central clearing service must be applied to the OTC derivatives processing. The OTC derivatives constitute more than 90% of the global derivatives market. The cleared OTC volumes have been steadily increasing since 2007, so that currently 62% of the volume reported by dealers is cleared centrally (Bank for International Settlements 2016). This clearing obligation is having a major impact on the financial system, as CCPs have become the most systemically important market participants.

On the one hand, CCPs have the potential to decrease systemic risk in OTC markets, when applied comprehensively (Lewandowska 2015). On the other hand, CCPs may themselves concentrate risk or potentially exacerbate the instability of financial economy in times of a downturn.

The aim of this paper is to assess the impact the CCP risk management practices (like margin requirements and haircuts) had, in the investigated timeframe, on procyclicality in the financial markets. In order to achieve this goal, empirical data from a leading European clearinghouse was analyzed in depth. Broadly speaking, procyclicality is understood as mutually reinforcing interactions between the financial and real sectors of the economy that tend to amplify business-cycle fluctuations and cause or exacerbate financial instability (Committee on the Global Financial System 2010).

A CCP interposes itself between counterparties to a trade, becoming the seller to the buyer and the buyer to the seller. Therefore, a CCP has a neutral position regarding the market risk of the cleared position. However, the CCP becomes exposed to this market risk if any of its members has defaulted. As the CCP guarantees the contract performance to non-defaulting party, it has to protect itself against any losses from counterparty default. Hence, CCPs collect collateral (margin) from members for their cleared positions. Generally, and regardless of the risk methodology applied, all margining systems contain backward- and forward-looking elements. The initial margin is a forward-looking element that aims to cover any losses that occurred in the period between member default and liquidation of the respective portfolio. Members have to post the initial margin when the CCP accepts the bilateral trades for clearing. However, the CCP collects variation margin that reflects the daily change in market value of the contracts, i.e., the daily gain or loss of a contract due to market movement. CCPs allow members to cover the initial margin requirement via cash or non-cash collateral, whereas the variation margin can only be covered using cash. The clearinghouse applies haircuts on non-cash collateral or on cash in foreign currency in order to accommodate for fluctuations in market prices and to protect itself against the envisaged loss in the value of the collateral. A haircut is a valuation discount on deposited securities, or on cash in foreign currency. In other words, the deposited collateral is not taken into account at 100% face value.

Haircuts are regularly calibrated to guarantee a high confidence level for extreme market conditions, and may be an effective microprudential instrument (protecting a CCP and its members from loss). However, in the existing research, a hypothesis has been put forward that margins and haircuts imposed by CCPs may have a procyclical impact (Murphy *et al.* 2014; Committee on the Global Financial System 2010) and may adversely affect the stability of the financial system as a whole. However, there is little or no empirical evidence to back it up.

The procyclicality related to margin requirements and haircut may be amplified by the reduction in overall margin requirements and haircuts in phases of growth and low-volatility markets as well as the tendency of margin requirements (and haircuts) to rise in periods of market stress, when volatility is also rising. This could impose an additional liquidity pressure on the already stressed markets, leading to defaults of market participants.

The procyclicality resulting from risk management practices can be an issue for both bilateral markets and cleared ones, as in both cleared and uncleared trading regimes volatility-sensitive risk models are used to calculate margin requirements. As shown in Murphy *et al.* (2014), all commonly used risk models prove some degree of procyclicality. However, as the recent financial market reform makes the clearing of OTC markets via CCPs mandatory, the procyclicality of margins imposed by CCPs is of particular concern. One reason is that CCP margin calls are unilateral: a CCP makes a call, and all its members must meet it; otherwise they are declared to be in default.

Typically, in the CCP risk management systems, the increasing asset prices and increasing market value of the cleared portfolio have no direct influence on the margin requirements posed by the CCP. However, price volatility is a major factor in the margining models. In the phase of economic growth, increasing prices are typically associated with lower price volatility. When a low volatility is factored in the margining models, the CCPs would typically reduce the margin requirement. This leads to the freeing-up of resources of clearing members (CMs) for further investments. Under these circumstances, and if the market participants' risk appetite spurs further expansion, procyclicality may occur. Two additional effects can be observed in the up cycle. First, a CCP typically reacts in the phases of growth by reducing haircuts as the volatility of prices of non-cash collateral decreases. Second, the increasing asset prices have an impact on the value of non-cash collateral posted at CCPs. The value of collateral increases, making it possible for CMs to use the excess collateral for further investment or the collateralization of further transactions. Both effects may incentivize further expansion in the growth phases.

In times of high volatility of asset prices, CCPs will typically increase the margin requirement and haircuts. Clearing members have to post additional collateral for their cleared portfolios. In stressed markets, this may lead to liquidity shocks. The resulting liquidity crunch may cause fire sales (i.e., banks try to sell a large amount of financial assets in a short period of time) which exacerbate the crisis further. Nevertheless, haircuts depend not only on price volatility but also on credit risk of a security issuer and liquidity risk of the posted collateral.

The concerns of the regulators with regard to the procyclical features of the CCP practices regarding margins and haircuts are reflected in the recent financial market reforms introduced via the European Market Infrastructure Regulation (EMIR) and via the Dodd-Frank Act of the US Senate. Apart from the obligation imposed by EMIR to clear all standardized OTC derivatives via a CCP, the regulatory technical standards (RTS) for CCPs detailed in EMIR, as stated in Articles 28 and 41 (EUR-Lex 2012), require CCPs to select a margin and haircut policy so that it limits procyclicality. CCPs should avoid any disruptive step changes in margin requirements and, at the same time, establish a transparent and predictable procedure for adjusting margin requirements in response to changing market conditions.

The aim of this research is to investigate the risk management practice of a leading European CCP in context of its potential procyclical impact. We do not aim to test the CCP margin model based on its mathematical construction or regarding its potential procyclical features. Instead, our aim is to test the hypothesis of procyclicality based on unique empirical data that reflects both portfolio effects and the changes in the cleared volume. The credit crisis and European sovereign debt crisis are our reference periods.

The structure of this paper is as follows. Section 2 gives an overview of the related literature. In Section 3, CCP risk management practice is described in detail. Section 4 describes the available data set, research design and results. Section 5 provides the conclusion, research limitations and outlook.

2 RELATED LITERATURE

The existing theoretical studies propose stylized models on how haircuts and initial margin may contribute to a procyclical expansion of leverage and liquidity during the growth phase and accelerate de-leveraging and drying of liquidity during downturns.

Brunnermeier and Pedersen (2009) show that margins and haircuts have an impact on asset prices via the loss spiral and the margin spiral mechanisms. In the loss spiral, the traders' initial losses lead to funding constrains. As a response, the investors de-leverage their positions by selling assets, which causes a drop in asset prices. As prices move away from fundamentals, margin levels increase, thus worsening the funding conditions for the investors and so on. In the margin spiral, a fall in asset prices induces lenders to increase haircuts and initial margins as a risk management measure. When borrowers face capital constraints and drying liquidity, additional collateral postings may cause fire selling of assets into already falling markets. What is being recommended to the policymakers by the existing theoretical research is, however, unclear, as the explored models are highly simplified and of stylized nature. While the models focus on haircuts, many other lending terms are also relevant in determining the effective supply of leverage to market participants. For example, Ashcraft, Gârleanu, and Pedersen (2010) show that central banks' lending facilities mitigate leverage constraints during the crisis. Thus, while, in the models, credit supply invariably responds to adjustments in collateral haircuts, such effects may be less clear in the presence of other credit terms that are simultaneously adjusting to the dynamically changing situation. This caveat is particularly important to keep in mind when evaluating the implications of policies that target the level of haircuts and initial margins.

In one of the few empirical studies on margin setting by CCPs, Abruzzo and Park (2016) analyze the margining method used by the US clearinghouse of Chicago Mercantile Exchange (CME). They provide evidence that the margin setting of the CME Group is indeed sensitive to volatility, and it has a more procyclical impact in times of higher market volatility than in calm periods (as the CME does not immediately decrease margins when volatility drops). This implies that the most disruptive effects of increased margin can be observed when a shock appears after a long period of low volatility markets, as margins are increased from a lower level. Acharya and Viswanathan (2011) also support this thesis.

Murphy et al. (2014) propose two measures for assessment of the initial margin models regarding their contribution to procyclicality. The "peak-to-trough measure" is a ratio of the maximum initial margin required for a constant portfolio to the minimum margin required over a fixed observation period across a business cycle. The second metric is defined as the largest increase in margin over an n-day period for a constant portfolio over a fixed observation period. This measure captures the amount of extra margin that market participants would need to fund on a short-term basis. Murphy et al. conclude that all of the most common initial margin models are to some extent procyclical, as the margin requirement increases in times of higher volatility of asset prices and, is reduced when the volatility decreasing. The report of the Bank for International Settlements "The role of margin requirements and haircuts in procyclicality" identifies collateral haircuts and margining practices in OTC derivatives as one source of procyclicality in the financial system (Committee on the Global Financial System 2010). This report and other papers recently issued by regulators (European Systemic Risk Board 2015) reflect the consideration that macroprudential haircut and margin instruments should be introduced by CCPs, like minimum constant through-the-cycle margins and haircuts or countercyclical add-ons. A good overview of the regulatory requirements for clearinghouses regarding limiting the procyclicality can be found in Mai (2016).

Brumm et al. (2015) argue that the macroprudential tools aimed at reducing procyclicality should be broadly applied across products to be effective, as their broad application will stop any leakages to nonregulated products.

However, Goodhart et al. (2012) show, based on a simulation approach, that a countercyclical change of macroprudential haircuts results in a minor and ambiguous impact on welfare.

In addition, one should also not forget that the margin method used as a microprudential tool is to protect a CCP from loss in case of member default. Moreover, any macroprudential margin floors and haircut add-ons that lead to over-margining represent an additional cost for CMs, and may have an adverse impact when considered from the macroeconomic perspective.

This research aims to close the gap in the existing academic literature on CCP's margining and haircut practices as well as deliver empirical evidence for a policy recommendation.

3 RISK MANAGEMENT BY CENTRAL COUNTERPARTIES

3.1 Margining Process

Ordinarily, a CCP calls for margin once a day. The calculation of the required amount of collateral is based on the end-of-day security prices. Apart from this regular margin call, a CCP, if necessary, may call for intraday margin (Wendt 2006). Using real-time prices, a CCP calculates the position's value and evaluates the intra-day risk. In case of a margin shortfall, the CCP issues a margin call against the CM. The CM has an option to enter a risk-reducing trade, deliver security collateral (from e.g., a bond market) or provide additional cash (eventually entering the repurchase agreement (repo) market). When none of the above measures is taken within a predefined timeframe the CM is declared to be in default.

When the haircut applied to the price of a certain security increases dramatically, CMs who have pledged that security as collateral face a decline in the value of their portfolio. Given that the exposure to cleared products remains unchanged, the CMs' collateral portfolios might become insufficient to cover the margin requirements of the CCP. A clearing member has several options to adjust its collateral portfolio in the case of rising haircuts on some securities (see Figure 1). First, CMs significantly overfund their collateral account; they can rely on a buffer that is dampening the impact of haircut changes. If a clearing member is in this comfortable position, it can simply leave the structure of its collateral portfolio unchanged. Second, a clearing member could choose to substitute the security, subject to an increase in haircut, and either sell it or use it for repo contracts. Hence, if haircuts increase, we should observe a reduction in quantity (share) of that respective security. Third, the clearing member could supplement its portfolio by adding more securities to meet the increased margin requirements. Finally a CM could provide additional cash as collateral.

Figure 1. The relationship between a CCP margin call/haircut increase and a CM's collateral allocation decisions.

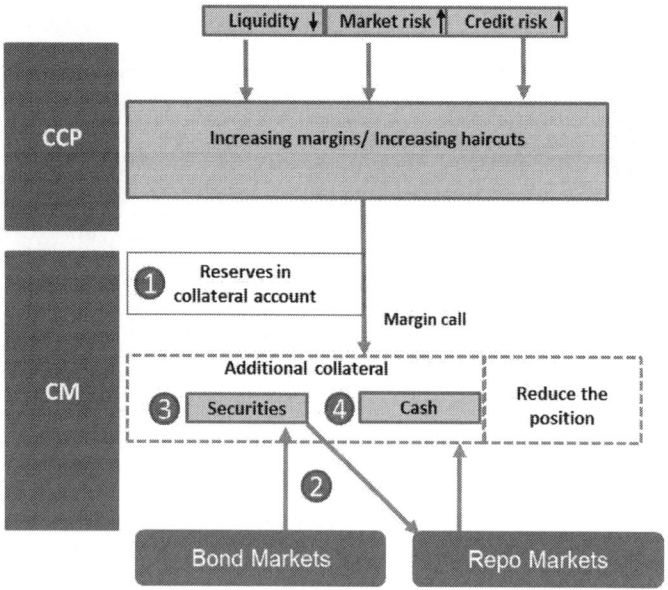

Source: own analysis.

3.2 Collateral Eligibility and Calculation of Haircuts

The assets accepted as collateral by clearinghouses are typically high-quality fixed-income securities (see European Central Bank (2013) for comparison of eligible collateral between clearinghouses). A few clearinghouses also accept equities. The level of the haircut for a given asset is driven mostly by the liquidity of the market for this asset, volatility of its price (market risk) and credit risk of a security issuer. CCPs can use different risk models to calculate haircuts and margin requirements.

4 RESEARCH DESIGN

4.1 Hypotheses

According to the definition of procyclicality, a link between higher margin requirements, diminishing collateral portfolio via higher haircuts and market stress should be empirically observable. Therefore, we hypothesize the following.

H1: total margin requirement (TMR) imposed by CCP and market stress are correlated.

H2: CCP haircuts and market stress are correlated.

The CCP risk practices are said to be procyclical when the conditional correlation is positive and exceeds 50%.

During the recent sovereign debt crisis, the haircuts on peripheral government bonds sharply increased, reducing their liquidity and amplifying the raise in the yields of these securities. Higher initial margins diminished the ability of leveraged investors to borrow, and tightened their funding constraint. Consequently, leveraged investors reduced their positions on the bonds with higher haircuts and shifted their portfolio towards securities with lower margins in order to relax their funding constraint (Molteni 2015). Based on this observation, we hypothesize that if haircuts increase, we should observe a reduction in quantity of that respective security in the collateral portfolio. We develop a test for the resulting scenario of the security dropout event, as stated above.

H3: securities with increased haircuts are dropped systematically from collateral portfolios.

As high-haircut securities are crowded out from the collateral portfolio, CMs may substitute them with a range of lower-haircut bonds, leading to diversification of their collateral portfolio. Therefore, we hypothesize the following.

H4: members diversify their collateral portfolio more in times of market stress as new securities are added to the collateral pool.

Based on the exploratory data analysis, we hypothesize that CMs systematically overfund their collateral accounts so that they can rely on a buffer that dampens the impact of haircut changes. The collateral buffer could act as a countercyclical break when CCPs increase margins under stress market conditions.

H5: clearing members systematically overcollateralize their positions at a CCP.

4.2 Data Description

The available data set, which is unique when compared with the existing research, encompasses the anonymized TMR for 263 CMs of a CCP between November 2005 and February 2015.[1] The collateral portfolio composition is given for each CM (ISIN, bond or stock, cash), along with the last available price of collateral (including haircuts). In addition, margin call amount for each CM is given for each day within the specified time frame. Generally, up to 263 clearing members and up to 1 617 000 unique bond and security ISINs (Figure 2) per day are included in our data set.[2]

The data for investigation of any procyclical effects should cover the full credit and business cycle. Our data set fulfils both criteria regarding the length of the analyzed time period (almost 10 years) and the interval between two data points (daily data).

---

[1] The CCP clears both listed and OTC derivatives.
[2] The analysis of the membership basis of the CCP shows that the number of new members and leaving CMs is balanced in our data set.

Figure 2. Number of unique ISINs (in thousands) in member collateral portfolios and CISS values.

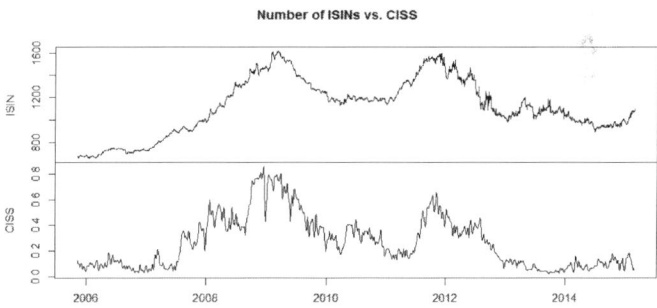

Source: own analysis.

On a regular basis, the European Central Bank is publishing an indicator of contemporaneous stress in the financial system: the Composite Indicator of Systemic Stress (CISS). The index, based on euro-area data, captures especially the effects of flight-to-quality and flight-to-liquidity by incorporating factors from securities markets (like volatilities, risk spreads and cumulative valuation losses). The CISS involves a large part of financial system: bank and non-bank financial intermediaries, money markets, equities and bonds markets as well as foreign exchange markets (Hollo, Kremer and Lo Duca 2012). We use CISS weekly data for the period 2005–2015 downloaded from the ECB's website (European Central Bank 2016).

We interpolate the weekly CISS values, using cubic spline interpolation method, in order to account for the daily data from the TMR aggregated through all CMs. Figure 3 shows the daily (interpolated) CISS index values and daily total margin requirement in trillion euros.

During the investigated period (November 2005–February 2015), the CCP applied a uniform margining methodology. The major change in the risk methodology came into force at the end of 2015.

Figure 3. TMR in trillion euros and daily CISS.

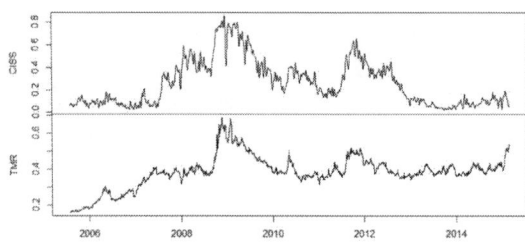

Source: own analysis.

Figure 4 shows the haircut index and daily CISS. The haircut index encompasses Italian, Spanish, Portuguese, Irish and Greek government bonds as they were mostly impacted in the recent European sovereign debt crisis. The index is equally weighted and includes all maturities.

In 2004, the CCP changed the haircut methodology from a static to dynamic calculation method. Since then, no major change in bond haircut methodology has been applied. Only the minimum haircut levels changed on a regular basis to reflect changes in risk.

Figure 4. Haircut index versus CISS.

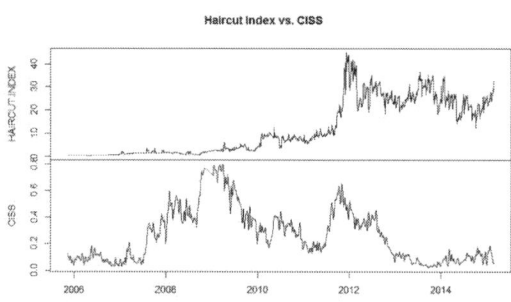

Source: own analysis

Figure 5 shows margin calls aggregated through all CMs per day.

In our analysis, we use daily returns, as opposed to end-of day values, of TMR and haircuts. We do this for two main reasons. First, just like the returns of an asset are a complete and scale-free summary of the investment opportunity, the returns of the TMR represent the scale-free size of the potential margin call. Second, return series are easier to handle than series of nominal values because the former have more attractive statistical properties.

Figure 5. Margin call in billion euros.

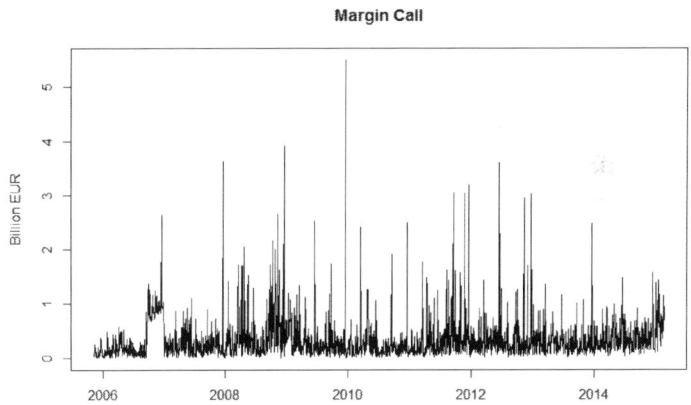

Source: own analysis.

Let P_t denote the value of the TMRs or haircut index at the end of trading day t. The log return is defined as $r_t = \ln(P_t / P_{t-1})$. The analysis of the plots of the daily log returns, squared returns and absolute value of returns for, respectively, daily TMR and CISS, weekly TMR and CISS, and the haircut index and CISS delivers evidence of volatility clustering (the plots are available on request). The volatility clustering characteristic for financial data refers to the observation that "large changes tend to be followed by large changes, of either sign, and small changes tend to be followed by small changes" (Mandelbrot 1963). In other words, volatility depends more on recent-past values than distant-past values.

141

Table 1. Summary statistics for daily and weekly TMR and CISS data.

Time series	Mean	Median	Min	Max	SD	Skew	Kurt	JB
Daily returns								
TMR	0.0005	0.0005	-0.1699	0.1059	0.0174	-0.1810	7.1754	5300
CISS	-0.0001	-0.0003	-0.4004	0.6769	0.0705	1.0745	15.1693	24000
Weekly returns								
TMR	0.0024	0.0032	-0.1484	0.1426	0.0329	0.0148	2.4866	120
CISS	-0.0009	-0.0062	-0.9251	1.2211	0.2638	0.4525	2.3381	130

Sample period is July 28, 2005–February 23, 2015 (giving 2451 daily observations) and August 5, 2005–February 20, 2015 for weekly data (giving 484 weekly observations). SD denotes standard deviation.

Tables 1 and 2 provide some standard summary statistics of the returns, along with the Jarque–Bera (JB) test for normality (Bera and Jarque 1980).[3]

Table 2. Summary statistics for daily haircut index and CISS.

Time series	Mean	Median	Min	Max	SD	Skew	Kurt	JB
Haircut index	0.0019	0.0000	-0.5219	0.5840	0.0777	-0.1768	14.2011	20000
CISS	-0.0003	-0.0005	-0.4004	0.6769	0.0711	1.1144	15.2993	23000

Sample period is November 8, 2005–February 23, 2015 giving 2336 daily observations.

---

[3] Under the null hypothesis, both the skewness and the excess kurtosis are zero. Any deviation from this increases the JB statistic.

The distribution of daily TMR and haircut index returns is clearly nonnormal, exhibiting negative skewness, pronounced excess kurtosis and high JB values. Part of this nonnormality is caused by the strong leptokurtosis during the subprime crisis and the European sovereign crisis. Weekly TMR and CISS returns have a distribution that is much closer to normal than daily returns.

Table 3. Results of MQ and LM test for Arch.

	Ljung-Box Statistics:			LM-test for ARCH		
p	1	5	10	1	5	10
Daily returns						
TMR	46.7 (0)	98.8 (0)	143.7 (0)	47 (0)	74 (0)	93 (0)
CISS	59.4 (0)	222.4 (0)	298.3 (0)	59 (0)	170 (0)	210 (0)
Haircut index	51.4 (0)	69 (0)	98.5 (0)	51 (0)	71 (0)	94 (0)
CISS*	56.2 (0)	210.8 (0)	283.5 (0)	56 (0)	160 (0)	200 (0)
Weekly returns						
TMR	8.8 (0.003)	24.53 (0)	39.86 (0)	8.8 (0.003)	18 (0.003)	35 (0)
CISS	18.3 (0)	65.2 (0)	109.3 (0)	18 (0)	42 (0)	55 (0)

*CISS daily is shown twice, based on different sample sizes.

Weekly TMR returns are calculated as the sum of daily returns from a given week. They display less volatility clustering than the daily returns. Further tests confirm this observation. Table 3 shows values of multivariate Ljung–Box Q-statistics (MQ), computed from daily and weekly squared TMR returns as well as squared daily haircut index returns (Tsay 2014). Also, the results of the Lagrange multiplier (LM) test for autoregressive conditional heteroscedasticity (ARCH) are presented in Table 3, for various values of p, i.e., lags (Engle 1982), calculated as in Tsay (2005,

143

pp. 101–102). There is clear evidence of volatility clustering in the daily and weekly returns. The LM test shows strong ARCH effects (especially for daily returns). Moreover, based on the results of the Ljung–Box statistics, the null hypothesis that the autocorrelations for lags 1 through p are all jointly zero can be rejected.

The augmented Dickey–Fuller test returns large negative numbers, so the hypothesis that there is a unit root can be rejected (Banerjee et al. 1993). Further, the results of the Kwiatkowski–Phillips–Schmidt–Shin (KPSS) test let us assume that the investigated time series are trend stationary (Kwiatkowski et al. 1992).

4.3 Methodology

Financial time series that exhibit time-varying volatility clustering are often evaluated with generalized autoregressive conditional heteroscedasticity (GARCH) models. GARCH models allow us to estimate current and future levels of volatilities based on historical data. These models capture the nonlinear dynamics in volatility and recognize that volatilities are not constant in time; for instance, a particular volatility may be high or low, depending on the time period in question.

Engle (2002) proposed a dynamic conditional correlation (DCC GARCH) model, which can be estimated using a two-step method based on the likelihood function. This model allows the simultaneous modeling of variances and conditional correlations of several time series. The estimation consists of two steps. First, the conditional variance of each univariate time series is estimated. Second, the standardized regression residuals obtained in the first step are used to model those conditional correlations that vary through time.

In the first step of the analysis, we apply a DCC GARCH model to the interpolated CISS values and aggregated margin requirements of all CMs. We do this in order to test our hypothesis of correlation between the TMR and systemic stress. The margin requirement is aggregated per day among all members. Ten members were removed from the sample, as they are state institutions exempted from posting margins. The weekly

CISS values were interpolated (using the cubic spline interpolation method) to obtain the daily values of the market stress index. For comparison, we estimate DCC GARCH parameters also based on the weekly CISS and weekly sums of TMR. The parameters of the applied DCC model are specified in Table 4.

Table 4. Parameters of the applied DCC (1,1) models.

	Daily TMR - CISS	Weekly TMR - CISS	Haircut Index - CISS
Estimation	2-step	2-step	2-step
Distribution	mvt	norm	mvt
Number of Parameters	16	16	16
Number of series	2	2	2

"MVT" denotes Student t distribution.

Analogously to an analysis of the correlation between market stress and the TMR, we perform an analysis of collateral haircuts and the CISS index. Here, we also use the interpolated CISS data.

It is a well-known fact that returns from financial market variables such as exchange rates or asset prices, measured over short time intervals, are much better fitted by non-Gaussian probability distributions. The same applies to margin requirements and haircuts that refer to the risks of financial assets. The empirical distribution of such returns is more peaked and has heavier tails than the normal distribution, which implies that significant changes in returns occur with a higher frequency than under normality. Therefore, it may be more appropriate to use a distribution that has fatter tails than the normal distribution. One of the most common fat-tailed error distributions for fitting GARCH models is the Student t distribution. Based on the results presented in Tables 1 and 2 (showing negative skewness, excess kurtosis and large JB values), we adopt the Student distribution for fitting the model of daily TMR–CISS and haircuts–CISS.

Different numbers of lags can be used as parameters of the GARCH models; however, Hansen and Lunde (2004) provide compelling evidence that it is difficult to find a volatility model that outperforms the simple GARCH (1,1). Therefore, we apply the first lags in the ARCH and GARCH processes.

Another stylized fact of financial volatility is that bad news tends to have a larger impact on volatility than positive news. That is, volatility tends to be higher in a falling market than in a rising market (see Black (1976) for an explanation of this "leverage effect"). Nelson (1991) proposed the exponential GARCH (EGARCH) model to allow for leverage effects.

Next, we take a closer look at the different effects of the collateral portfolio composition. We treat a dropout event as a trigger of a forthcoming fire sale. A dropout is the reduction of a given bond share in the collateral portfolio to zero, i.e., the bond is dropped completely from the collateral portfolio. In the first step of our analysis, we identify all dropout events for each ISIN and member. In our estimation window of thirty days preceding the dropout, we calculate the average haircut value for the given bond. We then test if the difference between the level of haircut at the date of a dropout event and the average from the preceding thirty days is larger than zero.

To test H4 regarding the diversification of collateral in the stress market conditions, we first calculate a number of distinct ISINs per day (both for bonds and equities). In the second step, we calculate the correlation between the number of ISINs and CISS. As we expect the correlation to be equally strong in both calm and stress markets, we calculate a Pearson's product-moment correlation coefficient.

For the analysis of potential overcollateralization, we compare the daily TMR for each member with the collateral portfolio value for that day (for the first time in the literature, including cash posted as collateral and taking collateral haircuts and FX haircuts on foreign currencies into account). In order to assess the extent of the collateralization, we calculate the daily ratios R of over/undercollateralization for each member:

$$R_{CM_i} = \frac{\sum_{j=1}^{l}((CV_{i,j} - TMR_{i,j})/TMR_{i,j})}{N},$$

where CM_i is CM i; j represents day; CV_{ij} is collateral value including haircuts of member i on day j; TMR_{ij} - total margin requirement of member i on day j; N - number of days in the data set; and $N = 1...l$.

Figure 6. Dynamic conditional correlation between CISS and TMR (daily data).

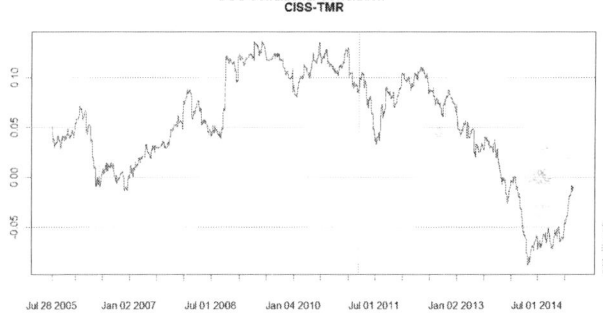

Source: own analysis.

4.4 Results

Figures 6 and 7 show the conditional correlation of CISS and aggregated Total Margin Requirement (based on the daily and, subsequently, weekly data). The obtained results reveal only a low average correlation level, which leads to rejection of H1 based on the definition of procyclicality in this research. In the investigated period, the procyclical impact of the TMR imposed on clearing members by the CCP could not be confirmed.

Interestingly, the obtained results seem to point to an amplification of dynamic conditional correlations during the periods of crisis which stretched from 7 August 2007 to 18 November 2012 (with short recovery periods in the first half of 2010 and 2011). The phases of market stress are identified by above-average values of the daily interpolated CISS index (i.e., above 0.262).

Figure 7. Dynamic conditional correlation between CISS and TMR (weekly data).

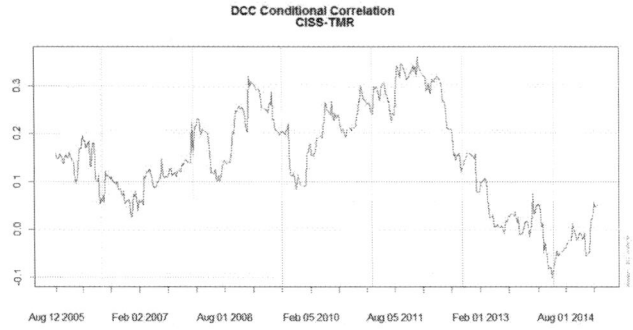

Source: own analysis.

The second interesting result is that the correlation between TMR and CISS becomes negative in 2013. This can be explained by the fact that the CCP incorporates historical values of high volatility in the margin model. The resulting margin requirement stays at a high level, whereas the current market volatility is actually falling.

Figure 8 shows the conditional correlation between CISS and the haircut index. The overall low level of dynamic conditional correlation leads to rejection of H2, according to the definition applied in this research. The haircut policy of the investigated CCP cannot be confirmed to cause a procyclical effect in the investigated time period.

However, the obtained results point to an amplification of the correlation during the periods of crisis. They suggest the correlations between haircuts and CISS have risen (by a different magnitude) in times of market stress, with characteristic correlation spikes. The sudden haircut increases may have a severe impact on clearing members in stressed markets and spur liquidity crunch when the external financing conditions deteriorate.

Figure 8. Conditional correlation between bond haircut index and CISS.

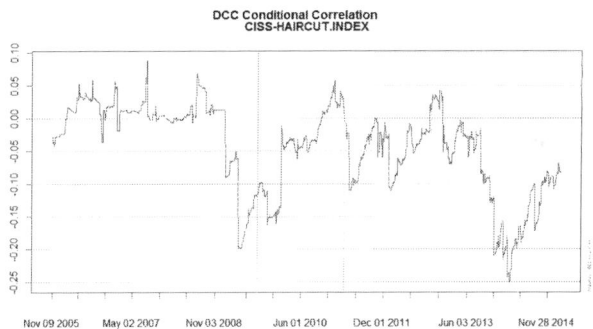

Source: own analysis.

Table 5 shows the estimated dynamic correlation coefficients for TMR and CISS as well as for CISS and Haircut Index. The results indicate that the correlations are significant at 10% level (for Haircuts/CISS) or better with dynamic conditional correlation parameters noted by dcca1 and dccb1. Notably, the sum of those coefficients is, in all cases, very close to one which indicates persistence of volatility in time.

Figure 9 shows dropout events per date. An extremely high number of these events (when members removed completely a given bond from their collateral portfolio) was observed starting 2012, which can be associated with the European sovereign debt crisis.

The haircut policy of the CCP was proven to be prone (only to a limited extent) to fire sales. Only 21% of the dropout events were driven by an increase of collateral haircuts during the thirty days preceding the event. H3 has been rejected.

However, the collateral portfolios become more diversified under the stress market conditions and less diversified in calm market times. The correlation between the CISS values and the number of unique ISINs (0.7682) was significant at 95% confidence interval. The empirical data supports H4.

Table 5. Results of the DCC GARCH (1,1) models for the dynamic conditional correlation between TMR and CISS and between CISS and the haircut index.

Coefficient	TMR-CISS (daily)	TMR-CISS (weekly)	HAIRCUTS-CISS
dcca1	0.004211** Std. Error: 0.001847 T-value: 2.27969	0.017323* Std. Error: 0.005342 T-value: 3.24248	0.008208*** Std. Error: 0.005009 T-value: 1.6385e+00
dccb1	0.994967* Std.Error: 0.001637 T-value: 607.96260	0.966710* Std.Error: 0.065318 T-value:14.80009	0.989131* Std.Error: 0.004737 T-value: .0883e+02

*, **, and *** denote statistical significance at the 1%, 5% and 10% levels.

H5, regarding systemic overcollateralization, was confirmed based on empirical data. As shown in Figure 10, only five members systematically undercollateralized their collateral portfolios (by a few percent of the TMR).[4] The remaining members maintained more collateral than required to cover the current TMR. In some cases, the average overcollateralization was very high, exceeding a thousand times the current margin requirement. Figure 11 shows the median of the under/overcollateralization ratios per day.

---

[4] Undercollateralization is only of a short-term nature. When a member has not sufficient collateral in his account to cover the margin requirement, CCP submits a margin call. The member has few hours to provide the required collateral, without being declared to be in default.

Figure 9. Number of bond dropout events per day.

Source: own analysis.

The results may be explained by the fact that some members do not actively manage their collateral accounts at the CCP to keep the operational effort low, or they keep more collateral than required by the CCP to reflect their internal assessment of the risk exposure. Figure 5 showing margin call makes it clear that a margin call may exceed the previous day TMR by several times.

Figure 10. Over/undercollateralization of member accounts.

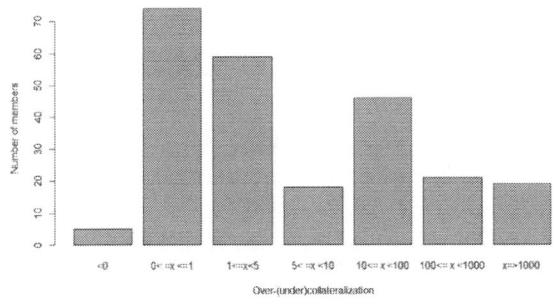

Source: own analysis.

151

Figure 11. Median of the under/overcollateralization ratios per day.

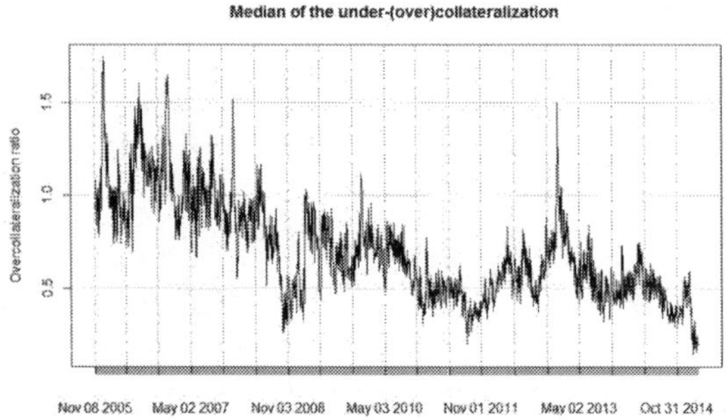

Median of the under-(over)collateralization

Source: own analysis.

5 CONCLUSION, RESEARCH LIMITATIONS AND OUTLOOK

5.1 Conclusion

A major policy concern in centrally cleared derivatives market is that margin requirements and collateral haircuts, imposed by CCPs, can sharply rise in times of stress, inhibiting trading and causing liquidity problems that exacerbate the crisis. This opinion is widely spread both in theoretical research and in the industry.

This research gives a first insight into the impact of CCPs' risk management practices, seen from the systemic risk perspective. A comprehensive data set we use spans almost ten years. Based on this data set, it cannot be statistically confirmed that, in the investigated period, the CCP risk practices caused a significant procyclical effect.

The historical data shows only a low average level of correlation between price volatility and the level of margins or haircuts in the investigated time frame. One possible explanations of the average low correlation levels is that the CCP already applies margin floors. However, the floors were imbedded in the applied CCP risk methodology and we do not possess the data required to extract them. Therefore, due to the lack of the possibility of further testing, we cannot definitely confirm the margin floors as a valid explanation.

The correlation between market stress and the level of margins or haircuts increases suddenly during periods of market stress. Nevertheless, whether the observed spikes of correlation could really spur a liquidity crunch for clearing members depends on the external financing conditions.

The dynamic conditional correlation between the total margin requirement and the stress index of the Eurozone, published by the European Central Bank, was proved to be a good metric of procyclicality, but requires further research in order to obtain a better understanding of how the CCP risk management practices could amplify business-cycle fluctuations.

Addressing procyclicality in the financial system is an essential component of strengthening the regulatory framework. Therefore, the regulators are considering the introduction of macroprudential tools, like higher minimum haircuts and margins or countercyclical add-ons. Having said that, we found out that systematic overcollateralization of open positions by clearing members (as observed in our data set) may already act as a countercyclical break. This result indicates that the burden of reasonably low, non-voluntary collateral floor on liquidity of clearing members would probably not be high. However, there might be some challenges in the implementation of the countercyclical breaks, e.g. the timing of the introduction of such a regulatory tool, determination of the appropriate level, and finally the question of whether different levels are feasible for different financial instruments.

Another interesting result of this research is that the negative correlation between the margin requirement and market stress appears after the periods of crisis. The negative correlation can be explained by the fact that the CISS index was sinking after the period of crisis, when markets recovered, but the CCP margin was not decreasing as the previous events (shocks from the crisis) were incorporated via stress scenarios into the margin model. Abruzzo and Park (2016) come to a similar conclusion.

Finally, the haircut policy of the CCP was not proven to be prone to fire sales, as suggested by the literature. Only some of the dropout events were motivated by an increase in haircuts. On the other hand, the collateral portfolios of the clearing members became more diversified in times of market stress than in the calm market. This finding suggests that new types of securities were added to the ones already present in the collateral portfolio when the clearing members needed to cover the increase in margin requirement under the stress market conditions.

5.2 Research Limitations and Outlook

As different CCPs use proprietary risk margining models, the transferability of our results on other clearinghouses is limited.

In the presented research, we abstract from the assessment how quickly and how strongly the CCP should react on the significant change in risk regime and what is the acceptable level of margin/haircut increase in a given time frame. The existing measures of procyclicality would allow comparing the risk management models between different clearinghouses when the required data would be available.

It was also out of scope of this study to analyze the direct impact of the minimum haircuts applied by the CCP. Such a research would require a simulation of the level of haircut, once with and once without the minimum haircut restriction as well as a simulation of the corresponding change in the collateral practices of the clearing members.

When formulating our hypotheses, we focused mostly on bond haircuts, leaving foreign exchange and equity haircuts out of our study. The limited number of events in our data set prevented us from a deeper analysis.

Moreover, for dropout events, we have not taken into account the potential time-lagged manner of haircut settings and collateral dropouts. It may be the case that the members who possess private information react faster (i.e., drop the bond from their portfolio faster) than the CCP increases the haircut. The dropout events are, therefore, only to a small extent explained by an increase in the CCP haircut. A further analysis of haircut setting by CCPs and member collateral practices could shed some light on this aspect.

REFERENCES

Abruzzo, N. and Park, Y.-H. (2016). An Empirical Analysis of Futures Margin Changes: Determinants and Policy Implications. *Journal of Financial Services Research*, 49 (1), 65–100.

Acharya, V. V. and Viswanathan, S. (2011). Leverage, Moral Hazard, and Liquidity. *Journal of Finance*, 66, 99-138.

Ashcraft, A., Gârleanu, N. and Pedersen, L.H. (2010). Two Monetary Tools: Interest Rates and Haircuts. *NBER Macroeconomic Annual*, 25, pp.143–180.

Banerjee, A., Dolado J.J., Galbraith, J.W. and Hendry, D. (1993). *Cointegration, Error Correction, and the Econometric Analysis of Non-Stationary Data*. Oxford: Oxford University Press.

Bank for International Settlements. (2016). *OTC derivatives statistics at end-June 2016*. http://www.bis.org/publ/otc_hy1611.htm (Accessed 11 Dec. 2016).

Bera, A., K. and Jarque C. M. (1980). Efficient tests for normality, homoscedasticity and serial independence of regression residuals. *Economics Letters*. 6 (3), 255–259.

Black, F. (1976). Studies in Stock Price Volatility Changes. In: *Proceedings of the Business Meeting of the Business and Economics Statistics Section, American Statistical Association*, 177–181.

Brunnermeier, M. K. and Pedersen, L. H. (2009). Market liquidity and funding liquidity, *Review of Financial Studies*, 22 (6), 2201–2238.

Brumm, J., Grill, M., Kubler, F. and Schmedders, K. (2015). Margin regulation and volatility. *Journal of Monetary Economics*, 75, 54–68.

Committee on the Global Financial System. (2010). *The role of margin requirements and haircuts in procyclicality*. CGFS Paper No. 34, http://www.bis.org/publ/cgfs36.pdf (Accessed 10 May 2015).

Engle, R. F. (1982). Autoregressive conditional heteroscedasticity with estimates of the variance of United Kingdom inflation. *Econometrica*, 50, 987–1007.

Engle, R. (2002). Dynamic conditional correlation: A simple class of multivariate generalized autoregressive conditional heteroskedasticity models. *Journal of Business and Economic Statistics*, 20 (3), 339–350.

EUR-Lex. (2012). Commission Delegated Regulation (EU) No 153/2013 December 2012 supplementing Regulation EU No 648/2012 of the European parliament and of Council with regard to regulatory technical standards on requirements for central counterparties.*Official Journal of the European Union*, L 52/41. (Accessed 11 Jun. 2016).

European Central Bank. (2013). *Collateral Eligibility Requirements*. https://www.ecb.europa.eu/pub/pdf/other/collateralframeworksen.pdf (Accessed 11 Jun. 2016).

European Central Bank. (2016). *Statistical Data Warehouse*. http://sdw.ecb.europa.eu (Accessed 11 Jun. 2016).

European Systemic Risk Board. (2015). *The efficiency of margining requirements to limit procyclicality and the need to define additional intervention capacity in this area*. https://www.esrb.europa.eu/pub/html/index.en.html (Accessed 11 Jun. 2016).

Goodhart, Ch., Kashyap, A., Tsomocos, D. and Vardoulakis, A. (2012). *Financial Regulation in General Equilibrium*. Chicago Booth Research Paper No. 11.

Hansen, P. R. and Lunde, A. (2004). A Forecast Comparison of Volatility Models: Does Anything Beat a GARCH(1,1) Model? *Journal of Applied Econometrics*, 20, 873–889.

Hollo, D., Kremer, M. and Lo Duca, M. (2012). *CISS - A Composite Indicator of Systemic Stress in the Financial System*. ECB Working Paper No. 1426.

Kwiatkowski, D., Phillips, P. C., Schmidt, P. and Shin, Y. (1992) Testing the null hypothesis of stationarity against the alternative of a unit root. *Journal of Econometrics*, 54 (1), 159–178.

Lewandowska, O. (2015). OTC Clearing Arrangements for Bank Systemic Risk Regulation: A Simulation Approach. *Journal of Money, Credit and Banking*, 47, 1177–1203.

Mai, E. (2016). *Regulatory requirements for limiting the procyclicality of the CCPs*. Mainstay presentation, http://www.mainstay-consulting.de/publications (Accessed 11 Jun. 2016).

Mandelbrot, B. (1963). The variation of certain speculative prices. *Journal of Business*, 36, 392–417.

Molteni, F. (2015). *Liquidity, Government Bonds and Sovereign Debt Crises*. CEPII Working Paper No. 32.

Murphy, D., Vasios M. and Vause, N. (2014). *An investigation into the procyclicality of risk-based initial margin models*. Bank of England Financial Stability Paper No. 29.

Nelson, D. B. (1991). Conditional heteroskedasticity in asset returns: A new approach. *Econometrica*, 59, 347–370.

Tsay, R. S. (2005). *Analysis of Financial Time Series* (2nd ed.), Hoboken (NJ): Wiley-Interscience, ISBN: 9780471690740.

Tsay R, S. (2014). *Multivariate Time Series Analysis with R and Financial Applications*. Hoboken (NJ): John Wiley & Sons, ISNB 13: 9781118617908.

Wendt, F. (2006). *Intraday Margining of Central Counterparties*. Netherlands Central Bank Working Paper.

Deutsche Zusammenfassung

Nachhandel von außerbörslich gehandelten Derivaten

- IT-Lösungen unter neuem regulatorischen Paradigma -

Olga Lewandowska

Deutsche Zusammenfassung

Inhaltsverzeichnis

1 EINLEITUNG **161**
    1.1 Einordung des Themas und Ziel der Dissertation 161
    1.2 Hintergrund 163
    1.3 Forschungsfragen und Struktur der Dissertation 167

2 FORSCHUNGSGEGENSTAND **171**
    2.1 OTC-Derivate und die Risiken im Derivate-Nachhandel 171
    2.2 Organisation der OTC-Derivatemärkte und Nettingmodelle im Nachhandel 172
    2.3 Forschung zum Thema OTC-Clearing 177

3 FORSCHUNGSMETHODEN **184**
    3.1 Quantitative Umfrage 184
    3.2 Die numerische Simulation der OTC-Derivatemärkte ... 186
    3.3 Fallstudie 188
    3.4 Empirisch-quantitative Analyse 189

4 ERGEBNISSE **190**
    4.1 Ergebnisse aus Artikel 1. 190
    4.2 Ergebnisse aus Artikel 2. 192
    4.3 Ergebnisse aus Artikel 3. 194
    4.4 Ergebnisse aus Artikel 4 195

5 BEITRAG ZUR FORSCHUNG UND PRAXIS **196**
    5.1 Beitrag zur Forschung 196
    5.2 Beitrag zur Praxis 198

6 LIMITATIONEN UND WEITERE FORSCHUNG 199
    6.1 Limitationen 199
    6.2 Weitere Forschung 202

Deutsche Zusammenfassung

1 EINLEITUNG

1.1 Einordung des Themas und Ziel der Dissertation

Die Untersuchung des Themas des Nachhandels von außerbörslich gehandelten Derivaten (engl. Over-The-Counter, OTC-Derivaten) setzt eine Überschneidung der Disziplinen Finanzwirtschaft und Informationstechnologie voraus. Die wichtigsten finanzwirtschaftlichen Themen in diesem Zusammenhang sind die industrielle Organisation der Finanzmärkte, die Finanzmarktregulierung und -stabilität sowie das Risikomanagement in den beteiligten Institutionen wie Clearinghäusern und Banken. Die Thematik der Informationstechnologie spiegelt sich in der Betrachtung des neuen Nachhandelsmodells für außerbörslich gehandelte Derivate als eine IT-Innovation.

OTC-Derivate sind Finanztransaktionen, die traditionell bilateral ausgehandelt und außerhalb von regulierten Märkten wie Börsen abgeschlossen werden. Sie weisen oft individuelle Vertragsgestaltungen wie Kündigungsklauseln, Leistungsbeschreibungen oder Sicherheitsleistungen auf. Gibson und Murawski (2006) beschrieben OTC-Derivatemärkte als typischerweise dezentralisiert, informell, nur geringfügig beaufsichtigt und reguliert, geregelt vor allem durch die Marktdisziplin. OTC-Derivatemärkte sind ein informales Netzwerk von bilateralen Handelsbeziehungen. Im Vergleich zu den OTC-Derivatemärkten sind die Börsen als Handels- und Marktplätze zentralisiert, formell und durch die Börsenaufsicht stark reguliert. Das Verlustrisiko infolge eines Ausfalls der Gegenpartei wird für börsengehandelte Instrumente in einem Clearinghaus vergemeinschaftet. Im Gegensatz dazu war das Ausfallrisiko in den OTC-Derivatemärkten traditionell nicht geteilt. Ohne Informationsasymmetrie und Moral Hazard-Probleme führt die Vergemeinschaftung des Verlustes zu einem Wohlfahrtsgewinn, da die erwarteten Kosten des Ausfalls aufgrund der Skalenvorteile reduziert werden. Private Information ist jedoch von größerer Bedeutung in den OTC- als in börsengehandelten Transaktionen, da die Bewertung der OTC-Derivate oft proprietäre und speziali-

Deutsche Zusammenfassung

sierte mathematische Modelle benötigt. Skalenvorteile waren in den OTC-Märkten traditionell eher durch die Herausbildung der großen Dealer-Firmen als durch ein Clearinghaus erschlossen (Pirrong 2009). Die wichtigste mikroökonomische Fragestellung bezüglich des Nachhandels für OTC-Derivate betrifft die von den Regulatoren vorgeschriebene Zentralisierung der Finanzmarktinfrastruktur durch die Migration der Abwicklung von den bilateralen Beziehungen zwischen Banken zu den zentralen Clearinghäusern. Sowohl die Zentralisierung als auch die mögliche Konsolidierung der Clearing-Infrastruktur führen zur Konzentration des Risikos in den Hauptinstitutionen und begründen implizit den erhöhten Bedarf an Regulierung und Aufsicht der Marktinfrastrukturdienstleister in dieser Netzindustrie. Die Thematik des Risikomanagements spielt eine eminente Rolle für Clearinghäuser und Clearing-Mitglieder und betrifft nicht nur das erwähnte Ausfallrisiko (Kontrahentenrisiko[1]), sondern auch das Liquiditäts-, das operationelle und das Marktrisiko.

Aufgrund der komplexen Natur von OTC-Derivaten kann ein Nachhandelsmodell für diese Finanzinstrumente als eine Informationstechnologie-basierte Innovation betrachtet werden. Mahnke, Overby und Özcan (2006) definieren eine IT-basierte Innovation als etwas, das „Hardware und/oder Software mit Business-Funktionen verbindet, um ein neues Verfahren, neue Produkte oder neue Dienstleistungen zu generieren". In diesem Zusammenhang ist die Berechnung von Sicherheiten für komplexe OTC-Derivate besonders herausfordernd. Die Fortschritte in der Informationstechnologie erlauben, die Preis- und Positionsänderungen in Echtzeit zu verfolgen und diese Informationen in die Risikomanagementwerkzeuge einfließen zu lassen. Somit kann ein Clearinghaus für OTC-Derivate als eine IT-Innovation gedeutet werden.

---

[1] Unter dem Kontrahentenrisiko eines Derivatgeschäftes versteht man das Ausfallrisiko im Rahmen einer Vertragsbindung zwischen mindestens zwei Parteien, also die Gefahr, dass einer der Vertragspartner seinen Verpflichtungen aus dem OTC-Derivat nicht mehr nachkommt.

Deutsche Zusammenfassung

Während in den letzten Jahren der Wertpapierhandel zum Thema zahlreicher akademischer Studien wurde (Easley und O'Hara 1987; Madhaven 2000; Campbell 2002; Stoll 2003), ist der Nachhandel von Finanztransaktionen bis heute weniger erforscht. Insbesondere im Bereich der Nachhandelsverarbeitung von außerbörslich gehandelten Derivaten ist die Anzahl der Publikationen geringer, obwohl mit einer steigenden Tendenz.

Der Fokus dieser Dissertation liegt auf dem Clearing von OTC-Derivaten. Clearing wird verstanden als die Verrechnung und das Prozessieren von Forderungen, Verbindlichkeiten und Verpflichtungen aus Wertpapier- und Termingeschäften, typischerweise auf Netto-Basis, für den Austausch der Finanzinstrumente oder des Geldes (BIS 2003). Ziel der Arbeit ist, die Thematik des Nachhandels aus verschiedenen Perspektiven zu erörtern. Hierzu wird das Kontrahenten-Risiko sowie das operationelle und systemische Risiko im Nachhandel von OTC-Derivaten untersucht. Die vorliegende Dissertation beschäftigt sich mit der zentralen Forschungsfrage, inwiefern ein Clearinghaus einen Beitrag zur Verbesserung des Nachhandels in den OTC-Märkten unter den oben genannten Risiko-Gesichtspunkten leisten kann und somit zur generellen Finanzmarktstabilität beiträgt.

Der erste Abschnitt dieser Zusammenfassung beschreibt kurz den Hintergrund, die Forschungsfragen und die Struktur der Dissertation. Der zweite Abschnitt konkretisiert den Forschungsgegenstand. Im dritten Abschnitt werden die verwendeten Forschungsmethoden genauer dargestellt. Der vierte Abschnitt skizziert die Kernergebnisse der einzelnen Artikel. Die Darstellung des Beitrags der Dissertation zur Forschung und Praxis sowie der Ausblick schließen die Arbeit ab.

1.2 Hintergrund

Bis vor der Finanzkrise 2007-2009 beschrieben die Autoren vor allem die Hauptmerkmale verschiedener Abwicklungsmodelle und analysierten deren historische Entwicklung (Moser 1998; Kroszner 1999; Bliss und Steigerwald 2006; Kroszner 2006). Gleichzeitig wurden die ökonomischen

Konsequenzen von Nachhandelsmodellen analysiert (Ripatti 2004; Bergman et al. 2004; Bliss und Kaufmann 2005). Erst als die Finanzkrise den Mangel an adäquater OTC-Nachhandelsinfrastruktur und die Risiken in den OTC-Derivatemärkten offenbarte, ist das Interesse am Thema OTC-Clearing sowohl in den akademischen Kreisen als auch unter den Regulatoren wesentlich gestiegen.

Unter den politischen Entscheidungsträgern in Europa und in den USA herrscht die Meinung vor, dass der OTC-Handel mit Derivatekontrakten erheblich zur letzten Finanzkrise beigetragen hat (Financial Crisis Inquiry Commission 2011), insbesondere da die Lehman Brothers Investment Bank als einer der wichtigsten Akteure in den OTC-Derivatemärkten galt und infolge der Marktturbulenzen insolvent wurde. Während des Niedergangs von Lehman Brothers gab es keinen Zentralen Kontrahenten für den größten Teil seines Portfolios, der als Sicherung zwischen Bank und Gegenparteien agieren konnte. Dadurch wurde eine Kettenreaktion von weiteren Insolvenzfällen hervorgerufen (dieser Dominoeffekt ist bekannt als „Systemisches Risiko").

Ein Zentraler Kontrahent (*Zentrale Gegenpartei*, engl. *Central Counterparty, CCP*) tritt als Vertragspartei zwischen den an einem Handelsgeschäft beteiligten Parteien auf. Er fungiert als Verkäufer für jeden Käufer und als Käufer für jeden Verkäufer. Da der CCP zur Vertragspartei für beide Clearing-Mitglieder wird, muss er für alle zukünftigen Verpflichtungen aus dem Finanzkontrakt aufkommen. In der Rolle des unabhängigen Risikomanagers setzt der CCP verschiedene Schutzmechanismen ein, um den Verlust im Falle des Ausfalls eines Clearing-Mitglieds zu minimieren. Dies wird genauer im Kapitel 2.2 erläutert. Im Regelfall wird ein OTC-CCP zum Kontrahenten für zwei Clearing-Mitglieder infolge des Novation-Prozesses.

Die *Novation* von Kontrakten, d.h. der Prozess der Übertragung bilateraler Verträge zwischen den Marktteilnehmern auf einen Zentralen Kontrahenten, schafft die Grundlage für das zentralisierte Risikomanagement (wie multilaterales Netting von Positionen, also die Verrechnung gegenseitiger Verpflichtungen von Teilnehmern an einem Clearingsystem, Sicherheitenmanagement und Verlustbeteiligung unter den

Mitgliedern) sowie das Prozessieren der Daten (Registrierung der Geschäfte und Reporting). Die Marktteilnehmer können potenziell davon profitieren, dass die bilateralen offenen Positionen zu einer einzigen Position (mit Zentraler Gegenpartei) reduziert werden, sodass weniger Kapital und Sicherheiten nötig sind, um das gleiche Geschäftsvolumen abzuwickeln.

Abbildung 1. Die Entwicklung des Marktanteils der durch CCP geclearten OTC-Derivate 2007-2017 (links), Bruttonominalwert des globalen Derivatemarktes im Dezember 2017 (rechts).[2]

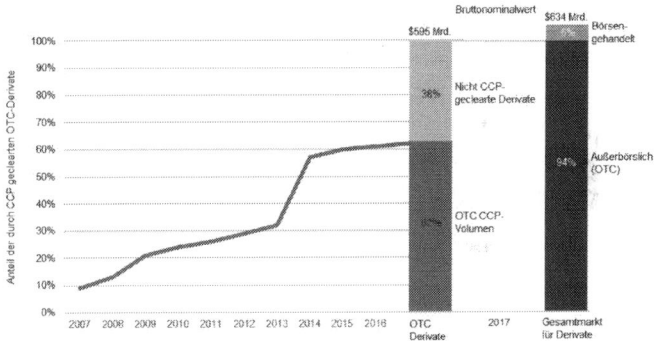

Quelle: eigene Darstellung basierend auf BIS (2018a); ISDA (2013), (2014) und (2016), um die doppelte Buchung durch Zentrale Gegenpartei bereinigt.

CCP-Clearing, eine Dienstleistung des Clearinghauses, ist seit Jahrzehnten das führende Abwicklungsmodell für börslich gehandelte Derivate, wie zum Beispiel Futures. In den OTC-Derivatemärkten wurde dagegen CCP-Clearing bis heute viel seltener eingesetzt. Durch die internationale Finanzkrise wurden vor allem die bilateral abgewickelten Märkte betroffen, wobei die CCP-Marktinfrastruktur für börslich gehandelte De-

---

[2] Clearing (Verrechnung) von OTC-Kontrakten durch CCP erhöht den Nennwert um 100 Prozent, weil das ursprüngliche Geschäft zwischen dem Käufer und dem Verkäufer des Finanzinstrumentes folglich in zwei voneinander unabhängige Geschäfte aufgeteilt wird. Aus diesem Grund sind in der zugrundeliegenden Statistik die geclearten Volumina für OTC-Zinsderivate und Kreditderivate korrekt um 50 Prozent reduziert.

rivate sich als widerstandsfähiger erwiesen hat. Kein CCP wurde während der Finanzkrise 2007-2009 zahlungsunfähig. Diese Tatsache lenkte die Aufmerksamkeit der Regulatoren auf eine Zentrale Gegenpartei für OTC-Derivatekontrakte („OTC-CCP").

Auf dem Gipfel in Pittsburgh im September 2009 haben sich die Regierungschefs der G20-Staaten zu Schlüsselreformen der OTC-Derivatemärkte verpflichtet (G20 2009). Nach der Finanzkrise wurden weltweit Regularien eingeführt, die die Stabilität und Transparenz der Märkte erhöhen sollten. Die Europäische Union setzt die G20-Vereinbarung zur Reform der Derivatemärkte vor allem durch die Verordnung über die europäische Marktinfrastruktur (kurz EMIR) um (Europäisches Parlament 2012). In den Vereinigten Staaten ist die Regulierung und Beaufsichtigung des Derivatemarktes über den Dodd-Frank Wall Street Reform Consumer Protection Act geregelt, der im Juli 2010 verabschiedet wurde (US Senate 2010). Übereinstimmend mit den G20-Vereinbarungen, im EMIR und im Dodd-Frank Act, wurden die folgenden Reformen geregelt. Soweit möglich sollen alle standardisierten OTC-Derivate über Börsen oder elektronische Plattformen gehandelt werden. Alle standardisierten OTC-Derivatekontrakte sollen über Zentrale Gegenparteien abgewickelt werden. OTC-Derivatekontrakte sollen an Transaktionsregister gemeldet werden, die die zentrale Sammlung und Verwaltung der elektronischen Aufzeichnungen von Derivatetransaktionsdaten übernehmen. Für nicht zentral abgewickelte Derivatekontrakte sollen höhere Kapitalanforderungen gelten.

Seit 2007 steigt das Volumen der OTC-Derivate, die durch CCPs gecleart werden. Die Abbildung 1 zeigt die Größe des globalen Derivatemarktes im Dezember 2017 und den Anstieg des Anteils des geclearten OTC-Derivatevolumens in den Jahren 2007-2017. Der Bruttonominalwert des globalen Derivatemarktes betrug Ende 2017 634 Mrd. US-Dollar, wobei der Anteil der außerbörslich gehandelten Kontrakte 94 Prozent davon ausmachte. Lediglich 6 Prozent der Kontrakte wurden an den regulierten Börsen gehandelt. Ende 2017 wurden rund 62 Prozent des Gesamtwerts aller OTC-Derivatekontrakte und Anlageklassen zentral über CCP gecleart.

Nach der Finanzkrise 2007-2009 ist das Interesse am Thema Nachhandel für OTC-Derivate unter akademischen Forschern gestiegen. Die neuesten Veröffentlichungen widmen sich vor allem der Auswirkung der jüngsten Reformen auf das Kontrahentenrisiko (Duffie und Zhu 2011; Arnsdorf 2012; Cont und Kokholm 2014; Kubitza, Pelizzon und Getmansky 2018) oder auf die systemweite Sicherheitennachfrage (Singh 2010; Sidanius und Zikes 2012; Heller und Vause 2012; Duffie, Scheicher und Vuillemey 2015; Vuillemey und Breton 2014). Die bestehende Forschung zum OTC-Clearing beschäftigt sich vor allem mit isolierten Faktoren. In dieser Dissertation wird der Nachhandel von außerbörslich gehandelten Derivaten aus der Perspektive des Kontrahenten-, operationellen und systemischen Risikos untersucht.

1.3 Forschungsfragen und Struktur der Dissertation

Diese kumulative Dissertation besteht aus vier wissenschaftlichen Veröffentlichungen, die sich mit Themen der Nachhandelsverarbeitung von OTC-Derivaten beschäftigen. Die Artikel und ihre Forschungsfragen werden im Folgenden vorgestellt.

Artikel 1[3] befasst sich mit den fördernden und hemmenden Faktoren für die Akzeptanz einer Zentralen Gegenpartei bei OTC-Marktteilnehmern. Zur Identifikation dieser Faktoren wurde ein Modell eingesetzt, das auf der Diffusionstheorie von Rogers basiert (Rogers 1995). Um die Relevanz der Faktoren zu ermitteln, wurde eine Umfrage unter Leitern von Clearingabteilungen in den Banken und Vermögensverwaltungsfirmen durchgeführt und unter Zuhilfenahme der Regressionsanalyse ausgewertet. Die Forschungsfrage ist: *„Welche Faktoren führen zur Akzeptanz des CCP-Clearings bei OTC-Marktteilnehmern?"*

---

[3] Lewandowska, O. (2010). Adoption of a Centralized Post-Trade Processing Market Infrastructure after the Credit Crisis. In: *Proceedings of the 16th Americas Conference on Information Systems (AMCIS 2010), Peru, Lima.*

Artikel 2[4] untersucht die Auswirkungen der neuesten Finanzmarktreformen wie EMIR und Dodd-Frank. In diesem Zusammenhang wurden vor allem die Konsequenzen der Clearingverpflichtung für standardisierte OTC-Derivate untersucht. Unter Einbeziehung der Netting-Effizienz[5] wird das Potenzial der verschiedenen Clearing-Modelle untersucht, das von OTC-Märkten ausgehende Kontrahentenrisiko zu senken. Darüber hinaus wird in diesem Artikel der Einfluss von OTC-spezifischen CCPs auf die Konzentration der Ausfallverluste und, implizit, auf das systemische Risiko untersucht. Diese Studie bedient sich einer numerischen Simulation als Basis für die Analyse und den Vergleich verschiedener Nachhandelsmodelle. Die Forschungsfrage ist: *„Was sind die Konsequenzen für das Kontrahentenrisiko in den Derivatemärkten, wenn OTC-Derivate durch CCP gecleart werden?"*

Im **Artikel 3**[6] wurde eine Fallstudie eines Clearinghauses für OTC-Derivate im Hinblick auf die durchgehende Datenverarbeitung (engl. straight through processing, STP) durchgeführt. Darin wird die STP-Rate im Nachhandelsprozess von Kreditderivaten vor und nach der Einführung eines Clearinghauses ermittelt. Darüber hinaus wird die CCP-Architektur für Kreditderivate mit all ihren Verbindungen zu externen Entitäten analysiert. Die Links zwischen dem Clearinghaus und den externen Dienstleistern werden im Hinblick auf das Optimierungspotenzial für die durchgehende Datenverarbeitung untersucht. Die Forschungsfrage ist: *„Wie kann das CCP-Modell bei der Übertragung auf die OTC-*

---

[4] Lewandowska, O. (2015). OTC Clearing Arrangements for Bank Systemic Risk Regulation: A Simulation Approach. *Journal of Money, Credit, and Banking*, 47 (6), 1177–1203.

[5] Die Netting-Effizienz ist hoch und der Nettingprozess effizient, wenn die erwartete Risikoexposition stark reduziert wird, indem die entgegengesetzten oder redundanten Positionen verrechnet werden.

[6] Lewandowska O. (2010). Is a Full Scale Straight Through Processing of OTC Derivatives Possible? A Straight Through Processing Potential of a Central Counterparty Clearing Model for Credit Default Swaps: An Exploratory Case. Paper presented at *FinanceCom, Germany, Frankfurt am Main*.

Derivatemärkte verbessert werden, sodass das operationelle Risiko minimiert wird?"

Basierend auf empirischen Daten eines führenden Europäischen Clearinghauses wird im **Artikel 4**[7] untersucht, ob und in welchem Umfang die prozyklischen Effekte der CCP-Risikomanagementpraktiken tatsächlich auftreten. Die Forschungsfrage ist: *„Welchen Einfluss hat die Einführung vom OTC-CCP auf das systemische Risiko in den Derivatemärkten, insbesondere durch die Risikomanagementpraktiken der CCPs?"*

Die Abbildung 2 illustriert den Zusammenhang zwischen den Artikeln der kumulativen Dissertation und den gewählten Forschungsmethoden. Im Zentrum dieser Dissertation steht die Studie über die Einführung einer Zentralen Gegenpartei in die OTC-Märkte (Artikel 1). Die Konsequenzen der Adoption des OTC-CCPs wurden in den einzelnen Artikeln in Detail analysiert: der Einfluss auf das Kontrahentenrisiko im Artikel 2, der Einfluss auf das operationelle Risiko im Artikel 3, der Einfluss auf das systemische Risiko im Artikel 4. Darüber hinaus werden im Artikel 2 im Markt koexistierende Nachhandelslösungen modelliert, die als Basis für den Vergleich mit dem OTC-CCP dienen.

Für die Forschungsfragen, die in den Publikationen der vorliegenden Dissertation adressiert wurden, eignen sich unterschiedliche Forschungsmethoden. Die Faktoren, die die Annahme der CCPs in den OTC-Derivatemärkten durch die Marktteilnehmer beeinflussen, wurden in einer quantitativen Umfrage und auf Basis eines Kausalmodells ermittelt (Artikel 1). Die Analyse der Auswirkungen des CCP-Clearings der OTC-Derivate auf das Kontrahentenrisiko basiert auf einer numerischen Simulation (Artikel 2). Die operationelle Effizienz der OTC-Derivatemarktinfrastruktur mit OTC-CCP wurde in einer qualitativen Forschung, anhand einer explorativen Fallstudie eines Clearinghauses für OTC-Derivate, analysiert (Artikel 3). Die Frage, ob die verwendeten Risi-

---

[7] Lewandowska, O. und Glaser F. (2017) The Recent Crises and Central Counterparty Risk Practices in the Light of Procyclicality: Empirical Evidence. *Journal of Financial Market Infrastructures*, 5 (3) 1–24.

komanagementpraktiken das systemische Risiko erhöhen, da die CCPs die Prozyklizität unterstützen, wurde mithilfe einer empirisch-quantitativen Analyse untersucht (Artikel 4)

Abbildung 2. Der Zusammenhang zwischen den Artikeln der kumulativen Dissertation und den gewählten Forschungsmethoden.

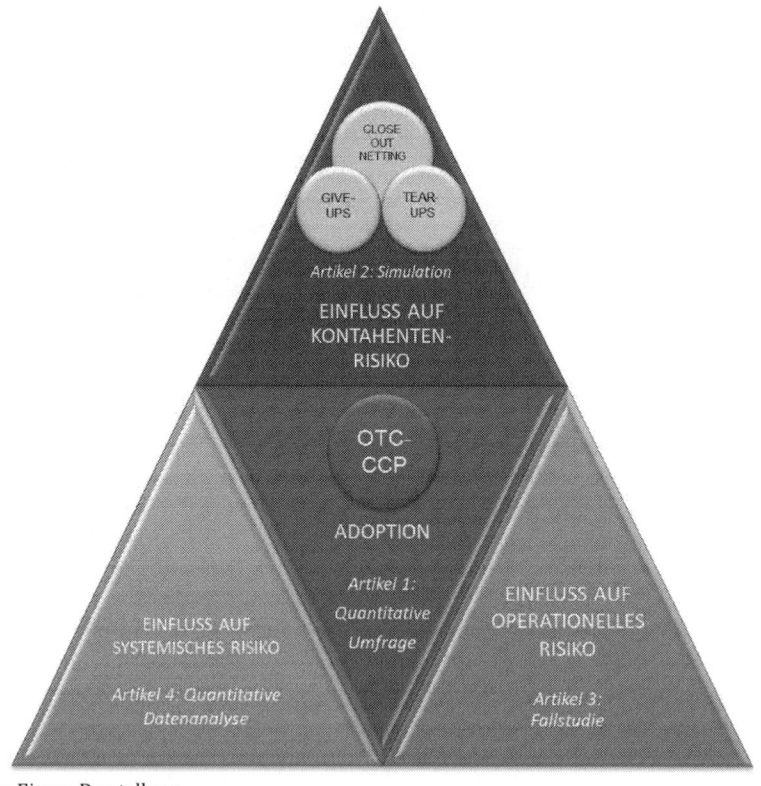

Quelle: Eigene Darstellung.

2 FORSCHUNGSGEGENSTAND

Im folgenden Kapitel wird der fachliche Kontext der vorliegenden Arbeit vorgestellt. Dazu werden die OTC-Derivate und Derivatemärkte charakterisiert und die Nachhandelsmodelle kurz beschrieben.

2.1 OTC-Derivate und die Risiken im Derivate-Nachhandel

Als Derivat wird ein Finanzinstrument bezeichnet, dessen Preis von der Preisentwicklung einer zugrunde liegenden Bezugsgröße, des sogenannten Basiswerts, abhängt. Basiswerte sind zum Beispiel Aktien, Aktienindizes, Staatsanleihen, Währungen oder Zinssätze. Derivative Finanzinstrumente können als unbedingte Termingeschäfte oder als Optionsgeschäfte ausgestaltet sein. Sie werden teils an Terminbörsen mit standardisierten Konditionen gehandelt, teils außerbörslich zu frei ausgehandelten Bedingungen. Preisänderungen im Basiswert führen in bestimmten Situationen zu erheblich stärkeren Preisänderungen des jeweiligen Derivates. Mit Derivaten kann man finanzielle Risiken absichern (Hedging), auf Preisänderungen spekulieren (Spekulation) oder Preisunterschiede zwischen Märkten ausnutzen (Arbitrage). Derivate ermöglichen industriellen Unternehmen, ihre Risikopositionen auf individuelle Weise abzusichern, was die Risikoaufnahme fördert und zum Wirtschaftswachstum beiträgt (Hull 2014).

Bei der Abwicklung von Derivaten und Aktien besteht ein wesentlicher Unterschied. Während die Verpflichtungen eines Käufers oder Verkäufers einer Aktie schon innerhalb von wenigen Tagen abgewickelt sind, kann sich die Lebensdauer eines Derivate-Kontrakts (die Dauer zwischen Abschluss und Ende des Kontraktes) über Jahrzehnte hinziehen. In dieser Zeit unterliegt die Kreditwürdigkeit der Gegenpartei typischerweise wesentlichen Schwankungen. Sowohl die längere Lebensdauer der Transaktionen und die höhere Bedeutung des Kontrahentenrisikos, als auch die potenziell größere Unsicherheit bezüglich des Wertes des finalen Ausgleichs machen das Clearing von Derivaten weit komplexer als die Abwicklung von Aktien (Bliss und Steigerwald 2006).

Unter den OTC-Derivaten identifizierte man die Kreditausfallderivate (engl. credit default swaps, CDSs) als einen ursächlichen Teil der 2007 ausgelösten Finanzkrise (Greenspan 2008). Aus diesem Grund hatten auch die jüngsten Marktreformen diese Derivateklasse zum Ziel (Stulz 2009). Die Clearingpflicht wird für bestimmte Kreditderivate seit Februar 2017 sukzessive eingeführt (Bundesanstalt für Finanzdienstleistungsaufsicht 2017)[8]. CDSs ermöglichen die Trennung des Kreditrisikos von der zugrunde liegenden Kreditbeziehung und damit den separaten Handel dieses Risikos. Der Sicherungsnehmer überträgt nur das isolierte Kreditausfallrisiko auf den Sicherungsgeber. Gegen den Erhalt einer einmaligen oder bei längeren Laufzeiten ggf. annualisierten Prämie, leistet der Sicherungsgeber lediglich bei Eintritt eines vorab spezifizierten Kreditereignisses dem Sicherungsnehmer des Referenzaktivums eine Ausgleichszahlung.

Den größten Teil gehandelter OTC-Derivate stellen dagegen die Zinsderivate wie Zinsswaps (engl. Interest Rate Swaps) und Forward Rate Agreements dar, deren Basiswert ein Zins oder eine zinsbezogene Größe ist. Im ersten Quartal 2018 wurden ca. 60 Prozent der OTC-Zinsderivate durch CCPs gecleart (BIS 2018b).

2.2 Organisation der OTC-Derivatemärkte und Nettingmodelle im Nachhandel

Im Gegensatz zu standardisierten Derivaten wie Futures werden OTC-Derivate traditionell außerbörslich gehandelt und abgewickelt. Die Marktarchitektur von Börsen (mit zentralem Orderbuch) und OTC-Derivatemärkten unterscheidet sich grundsätzlich bezüglich (1) der Inter-

---

[8] Global werden ca. 28 Prozent der Kreditderivate durch CCPs gecleart (BIS 2018b). Bellia et al. (2017) erklären den relativ kleinen Marktanteil der geclearten Kreditderivate, für die zwar noch keine Clearingpflicht besteht, aber die für das CCP-Clearing geeignet sind (wie zum Beispiel Single Names CDSs); vgl. Ghamami und Glasserman (2017).

aktion der Orderströme, (2) des Marktzugangs und (3) der Rolle der Intermediäre:

1. In den OTC-Derivatemärkten ist der Orderfluss generell von bilateraler Natur. Die Transaktionen werden zwischen zwei Vertragsparteien verhandelt und der Abschluss findet typischerweise telefonisch statt.
2. Der Marktzugang ist segmentiert und Endkunden handeln nicht direkt miteinander, sondern benutzen Intermediäre.
3. Die Intermediation in OTC-Derivatemärkten übernehmen typischerweise große internationale Banken, die beide Seiten des Marktes abdecken, d.h., sie sind gleichzeitig Käufer und Verkäufer von Kontrakten für die jeweiligen Kunden (Li und Schürhoff 2014) und gehören somit zur sogenannten „Sell-Side".[9]

Die Nachhandelsmodelle, die sich in OTC-Derivatemärkten entwickelt haben, unterscheiden sich vor allem im Netting von Handelspositionen. Es ist zwischen bilateralem und multilateralem Netting zu differenzieren. Bilaterales Netting bezieht sich auf eine Form des Nettings zwischen zwei Vertragsparteien und innerhalb eines vertraglich vereinbarten Verrechnungsverfahrens, während multilaterales Netting unter mehreren Vertragsparteien innerhalb eines institutionalisierten Abrechnungssystems stattfindet.

Innerhalb des bilateralen Nettings unterscheidet man zwischen dem *Close-out Netting* und dem *Prime-Brokerage*-Modell. Formen des multilateralen Nettings umfassen die *Portfolio Compression* und das *CCP-Clearing* (BIS 2007).

In einem *Close-out Netting* (Close-out bedeutet im Englischen „ausbuchen" der bisherigen Forderungen) werden alle unter einem Aufrechnungsvertrag laufenden Geschäfte in allen Anlageklassen aufgrund der

---

[9] Unter Sell-Side werden Finanzinstitutionen (vor allem große, international agierende Banken) verstanden, die Dienstleistungen für institutionelle Investoren wie Asset Managers, Hedge Funds oder kommerzielle Hedgers und Unternehmen anbieten, d.h. für „Buy-Side", Kundenseite (Harris 2003).

darin enthaltenen Close-out Netting-Klausel beendet. In der Close-out-Klausel vereinbaren die am Netting beteiligten Parteien, dass bei Eintritt eines definierten Ereignisses, wie z.b. der Insolvenz, die gegenseitigen Geschäfte genettet werden und damit eine unverzügliche Abrechnung inklusive abschließendem Saldoausgleich stattfindet (Bergman *et al.* 2004).

Ein weiteres Nachhandelsmodell ist das sogenannte *Prime-Brokerage-Give-ups* Modell. Es ermöglicht einem Kunden, die Liquidität von mehreren Handelsausführungs-Dealern zu nutzen und gleichzeitig eine Kreditbeziehung, Sicherheitenaustausch und Settlement nur mit einer Entität – dem Prime-Broker einzugehen (New York Fed 2005). Kundenpositionen und Sicherheiten können so vom Prime-Broker verrechnet werden.

Der *Portfolio Compression Service (tear-ups, Portfoliokomprimierung)* basiert auf multilateraler Terminierung von offenen Positionen. Das Ziel der Tear-ups ist es, die redundanten Portfoliopositionen zu terminieren oder sie mit neuen Positionen zu ersetzen, sodass die bilateralen Bruttopositionen reduziert werden, aber die Gesamtnettoposition des Marktteilnehmers unverändert bleibt (ISDA 2012).

Die zentrale Bedeutung der Sell-Side Dealer in ihrer Doppelrolle als Prime-Brokers (d.h. Nehmer des Kontrahentenrisikos) und Market Makers (d.h. Produktstrukturierer und Liquiditätsanbieter) ist ein typisches Merkmal von OTC-Derivatemärkten. Der Handel zwischen Banken im Inter-Dealer-Markt repräsentiert den größten Teil der OTC-Handelsaktivität. In den Dealer-Kunden-Märkten handeln die gleichen Dealer mit Investoren (Buy-Side) und anderen kleineren Banken. Die beschriebenen Handelsbeziehungen führen zu einer Marktstruktur, die hochkonzentriert ist, d.h. bei der der größte Teil des Handelsvolumens auf eine geringe Anzahl von Marktteilnehmern konzentriert ist. Diese Marktstruktur spiegelt sich auf der Clearingebene wider. Wenn die Dealer als Prime-Brokers fungieren, entstehen widergespiegelte Geschäfte zwischen dem Prime-Broker und dem Kunden, sowie zwischen dem Handelsausführungs-Dealer und dem Prime-Broker.

Abbildung 3. Bilaterale Positionen (a), Netting durch Portfoliokomprimierung (b) und Netting durch CCP (c).

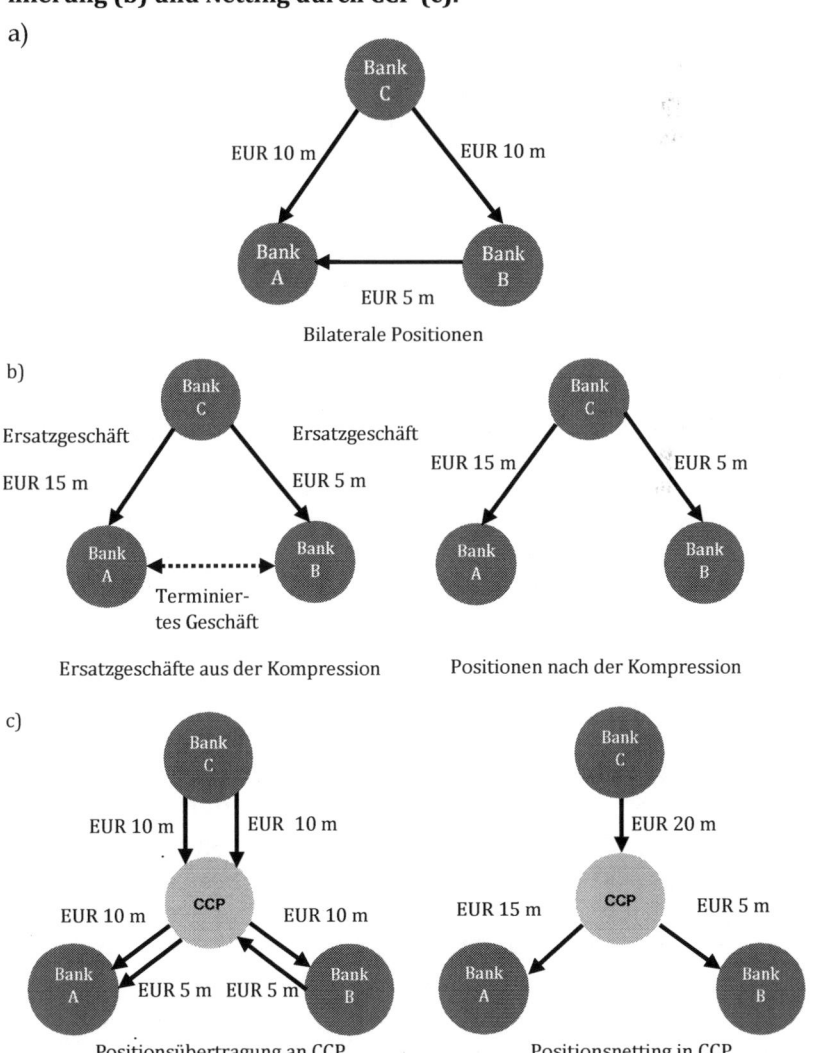

Quelle: eigene Analyse basierend auf Rehlo und Nixon (2013).

CCP-Clearing basiert auf multilateralem Netting von Kontrakten der Clearing-Mitglieder in allen Anlageklassen. Durch die *Novation* von bilateralen Positionen kann die Zentrale Gegenpartei Geschäfte verrechnen. Wie in der Abbildung 3 dargestellt, werden bilaterale Handelsbeziehungen in den OTC-Derivaten durch die Position der Kontrahenten zu einem CCP ersetzt. In der heutigen Praxis haben nur Sell-Side-Marktteilnehmer einen direkten Zugang zum Clearinghaus, während die Buy-Side-Kunden den indirekten Zugang durch „direkte" Clearing-Mitglieder nutzen. In den anderen als CCP-Clearingmodellen riskieren die Geschäftsparteien, dass der Kontrahent nach dem Abschluss einer Transaktion insolvent wird. Wohingegen beim CCP-Clearing der CCP vertraglich verpflichtet ist, die Forderungen gegenüber den nicht ausfallenden direkten Clearing-Mitgliedern zu decken, wenn der Käufer oder der Verkäufer eines Kontrakts zahlungsunfähig wird (Pirrong 2011).

CCPs verwalten das Kontrahentenrisiko mithilfe einer Reihe von Maßnahmen. Unter anderem erheben sie Sicherheitsleistungen („*Margin*") von ihren Mitgliedern. Eine Zentrale Gegenpartei erhebt Anfangseinschuss-Zahlungen (engl. *Initial Margin*), um die Verluste im Wert der offenen Positionen mit einem ausgefallenen Kontrahenten zu decken. Die Verluste können potenziell auftreten, bevor die Position zu marktüblichen Preisen ersetzt werden kann. Es ist wichtig zu beachten, dass ein Clearinghaus die *Initial Margin* zum Zeitpunkt des Clearings eines Kontaktes verlangt und über die gesamte Lebensdauer des Kontraktes hält, um die Risiken des zugrunde liegenden Geschäfts abzusichern. Zur weiteren Risikoreduktion und Absicherung wird in der Regel durch den CCP die Barwertänderung der Derivatepositionen in regelmäßigen Zeitabständen (z.B. täglich) berechnet und zwischen den Teilnehmern durch die Einziehung der sog. *Variation Margin* ausgeglichen. Der CCP fungiert in diesem Fall als Vermittler und übergibt die *Variation Margin* zwischen den ursprünglichen Kontrahenten der Transaktion (Sidanius und Zikes 2012).

Die CCPs erlauben, dass Mitglieder ihren Margin-Anforderungen mit Bargeld oder Wertpapieren nachkommen. Da Wertpapiere den üblichen Marktpreisschwankungen aufgrund der Änderung von Marktvariablen, wie zum Beispiel Zinssätzen, unterliegen, schützt sich der CCP mit sogenannten *Haircuts* gegen potenzielle Verluste im Wert der Sicherheiten. Ein *Haircut* ist ein Bewertungsabschlag auf die von den Mitgliedern als Anfangseinschuss hinterlegten Wertpapiere (oder auf Bargeld in Fremdwährung). Mit anderen Worten, ein Wertpapier, das als Sicherheit hinterlegt wird, wird nicht zu 100 Prozent berücksichtigt. Ein Abschlag von 5 Prozent bedeutet beispielsweise, dass ein Marktteilnehmer zur Erfüllung einer anfänglichen Marge von 95 Mio. EUR in Geld, 100 Mio. EUR in Wertpapieren zu hinterlegen hat.

Die Verteilung des Ausfallverlustes unter den Clearing-Mitgliedern ist eine weitere Prozedur in der Risikomanagement-Praxis der CCPs. Im Falle einer Zahlungsunfähigkeit eines Mitglieds und wenn die von ihm hinterlegten Sicherheiten nicht ausreichen, um den entstandenen Verlust zu decken, greift der CCP auf den Ausfallfonds (engl. default fund oder clearing fund) des ausfallenden Mitglieds zurück. Wenn diese Ressourcen ebenfalls nicht ausreichen, wird der Verlust auf andere Clearing-Mitglieder verteilt. Dabei nutzt der CCP die bestehenden Ressourcen und Maßnahmen, typischerweise in der folgenden Reihenfolge (Deutsche Börse 2014):

1. Netting der Positionen des ausgefallenen Clearing-Teilnehmers
2. Verkauf von Sicherheiten des ausgefallenen Clearing-Teilnehmers
3. Beitrag des ausgefallenen Teilnehmers zum Ausfallsfonds
4. Beiträge des CCPs (Eigenkapital/Sicherheiten des CCPs)
5. Verbleibender Ausfallfonds der nicht ausgefallenen Teilnehmer
6. Verbleibendes Eigenkapital des CCPs

2.3 Forschung zum Thema OTC-Clearing

Eines der wichtigsten Themen in der Clearing-Literatur nach der Finanzkrise 2007-2009 sind die Auswirkungen der neuen Marktreformen auf das systemische Risiko des gesamten Finanzsystems. Hier sind drei Forschungsströmungen zu erkennen: i) zum Einfluss der Clearingpflicht von OTC-Derivaten auf die *Netting-Effizienz* und die *Verlustverteilung* unter den nicht insolventen Mitgliedern im Falle des Ausfalls eines Clearing-Mitgliedes, ii) zur Auswirkung der jüngsten Finanzreformen auf die *Sicherheitennachfrage* in den Finanzmärkten, iii) zur Auswirkung von CCP-*Risikomanagementpraktiken* sowie der *Konsolidierung* unter CCPs auf die Finanzmärkte und ihre Akteure.

i) Bezüglich des ersten Punktes unterstützt die bestehende Literatur die These, dass die Clearingpflicht unter EMIR und Dodd-Frank zur Steigerung des Kontrahenten- und des systemischen Risikos in den OTC-Derivatemärkten (in mehreren plausiblen Fällen) beitragen kann. Der negative Einfluss ist vor allem damit begründet, dass die Netting-Effekte zwischen Produkten zerstört werden können, wenn ein Teil des Portfolios zentral und ein Teil bilateral gecleart wird (Duffie und Zhu 2011; Cont und Kokholm 2014). Diese Befürchtung entstammt der Überlegung, dass nicht-standardisierte OTC-Derivate außerhalb der Clearinghäuser auch in der Zukunft bilateral abgewickelt werden, weil ein Clearinghaus nur die standardisierten Anlageklassen abwickeln kann. Darüber hinaus senkt die Koexistenz mehrerer CCPs die Netting-Effizienz, weil Marktteilnehmer und deren Portfolios auf mehrere CCPs aufgeteilt werden und keine Verrechnung zwischen CCPs stattfindet (Duffie und Zhu 2011; Heath, Kelly und Manning 2013). Diese Effekte können jedoch durch die Herstellung von Verbindungen zwischen den Clearinghäusern gemildert werden (Cox, Garvin und Kelly 2013; Anderson, Dion und Perez Saiz 2013).

Zusammenfassend kann man sagen, dass zwei Faktoren für das Gesamtergebnis der letzten Marktreformen entscheidend werden: das Profil der Handelsaktivitäten der Marktteilnehmer und der Grad der Fragmentierung innerhalb der Clearingindustrie über Länder und Produkte hinweg.

Kubitza, Pelizzon und Getmansky (2018) beziehen das systematische Risiko, verstanden als Korrelationen zwischen und innerhalb von Derivate-Klassen, in das Modell von Duffie und Zhu (2011) ein. In Anwesenheit des systematischen Risikos steigt die Mindestanzahl an Marktteilnehmern, die an einem Ein-Anlageklasse-CCP teilnehmen müssen, um die Vorteile des multilateralen Nettings zu erreichen. Wenn die Besicherung der nicht zentral abgewickelten Kontrakte höher als der CCP-Initial-

Deutsche Zusammenfassung

Margin ist[10], steigt die Mindestanzahl an Clearing-Mitgliedern weiter. Für ausreichend extreme Realisierungen von Marktstressszenarios sichert ein CCP, verglichen mit einem bilateralen Clearing, keine Reduktion des Kontrahentenrisikos. Die Empfehlung für die Regulatoren ist, dass die Margin-Anforderungen für zentral und nicht zentral abgewickelte OTC-Derivate angeglichen werden sollen (weil sie ein entscheidender Faktor auch in einem globalen CCP sind). Darüber hinaus unterstützen die Autoren die Revision der Marktinfrastrukturreformen und die Möglichkeit des Aufhebens der Clearingpflicht in extremen Marktstresssituationen (ESRB 2017b; FSB 2017).

Es wurden verschiedene Forschungsmethoden angewandt, um die *Netting-Effizienz* von unterschiedlichen OTC-Clearingmodellen zu untersuchen. Sowohl Duffie und Zhu (2011) als auch Kubitza, Pelizzon und Getmansky (2018) stellen ein Modell der durchschnittlichen Exposition von Marktteilnehmern vor. Garratt und Zimmerman (2015) erweitern die Arbeit von Duffie und Zhu durch die Anwendung der Netzwerktheorie. Dies ermöglicht ihnen, die Heterogenität der Agenten in das Modell zu integrieren. Die Schlussfolgerung aus dem Artikel von Garratt und Zimmerman (2015) ist jedoch ähnlich wie bei der oben erwähnten Arbeit von Duffie und Zhu: Es ist unwahrscheinlich, dass sich durch die CCPs die *Netting-Effizienz* erhöhen wird, wenn die Struktur des Netzwerks sich auf nur einige wenige wichtige Knotenpunkte (dies entspricht einer Marktstruktur mit wenigen dominierenden Derivatehändlern) stützt.

Im Artikel 2 dieser Dissertation wird die Heterogenität zwischen dem Zentrum des Netzwerks (große Derivate-Dealer) und der Peripherie (Buy-Side-Kunden) dadurch reflektiert, dass verschiedene Marktsegmente modelliert und die Positionen der Marktteilnehmer für Prime-Broker-Give-ups und den CCP entsprechend transformiert werden. Auf diese

---

[10] Die Besicherungspflicht für nicht zentral abgewickelte Kontrakte tritt schrittweise bis 1. September 2020 in Kraft (BIS 2015). Im Artikel 2 der vorliegenden Arbeit werden die bilateralen Margin-Anforderungen in die Analyse der Verlustverteilung unter den Clearing-Mitgliedern einbezogen. Vor der Finanzkrise 2007-2009 war die Besicherung in den bilateralen OTC-Derivate Märkte nicht üblich.

Weise werden die Vorteile der Modellierung der Netzwerkdynamik auch in dieser Dissertation erreicht. Darüber hinaus erlaubt die Modellierung der Marktsegmente und etablierten OTC-Nachhandelsmodelle wie Tear-ups und Prime-Broker-Give-ups zusätzliche Erkenntnisse, die in einem Vergleich mit rein bilateralem Clearing nicht möglich sind.

Jackson und Manning (2007) tragen zur Diskussion bezüglich der *Verlustverteilung* unter verschiedenen Nachhandelsmodellen bei und zeigen, dass, beim Betrachten von nur genau einer Anlageklasse, die Verluste nach dem Ausfall eines Clearing-Mitglieds unter CCP-Clearing weniger konzentriert sind als bei einem anderen Clearing-Modell, dem sogenannten Ring-Clearing, das *Tear-ups* ähnlich ist.

Kubitza, Pelizzon und Getmansky (2018) weisen darauf hin, dass die *Verlustverteilung* bei CCP-Clearing zu verzerrten Anreizen für die Marktteilnehmer mit eindimensionaler Portfolioausrichtung führen kann. CCP-Clearing bietet mehr Vorteile für Derivatehändler mit gehegten Portfolien als, zum Beispiel, für Asset Manager, deren Kontahentenrisiko stärker mit dem systematischen Risiko korreliert. Letztere wären nach dem Ausfall eines Clearing-Mitglieds mehr am Verlust beteiligt als erstere; es sei denn, der OTC-CCP sorgt mit einer Verlustverteilungsmethode für eine entsprechende Umverteilung des Verlustes an die Clearing-Mitglieder.

Auch Pirrong (2009) weist auf verschiedene Umverteilungseffekte von CCP-Clearing in den OTC-Derivatemärkten hin, wie zum Beispiel darauf, dass ein CCP die Positionen der Kunden garantiert. Somit werden die nicht-direkten CCP-Mitglieder gegen das Ausfallrisiko des direkten Clearing-Mitglieds abgesichert, ohne dass die Kunden in den Ausfallfonds einzahlen und die Kosten der Absicherung tragen.

Im Artikel 2 dieser Dissertation wurde gezeigt, dass die Verlustvergemeinschaftung unter einem CCP, der mehrere Anlageklassen nettet, das systemische Risiko effektiv reduzieren kann. Dieses Ergebnis ist besonders relevant, da die Prime-Broker-Give-ups eine sehr starke Konzentration der Verluste bei einzelnen Marktteilnehmern verursachen.

Deutsche Zusammenfassung

ii) Die neuesten Studien zum Thema CCP für OTC-Derivate untersuchen explizit die potenzielle Änderung der *Sicherheitennachfrage*[11] durch die Clearingpflicht, wobei die meisten Modelle einen Anstieg in der *Sicherheitennachfrage* vorhersagen (Singh 2010; Pirrong 2012; Vuillemey und Breton 2014). Singh (2010) argumentiert, dass die *Sicherheitennachfrage* durch Clearingpflicht angetrieben werden kann, da zum einen nicht alle bilateralen OTC-Positionen vor der Finanzkrise abgesichert waren und zum anderen die Banken in den OTC-Derivatemärkten die Sicherheiten mehrfach ansetzen dürfen (engl. *rehypothecation*). Unter CCPs ist die Weiterverpfändung aller Positionen und Sicherheiten nicht erlaubt, sodass die Banken möglicherweise gezwungen sind, mehr Kapital bereitzustellen. Auch Pirrong (2012) argumentiert, dass Margin-Anforderungen unter CCPs sowie höhere Sicherheitenanforderungen für nicht zentral gecleate OTC-Kontrakte unter EMIR und Dodd-Frank die systemweite Sicherheitennachfrage steigen lassen werden. Duffie, Scheicher und Vuillemey (2015) unterstützen die These, dass eine globale Sicherheitennachfrage maßgeblich durch die Anwendung von Anfangseinschuss-Zahlungen für Derivate-Dealer erhöht wird. Das CCP-Clearing reduziert aber die Sicherheitennachfrage, unter der Bedingung, dass der Grad der Fragmentierung innerhalb der Clearingindustrie gering ist.

iii) CCPs werden durch die neuesten Marktreformen zu den systemisch wichtigsten Marktteilnehmern. Deswegen steigt zunehmend das Interesse von Regulatoren und akademischen Forschern an den *Auswirkungen der Risikomanagementpraktiken* der CCPs auf die Marktteilnehmer und die gesamtwirtschaftliche Entwicklung sowie an den Konsequenzen der *Konsolidierung* unter CCPs. Einerseits werden die CCP-spezifischen Sanierungs- und Abwicklungspläne analysiert, andererseits werden Margen und Sicherheitsabschläge, ein Teil der Riskomanagementpolitik der CCPs, zunehmend im Kontext der Prozyklizität der Finanzmärkte untersucht. Nichtsdestotrotz ist die empirische Forschung zu CCP-

---

[11] In der vorliegenden Arbeit wird die Netting-Effizienz als wichtigster zugrunde liegender Faktor für die Sicherheitennachfrage betrachtet und untersucht.

Risikomanagementpraktiken für OTC-Derivate selten. Ein Erklärungsansatz wäre, dass die umfassenden Daten über Sicherheitsabschläge und Margin-Anforderungen nicht öffentlich verfügbar sind. In einer der wenigen empirischen Studien über CCP-Margen analysieren Abruzzo und Park (2016) die Margining Methode des US-Clearinghauses der Chicago Mercantile Exchange (CME).[12] Sie belegen, dass die Methode der CME zur Berechnung der Margen in der Tat volatilitätssensibel ist. Darüber hinaus hat sie eine stärker *prozyklische Wirkung* in Zeiten höherer Marktvolatilität als in ruhigen Zeiten (die CME senkt nicht sofort die Margen, wenn die Volatilität sinkt). Dies bedeutet, dass die meisten störenden Auswirkungen einer erhöhten Marge dann vorkommen, wenn eine Krise nach einer langen Periode ruhiger Märkte eintritt, da die Einschussanforderungen von einem niedrigeren Niveau erhöht werden. Auch Acharya und Viswanathan (2011) sowie Murphy, Vasios und Vause (2014) unterstützen diese These.

Die bestehenden theoretischen Studien beschreiben in stilisierten Modellen, wie Sicherheitsabschläge und Margen zu einer prozyklischen Erweiterung der Hebelwirkung und Liquidität während der Wachstumsphase beitragen und in der Abschwungphase De-Leveraging und Austrocknung von Liquidität beschleunigen (Brunnermeier und Pedersen 2009). Eine Empfehlung aus der bestehenden theoretischen Forschung für die politischen Entscheidungsträger ist jedoch unklar, da die Modelle stark vereinfacht und von stilisierter Natur sind. Während die Modelle sich auf Margen und Sicherheitsabschläge konzentrieren, sind viele andere Kreditkonditionen für die Marktteilnehmer wichtig (zum Beispiel die Kreditfazilitäten der Zentralbanken, siehe Ashcraft, Gârleanu und Pedersen 2010).

---

[12] Im Artikel 4 dieser Dissertation werden dagegen nicht die Margen für die von den Forschern ausgewählten Finanzinstrumente, sondern die zehnjährige Historie der empirischen Margen und Sicherheiten für reale Portfolien aller Clearing-Mitglieder analysiert.

Deutsche Zusammenfassung

Ein wichtiger Aspekt des *Risikomanagements* im Clearinghaus sind die CCP-Sanierungs- und Abwicklungsmechanismen. Sie sollten so entworfen werfen, dass sie die erwarteten Kosten für alle Marktteilnehmer inklusive der Clearing-Mitglieder, CCP-Betreiber, Endkunden und Steuerzahler minimieren (Duffie 2015). Elliott (2013) fasst die von den CCPs implementierten Strategien zusammen. Cerezetti *et al.* (2017), Avellaneda und Cont (2013) sowie Vicente *et al.* (2015) entwickeln Abwicklungsstrategien, die gleichzeitig Marktrisiko und Liquidationskosten berücksichtigen. Heath, Kelly und Manning (2015) analysieren die Konsequenzen eines *Variation Margin Haircutting*.

Krahnen und Pelizzon (2016) weisen darauf hin, dass die Skaleneffekte im Betrieb vom CCP zur *Konsolidierung* zwischen CCPs oder sogar zum Monopol führen können. Ein solches Monopol stellt ein ultimatives Kontrahenten- und systemisches Risiko für den gesamten Finanzsektor dar. Die Insolvenz eines Clearinghauses würde potenziell eine Rettungsaktion seitens der Regierung verlangen. Die Autoren erkennen, dass, solange noch kein Monopol entstanden ist, die CCPs mit geringen Margin-Anforderungen um die Marktanteile konkurrieren. Die Autoren – sowie Friedrich und Thiemann (2018) – empfehlen deswegen eine supranationale Aufsicht der CCPs und eine Regulierung der Abwicklungsmechanismen der CCPs.

Wie bereits hervorgehoben, wurden bislang in der Literatur in erster Linie einzelne Aspekte im Rahmen wissenschaftlicher Forschungen untersucht. Die aktuelle Dynamik in der Nachhandelsindustrie zeigt die Notwendigkeit einer umfassenden Sicht auf die Clearinghäuser, da ein einheitlicher Ansatz für ihre Regulierung wünschenswert ist. Dazu sollten, wie in der vorliegenden Arbeit, nicht nur die Risikopraktiken der Clearinghäuser, sondern auch ihre operationellen und IT- Aspekte erforscht werden.

3 FORSCHUNGSMETHODEN

Während für Artikel 1, 2 und 4 ein quantitativer Forschungsansatz geeignet ist, wurde für die Forschungsfragen des Artikels 3 ein qualitativer Forschungsansatz, genauer: eine explorative Fallstudie ausgewählt. Nachfolgend werden die verwendeten Forschungsansätze näher erläutert.

3.1 Quantitative Umfrage

Für die im Artikel 1 adressierte Forschungsfrage (*Welche Faktoren führen zur Akzeptanz des CCP-Clearings bei OTC-Marktteilnehmern?*) ist ein quantitativer Ansatz zielführend, da er erlaubt, die Stärke der Faktoren zu messen, die die OTC-CCP-Akzeptanz beeinflussen. Im ersten Schritt wurde ein Kausalmodell entwickelt und als Strukturgleichungsmodell operationalisiert.

Ein Kausalmodell ist eine theoretisch-hypothetische Konstruktion der Abhängigkeitsbeziehungen in einem System mit mehreren Variablen. Ein Strukturgleichungsmodell erlaubt, die latenten Variablen zu modellieren. Eine latente Variable ist eine Variable, die nicht direkt gemessen werden kann, aber nach der Hypothese den beobachteten Variablen zugrunde liegt. Gemessen wird die latente Variable durch mehrere manifesten Variablen, die direkt beobachtbar sind.

Um das Kausalmodell zu evaluieren, wurde eine Umfrage unter Leitern der Clearingabteilungen in den Banken durchgeführt. Die Ergebnisse der Umfrage wurden unter Verwendung der Methode der partiellen kleinsten Quadrate (engl. Partial Least Squares, PLS) analysiert (Chin 1998).

Um ein Strukturgleichungsmodell abzuschätzen, stehen alternative Ansätze zur Verfügung, aber schließlich wurde der komponentenbasierte Ansatz der PLS-Methode statt der Kovarianz-basierten Alternativen wie LISREL (Chin 1998) gewählt. Das hatte verschiedene Gründe. Kovarianzbasierte Methoden konzentrieren sich darauf, wie gut die verfügbaren Daten zu einem bekannten, bereits akzeptiertem Kausalmodell passen. Die PLS-Regression zielt dagegen auf die Vorhersage und die Minimierung der Restvarianz der abhängigen Variablen. Daher ist die PLS-Methode für neue kausale Modelle, die vorher nicht durch entsprechende Forschung hinreichend validiert wurden (wie das OTC-CCP-Adoption-Modell), eher geeignet. Darüber hinaus, im Gegensatz zu Kovarianz-basierten Methoden, macht PLS keine Annahme über die Verteilung der Messdaten und erfordert nur kleinere Stichprobengrößen (Chin 1998).

Für die Forschung im Artikel 1 wurde das Regressionsmodell gewählt, um die Beziehung zwischen OTC-CCP-Akzeptanz und verschiedenen Aspekten des CCPs zu untersuchen. Das PLS wurde eingesetzt, um sowohl die Parameter des Mess- als auch des Strukturmodells zu schätzen. PLS ist die am besten geeignete Analysemethode für diese Studie, weil es explorative Forschung unterstützt und nur kleine Mindestanforderungen an die Stichprobengröße legt.

Wie bereits erwähnt, wird das CCP-Clearing für OTC-Derivate als eine IT-basierte Innovation verstanden. Die wissenschaftliche Forschung hat zahlreiche Theorien und Modelle entwickelt, um die Einflussfaktoren auf die Akzeptanz einer Technologie-Innovation zu erklären. Zu den einflussreichsten zählt die sogenannte „Diffusion of Innovation"-Theorie von Rogers (Rogers 1995). Diese Theorie basiert auf den wahrgenommenen Attributen der Innovation wie relativer Vorteil, Kompatibilität, Komplexität, Überprüfbarkeit und Beobachtbarkeit. Das zugrunde liegende Modell dieser Arbeit ist eine Erweiterung der Innovationstheorie und nutzt die ersten drei genannten Innovationsattribute. Tornatzky und Klein (1982) zeigen in einer Meta-Analyse von 75 Studien, dass von den fünf Innovationsattributen in den meisten Fällen lediglich drei – nämlich relativer Vorteil, Kompatibilität und Komplexität – eine hinreichend signifikante Modellierung der Akzeptanz einer Innovation erlauben.

Obwohl die Theorie von Rogers sich als eine praktikable Rahmenbedingung für die Prüfung der Übernahme der Innovation erwiesen hat (Dwivedi et al. 2008), ist es notwendig, zusätzliche Faktoren zu integrieren, die bei der Erläuterung der Kontexteffekte helfen. Im Modell wurden zwei moderierende Effekte vermutet. Darüber hinaus wurden die im Clearing bestehenden Skaleneffekte und die „Produktstandardisierung" als zusätzliche latente Variablen berücksichtigt.

Die Auswertung des Messmodells basiert auf der Bewertung der Beladungsfaktoren, Diskriminanzanalyse, Konvergenzvalidität und Reliabilität des Konstrukts. Das Strukturmodell wurde hinsichtlich R^2 und Pfadkoeffizienten geprüft, deren Signifikanz durch Bootstrapping mit 500 getesteten Proben bestätigt wurde. Die Diskriminanzvalidität des Modells wurde bestätigt, ebenso wie dessen prädiktive Relevanz (Schloderer, Ringle und Sarstedt 2009).

3.2 Die numerische Simulation der OTC-Derivatemärkte

OTC-Derivatemärkte sind intrinsisch intransparent. Daher sind die Marktdaten, die die echten Handelspositionen der Kontrahenten reflektieren und die Auswirkungen des Nachhandelsmodells auf die Netting-Effizienz untersuchen lassen, nicht verfügbar. Infolgedessen kann die im Artikel 2 behandelte Forschungsfrage (*Was sind die Konsequenzen für das Kontrahentenrisiko in den Derivatemärkten, wenn OTC-Derivate durch CCP gecleart werden?*) nicht auf realen empirischen Daten basierend beantwortet werden. Aus diesem Grund wurde die numerische Simulation als geeignete Methode identifiziert, um diese Forschungsfrage zu adressieren.

Die Simulation ist ein häufig verwendetes und vorteilhaftes Verfahren in der Forschung der Finanzmärkte (Grunenberg, Kunzelmann und Weinhardt 2004). Der Vorteil der Computersimulation ist, dass sie einen tiefen Einblick in die hochkomplexen Wechselwirkungen, z.B. in den OTC-Derivatemärkten, ermöglicht (siehe LeBaron 2006). Eine Computerbasierte Simulation kann als eine Software-Implementierung eines formalen Modells angesehen werden (Zeigler 1976; Sauerbier 1999). Eine Simulation ermöglicht die Untersuchung einer größeren Reihe von Szenarien, als dies bei einem rein analytischen Ansatz möglich wäre. Diese Methode erlaubt einen quantitativen Vergleich der unterschiedlichen Nachhandelsmodelle und die Untersuchung von einigen komplexen Wechselwirkungen, wie z.B. die Auswirkungen der Heterogenität im Handelsverhalten auf verschiedene Nachhandelsmodelle. Sie ermöglicht die Wiederholbarkeit genau des gleichen Szenarios mit verschiedenen Parametern, um die Auswirkungen eines einzelnen Faktors auf das Ergebnis beurteilen zu können. In dieser Dissertation sind die Anzahl von Anlageklassen und die Anzahl von teilnehmenden Agenten bei gegebenem Nachhandelsmodell die wichtigsten Parameter.

Die Simulationsumgebung – dargestellt im Artikel 2 – basiert auf einer Matrizenrepräsentation der Nettohandelspositionen zwischen den Marktteilnehmern. Im Modell sind die Agenten heterogen und unterscheiden sich bezüglich des Handelsverhaltens, d.h., es gibt Sell-Side und Buy-Side Agenten.

Im ersten Schritt der Analyse wird die Matrize von Handelspositionen zwischen den Marktteilnehmern in einer bestimmten Anlageklasse in vier Untermatrizen zerlegt, die unterschiedliche Marktsegmente repräsentieren. Vier verschiedene Nachhandelsmodelle werden dargestellt, indem die Matrizen transformiert werden. Die Vergleichskenngröße ist hierbei die Netting-Effizienz, die misst, inwieweit die Nettohandelspositionen der Marktteilnehmer reduziert werden.

Für den zweiten Teil der Analyse werden die Verluste, die nach dem Ausfall eines Clearing-Mitglieds entstehen, modelliert (Bates und Crain 1999). Die Wiederherstellungskosten entstehen nur dann, wenn ein Ausfall gleichzeitig mit einer nachteiligen Preisbewegung auftritt und die gesammelten Sicherheiten übersteigt. Das Verlust-Konzentrationsverhältnis wird definiert durch den Anteil maximaler Wiederherstellungskosten im Vergleich zur Summe aller Verluste aller Agenten im gegebenen Szenario.

Generell werden die Matrizen der bilateralen Handelspositionen für eine variable Anzahl von Agenten in variabler Anzahl der Anlageklassen (wie z.B. Zinsderivate oder Rohstoffderivate) erzeugt. Für die Analyse der Ausfallverlustverteilung werden zusätzlich die Preisänderungen, Einschussanforderungen und Ausfälle der Clearing-Mitglieder modelliert.

Um die Netting-Effizienz von unterschiedlichen Clearing Nachhandelsmodellen zu vergleichen, wird in den Simulationsläufen eine Reihe von Netting-Effizienzkennzahlen für eine bestimmte Anzahl von Anlageklassen und Agenten für jedes der analysierten Nachhandelsmodelle bestimmt. Die Simulationsläufe für die Verlust-Konzentrations-Analyse liefern die Kennzahlen für jedes Nachhandelsmodell und in Abhängigkeit von der Anzahl der Agenten.

3.3 Fallstudie

Für die im Artikel 3 (Wie kann das CCP-Modell bei der Übertragung auf die OTC-Derivatemärkte verbessert werden, sodass das operationelle Risiko minimiert wird?) adressierte Forschungsfrage wurde eine Fallstudienmethode ausgewählt. Eine Fallstudie wird bevorzugt, wenn „Wie"-, „Warum"- oder „Was"-Fragen mit einem erklärenden Charakter beantwortet werden sollen (Yin 2003a). Als Forschungsmethode wurde eine Fallstudie gewählt, da sie einen explorativen Einblick in den aktuell nur marginal erforschten Bereich des Nachhandels mit OTC-Derivaten erlaubt. Eisenhardt (1989) behauptet: „Fallstudien sind gut für neue Forschungsbereiche geeignet, für die bestehende Theorien inadäquat scheinen". Dazu sind die Fallstudien dann als Methode geeignet, wenn ein zeitgenössisches Phänomen in einem realweltlichen Kontext untersucht werden soll (Yin 2003a), was auf die Verarbeitung von OTC-Derivaten zutrifft. Fallstudien sind im Bereich der Informationssysteme eine der am häufigsten verwendeten qualitativen Forschungsmethoden (Orlikowski und Baroudi 1991).

Die Einzelfallstudie gilt als eine potenziell reiche und wertvolle Quelle für Daten, geeignet für die Erkundung der Beziehungen zwischen Variablen in ihrem jeweiligen Kontext (Benbasat, Goldstein und Mead 1987). Remenyi *et al.* (1998) argumentieren, dass es unerlässlich ist, bei der Durchführung einer Einzelfallstudie die Gültigkeit der Ergebnisse zu prüfen. Denzin (1989) nennt es eine „Datenquellen-Triangulation", was bedeutet, dass mehrere Quellen von Beweismitteln verwendet werden sollten. Um die notwendige Strenge zu erreichen, ist es wichtig, die Forschungsfrage und die Einheit der Analyse in der Entwicklung und Vorbereitungsphase explizit und richtig zu definieren. Wie die Feldstudien verwenden die Fallstudien typischerweise Fragebögen, kodierte Interviews oder systematische Beobachtungen als bevorzugte Techniken zur Datenerfassung (Yin 2003b).

Die Datenerfassungstechniken, die in dieser Dissertation verwendet wurden, sind semi-strukturierte Interviews und Dokumentenanalysen. Semi-strukturierte Interviews verbessern die allgemeine Qualität und erlauben den Forschern, Fragen und Antworten zu klären und die neuen Dimensionen eines Phänomens zu entdecken. Yin (2003a) argumentiert, dass die Dokumentation ergänzend verwendet werden sollte, um die Daten aus anderen Quellen zu überprüfen.

Es wurde mit der Überprüfung aller relevanten Unterlagen vom Clearing-Service für Kreditderivate begonnen, bevor die Gestaltung eines Fallstudienprotokolls stattgefunden hat. Technische Systemspezifikationen und funktionale Prozessbeschreibungen, Kundenpräsentationen sowie Feldnotizen wurden in einer Fallstudien-Datenbank gesammelt.

Interviews mit wichtigen Mitarbeitern in verschiedenen Positionen innerhalb der Organisation und des Projekts wurden durchgeführt. Die Befragten waren die IT- und Business-Manager sowie zahlreiche Business- und IT-Analysten des Clearinghauses. Interviews wurden aufgezeichnet und transkribiert. Informationen wurden auch aus Sekundärquellen aus dem Intranet bezogen. Die Genauigkeit aller Daten wurde durch darauffolgende Treffen und den Austausch von Dokumenten per E-Mail überprüft.

3.4 Empirisch-quantitative Analyse

Für die im Artikel 4 adressierte Forschungsfrage („Welchen Einfluss hat die Einführung vom OTC-CCP auf systemisches Risiko in den Derivatemärkten, insbesondere durch die Risikomanagementpraktiken der CCPs?") wurde ein empirischer Ansatz gewählt. Während zahlreiche Studien in Bezug auf die Dynamik des Handels in den Finanzmärkten empirische Analyse einsetzen (Biais, Hillion und Spatt 1995; Madhavan, Richardson und Roomans 1997), wird diese Methode im Post-Trading-Bereich nur selten angewandt. Ein Erklärungsansatz wäre hier ein begrenzter Zugang für die Forscher zu proprietären Daten von CCPs und deren Clearing-Mitgliedern.

Artikel 4 basiert auf einer umfangreichen Datenmenge, die von einem führenden Europäischen Clearinghaus zur Verfügung gestellt wurde. Sie umfasst die täglichen Margen-Anforderungen sowie Sicherheitsabschläge von 262 Clearing-Mitgliedern über einen Zeitraum von zehn Jahren.

Eine erste explorative Datenanalyse hat gezeigt, dass sich die Volatilität der Margen/Sicherheitsabschläge im Zeitverlauf geändert haben könnte. Eine solche sich zeitlich verändernde Volatilität ist für Finanzmärkte charakteristisch und kann mit verallgemeinerten autoregressiven Modellen bedingter Heteroskedastizität (GARCH) analysiert werden (Bollerslev 1986). Eine Erweiterung ist das von Engle (2002) vorgeschlagene Modell der dynamischen bedingten Korrelation (DCC GARCH). Eine Schätzung des Modells erfolgt in zwei Schritten. Im ersten Schritt wird der univariate GARCH-Prozess geschätzt, im zweiten Schritt wird die Schätzung der dynamischen Korrelationsstruktur darauf aufgebaut. Es handelt sich hierbei um ein anerkanntes Modell, das häufig im Bereich der Vermögensverwaltung angewandt wird, wo Korrelationen einen wichtigen Faktor bei der Bewertung oder Absicherung strukturierter Finanzinstrumente darstellen.

4 ERGEBNISSE

Im nachfolgenden Abschnitt werden die wichtigsten Ergebnisse der vier Forschungsartikel, aus denen diese kumulative Dissertation besteht, erläutert.

4.1 Ergebnisse aus Artikel 1: Adoption of a Centralized Post-Trade Processing Market Infrastructure after the Credit Crisis.

Basierend auf der Diffusionstheorie von Innovationen zielt diese empirische Studie im Bereich des OTC-Clearings darauf ab, die Faktoren zu identifizieren, die die Einführung des CCP-Clearings für OTC-Derivate beeinflussen.

Die Methode der PLS-Regression wurde angewandt, um die Ergebnisse einer Umfrage unter Leitern der Clearingabteilungen in den Banken

Deutsche Zusammenfassung

und Vermögensverwaltungsfirmen zu evaluieren. Die empirische Analyse hat bestätigt, dass Kompatibilität mit bestehenden Nachhandelsprozessen und der wahrgenommene relative Vorteil des OTC-CCPs bedeutend zur Adoption des CCP-Clearings für OTC-Derivate beitragen, wobei Komplexität kein signifikanter Prädiktor ist.

Die Ergebnisse stehen im Einklang mit den Beobachtungen über die CCP-Diffusion im OTC-Derivatemarkt (BIS 2007). Da die Marktteilnehmer in den letzten Jahren hohe Investitionen in den Nachhandelslösungen getätigt hatten und Verbindungen zu einer globalen Infrastruktur herstellten, ist die operative Kompatibilität zwischen bestehender Nachhandelsinfrastruktur für OTC-Derivate und CCP-Service von wesentlicher Bedeutung. Eine beschleunigte Akzeptanz von OTC-CCPs wurde nach den Turbulenzen der Finanzkrise von 2007-2009 beobachtet. Dies kann durch eine Erhöhung des wahrgenommenen relativen Vorteils der OTC-CCP (vor allem auf der Kontrahentenrisiko-Ebene) erklärt werden. Die kritische Anzahl der Teilnehmer wurde in der Studie mit starkem direktem Einfluss auf Akzeptanz des CCPs für OTC-Derivate bestätigt. Im Clearing bestehen Skaleneffekte im Netting, da mit steigender Anzahl der Clearing-Mitglieder die Netting-Möglichkeiten potenziell zunehmen. Deswegen ist das Erreichen der kritischen Anzahl der Marktteilnehmer und der Höhe der Volumina wesentlich für die OTC-CCP-Annahme und abhängig von den größten Derivate-Händlern.

Die Komplexität wurde in der Studie, anders als erwartet, nicht als ein signifikanter Faktor für die OTC-CCP-Adoption bestätigt. Die Begründung könnte die wahrgenommene relativ niedrige CCP-Margin-Anforderung sein, die sich aus dem zunehmenden Wettbewerb im Clearingbereich oder aus zunehmender Nutzung von Sicherheiten im bilateralen Nachhandel ergibt.

Die „Produktstandardisierung" hat, wie die Studie zeigt, sowohl einen starken direkten Einfluss auf OTC-CCP-Adoption als auch indirekt auf das Verhältnis zwischen dem relativen Vorteil und der Adoption. Nichtstandardisierte Produktmerkmale behindern die Automatisierung von Nachhandel-Verarbeitungsprozessen. Der häufige Mangel an einem allgemein anerkannten Bewertungsmodell für nicht standardisierte Produkte erschwert hierbei das Risikomanagement zusätzlich. Daher ist die Standardisierung eine Voraussetzung für ein wirksames CCP-Clearing. Zusammenfassend lässt sich sagen, dass die Akzeptanz des CCP-Modells seitens der Marktteilnehme mit steigender Kompatibilität der Lösung für OTC-Derivate mit bestehenden OTC-Abwicklungsprozessen, steigender Wichtigkeit des Kontrahentenrisikos und fortschreitender Standardisierung der OTC-Kontrakte sowie der Beteiligung im CCP zunimmt.

4.2 Ergebnisse aus Artikel 2: OTC-Clearing Arrangements for Bank Systemic Risk Regulation: A Simulation Approach.

Dieser Artikel beschäftigt sich mit den Auswirkungen der jüngsten Finanzmarktreformen, die in den OTC-Derivatemärkten nach der Finanzkrise von 2007-2009 eingeführt wurden (vor allem mit der Clearingverpflichtung für OTC-Derivate). Der Artikel vergleicht den Status quo mit den simulierten Ergebnissen der vorgeschlagenen Reformen. Hierbei werden bestehende OTC-Clearing-Nachhandelsmodelle mit dem von den Regulatoren vorgeschlagenem CCP-Clearing-Modell verglichen.

Die Simulationsläufe der Netting-Effizienzanalyse liefern Ergebnisse für jedes Marktsegment. Im Sell-Side-to-Sell-Side-Marktsegment maximiert der OTC-CCP die Netting-Effizienz, verglichen mit Tear-ups (Close-out Netting), wenn zwei oder mehr Assetklassen gecleart werden (mehr als zwei Agenten am OTC-CCP teilnehmen). Die Netting-Effizienz steigt mit der Anzahl der beteiligten Agenten und der Anlageklassen, jedoch mit abnehmenden Grenzschritten.

Beim Vergleich von CCP-Clearing mit dem Prime-Broker-Modell, zeigt sich, dass die Verschiebung der Prime-Broker-Positionen der Sell-Side-Agenten zum Clearinghaus zu erheblichen Netting-Effizienzgewinnen für die Sell-Side führt. Der Buy-Side-Zugang zu einem CCP wirkt sich im Gegenteil sogar nachteilig auf die Sell-Side aus, da die Sell-Side-Agenten eine zusätzliche Belastung bei der Aufrechterhaltung segregierter Kundenpositionen haben.

Deutsche Zusammenfassung

Im Buy-Side-to-Sell-Side Segment liefern das Prime-Broker-Modell und ein CCP die gleiche Netting-Effizienz. Mit der Anzahl der teilnehmenden Sell-Side-Agenten sowie mit der Anzahl der Anlageklassen unter solchem Nachhandelsmodell steigt die Netting-Effizienz, jedoch mit abnehmenden Grenzschritten. Die Verschiebung der Kundenpositionen unter Prime-Brokerage zu einem CCP bietet keine Netting-Effizienzgewinne. Allerdings bringt das CCP-Clearing andere Vorteile für die Buy-Side-Kunden, da ihre Position von allen Sell-Side-Agenten abgesichert wird. Im Falle eines Ausfalls eines Clearing-Mitglieds kann der Buy-Side-Agent seine segregierte Position auf ein anderes Mitglied übertragen. Die Segregierung der Kundenpositionen stellt jedoch eine zusätzliche Belastung für Sell-Side-Agenten dar.

Die Ergebnisse der Verlust-Konzentrations-Analyse zeigen, dass im Vergleich zu den anderen Nachhandelsmodellen, bei einem CCP, die Ausfallverluste am wenigsten konzentriert sind. Außerdem werden die Verluste in größerem Umfang mit der zunehmenden Anzahl von CCP-Mitgliedern verteilt. Das systemische Risiko wird dadurch effektiv reduziert. Das Prime-Brokerage-Modell führt im Vergleich zu der höchsten Konzentration der Verluste, was die Fragilität der großen Derivate-Dealer bestätigt.

Die Ergebnisse zeigen, dass ein obligatorisches Clearing aller OTC-Derivate durch eine Zentrale Gegenpartei, im Vergleich zu bestehenden Clearing Nachhandelsmodellen, das systemische Risiko erheblich reduzieren würde, aber nur unter der Voraussetzung, dass die multilateralen Netting-Vorteile der CCP und die Verlustvergemeinschaftung weitgehend angestrebt werden. Um dieses Ziel zu erreichen, sollten die politischen Entscheidungsträger sicherstellen, dass die kritische Masse an Marktteilnehmern und Assetklassen dem obligatorischen Clearing unterliegt. Die Produktstandardisierung sollte weiter gefördert werden. Die Kundenpositionen sollten nicht vollständig aus dem Netting ausgeschlossen werden, indem geeignete Segregierungsmodelle von den Regulatoren unterstützt werden.

4.3 Ergebnisse aus Artikel 3: Is a Full Scale Straight Through Processing of OTC-Derivatives Possible? A Straight Through Processing Potential of a Central Counterparty Clearing Model for Credit Default Swaps: An Exploratory Case.

In diesem Artikel werden die Auswirkungen der Einführung eines OTC-Clearinghauses auf der operationellen Ebene untersucht. Insbesondere wird in der Studie die externe, d.h. branchenweite Straight Through Processing-Rate (STP-Rate) (Hee, Che und Huang 2003) vor und nach der Einführung eines Clearinghauses für Kreditderivate analysiert. Die externe STP-Rate wird im Artikel 3 als eine Herausforderung verstanden, die externen Partner im Finanzprozess für OTC-Derivate nahtlos zu verbinden: die Handelsplattformen, die Kontrakt-Bestätigungsplattformen, die Clearinghäuser und die anderen Dienstleistungsanbieter.

Das Ergebnis der Studie zeigt, dass der Beitrag des untersuchten Clearinghauses für Kreditderivate zur Erhöhung der STP-Rate in der Nachhandel-Wertschöpfungskette relativ gering war. Ein Clearinghaus zentralisiert die Funktionen wie Ereignis-, Positionen- und Sicherheitenmanagement. Nichtsdestotrotz waren die ersten zwei Funktionen bereits weitgehend in anderen Marktinstitutionen automatisiert, noch bevor der Zentrale Kontrahent für Kreditderivate eingeführt wurde. Zusammenfassend lässt sich sagen, dass die geringe Verbesserung der STP-Rate nach der Einführung des OTC-CCPs vor allem dank der Verbesserungen durch das zentralisierte Sicherheitenmanagment erfolgte.

Da eine hohe Nicht-STP- oder Ausnahmerate die erforderliche Mitarbeiterzahl signifikant erhöhen kann, sind die Kosten pro Geschäft eine implizite STP-Kennzahl (Best und Weth 2009). Die Senkung der Kosten pro Geschäft, die durch die Einführung eines Clearinghauses für den CDS-Markt verursacht wurde, wurde in der Studie auf 14 Prozent geschätzt.

Artikel 3 zeigt die Implementierungsanstrengungen auf, die geleistet werden müssen, um das CCP-Modell erfolgreich in den OTC-

Derivatemärkten einzusetzen. In der Studie wird ein Optimierungsvorschlag für die analysierte Clearinghaus-Architektur in Bezug auf ihr STP-Potenzial gemacht. Vor allem eine direkte Verbindung zwischen dem CCP und der Bestätigungsplattform würde erlauben, den Workflow zu vereinfachen und einen Echtzeit-Versand der bestätigten Geschäfte an den CCP zu ermöglichen.

4.4 Ergebnisse aus Artikel 4: The Recent Crises And Central Counterparty Risk Practices in the Light of Procyclicality: Empirical Evidence.

Ein aus Sicht der Regulierungsbehörden problematischer Zusammenhang in den zentral abgewickelten Derivatemärkten ist, dass CCP-Margen-Anforderungen und Sicherheitsabschläge in Zeiten einer Marktkrise stark steigen, den Handel hemmen und Liquiditätsdruck verursachen können und die Krise damit weiter verschärfen. Die im Artikel 4 dargelegte Forschung gibt einen Einblick in die prozyklischen Auswirkungen der Risikomanagementpraktiken der Zentralen Gegenparteien.

Die Literatur suggeriert, dass CCP-Riskomanagementpraktiken wie Margining und Sicherheitsabschläge den Wirtschaftszyklus verschärfen können (Brunnermeier und Pedersen 2009). Basierend auf der zehnjährigen Historie empirischer Daten eines der weltweit führenden Clearinghäuser wurde im Artikel 4 untersucht, ob und inwieweit die prozyklischen Effekte statistisch belegbar sind. Die Ergebnisse für den untersuchten Zeitraum, der die Finanzkrise 2007-2009 und die Europäische Staatsschuldenkrise (begonnen im Jahr 2010) mit einschließt, lassen die von der theoretischen Forschung aufgestellte Hypothese, dass die CCP-Risikomanagementpraktiken prozyklisch sind, nicht bestätigen. Die Ergebnisse zeigen nur ein geringes durchschnittliches Niveau der bedingten Korrelation zwischen Marktstress und CCP-Margin-Anforderungen einerseits und zwischen Marktstress und Sicherheitsabschlägen andererseits.

Die Dämpfung der Prozyklizität im Finanzsystem ist ein wesentlicher Bestandteil der Stärkung des regulatorischen Regelwerkes. Deshalb erwägen die Regulierungsbehörden die Einführung von makroprudenziellen Instrumenten, wie minimale Sicherheitsabschläge und Margen oder antizyklische Zuschläge. Im Artikel 4 wurde dagegen gezeigt, dass die systematische Übersicherung der offenen Positionen von Clearing-Mitgliedern (wie in den empirischen Daten beobachtet) bereits antizyklisch wirken kann. Darüber hinaus lässt sich feststellen, dass wenn die Märkte sich nach der Krise beruhigen, im CCP-Risikomanagementmodell die vorherigen Extremereignisse berücksichtigt werden, was zu einer antizyklischen Margin-Anforderung führt.

Überraschenderweise hat sich die CCP-Risikomanagementpraxis nicht als anfällig für Notverkäufe (engl. „fire sales") erwiesen, wie es in einigen theoretischen Modellen (z.B. Brunnermeier und Pedersen 2009) prognostiziert wird. Die Clearing-Mitglieder entfernten nur selten (in 20 Prozent der Fälle) die Wertpapiere aus dem Sicherheitsportfolio, wenn die Sicherheitsabschläge für diese Wertpapiere gestiegen waren. Die Sicherheitsportfolien der Clearing-Mitglieder unterliegen dagegen in den Zeiten des Marktstresses stärker der Diversifikation als während der ruhigen Phasen.

5 BEITRAG ZUR FORSCHUNG UND PRAXIS

In diesem Abschnitt werden die Auswirkungen der Ergebnisse dieser Dissertation auf die Theorie und Praxis erläutert.

5.1 Beitrag zur Forschung

Diese Arbeit erweitert die Forschung zu Nachhandelsmodellen auf verschiedenen Ebenen und in verschiedenen Bereichen.

Erstens wird in dieser Dissertation die Positionierung des OTC-CCPs als eine IT-ermöglichte Innovation (Mahnke, Overby und Özcan 2006) vorgenommen. Artikel 1 definiert das CCP-Clearing als eine digitale Innovation im Zusammenhang mit dessen Einsatz in den OTC-Derivatemärkten. In der bestehenden Literatur wurde OTC-CCP bisher lediglich als eine Risikomanagement-Institution betrachtet. Diese Studie

Deutsche Zusammenfassung

untersucht OTC-CCP als eine IT-basierte Neuerung und betrachtet dieses Nachhandelsmodell aus unterschiedlichen Perspektiven. Dadurch wird die Einführung des OTC-CCPs in einen neuen, über den Rahmen des reinen Risiko-Aspekts hinausgehenden Kontext gestellt. Die Positionierung des OTC-CCP als eine IT-ermöglichte Innovation ist ein äußerst vielversprechender Forschungsansatz, da er eine Vielzahl an Fragestellungen und weiteren Untersuchungen erlaubt, für die diese Dissertation eine wichtige Grundlage darstellt.

Zweitens wird die Entscheidung über die CCP-Adoption untersucht. Die Faktoren, die die Adoption von OTC-CCPs durch Marktteilnehmer beeinflussen, wurden im Artikel 1 analysiert. Der Beitrag zur Theorie hat drei Dimensionen. Die durchgeführte Umfrage erweitert die Adoptionstheorie auf die Domäne des OTC-Clearings, die vorher nicht in der Adoptionsforschung adressiert wurde. Darüber hinaus erweist sich das im Artikel 1 vorgestellte Forschungsmodell mit den Innovationsattributen, die die Einführung einer Innovation fördern oder verhindern, als erfolgreiche Erweiterung zentraler Aspekte der Theorie von Rogers zur Diffusion von Innovation (Rogers 1995). Dies ist ein vielversprechender Vorschlag für die weitere Forschung, weil zwei der drei von Rogers aufgestellten hypothetischen Beziehungen bestätigt werden konnten. Auch konnten die Konstrukte wie relativer Vorteil, Kompatibilität, kritische Masse und Produktstandarisierung als substanzielle Prädiktoren der Adoption des OTC-CCPs bestätigt werden.

Drittens erweitert der Artikel 2 die akademische Forschung zu Nachhandelsmodellen, indem die OTC-Derivatemarkt-Struktur mit ihren wichtigsten Merkmalen (wie u.a. die zentrale Rolle der Derivaten-Dealer) und die darauf basierenden vier Nachhandelsmodelle explizit modelliert werden. Das entwickelte mathematische Modell erlaubt daher eine vergleichende Analyse der verschiedenen Nachhandelsmodelle in Bezug auf ihre potenzielle Netting-Effizienz. Das analytische Modell kann als Basis für die weitere Forschung benutzt werden, um weitere Merkmale und Aspekte, wie die Risikoreduktion oder die Eigenkapitalbelastung der verschiedenen Nachhandelslösungen, zu evaluieren. Das Modell liefert damit eine wissenschaftliche Grundlage und ein Modellierungswerkzeug zur Untersuchung weiterer möglicher struktureller Reformen des Finanzmarktes im Spannungsfeld von Stabilität und Liquidität.

Viertens wurden die Konsequenzen der unterschiedlichen Nachhandelsmodelle und Risikomanagementpraktiken der CCPs untersucht. Da die empirischen Daten zur Analyse der Konsequenzen der Clearingmodelle nicht verfügbar sind, zeigt die im Artikel 2 präsentierte Simulationsumgebung eine Möglichkeit auf, den Einfluss der Nachhandelsmodelle zu untersuchen. Die Ergebnisse der numerischen Simulation tragen zum tieferen Verständnis dessen bei, wie die komplexen Interaktionen der Marktteilnehmer auf der Mikroebene und die Clearingmodelle das systemische Risiko in den OTC-Derivatemärkten beeinflussen. Die empirische Datenanalyse im Artikel 4 erläutert den Einfluss der CCPs auf die Finanzmarktstabilität basierend auf einer hinreichend aussagekräftigen Datengrundlage und stellt damit einen wertvollen Beitrag zur Forschung im Bereich der Auswirkungen der Risikomanagmentpraktiken der zentralen Gegenparteien.

Schließlich fördert der Artikel 3 das Verständnis von Forschern bezüglich des STP-Potenzials eines Clearinghauses für OTC-Derivate. Basierend auf dem ausgewählten Fallstudiendesign, besteht der Beitrag des Artikels 3 zur Theorie darin, konkretes, kontextabhängiges Wissen in Bezug auf die Identifizierung neuer Phänomene und Trends im CDS-Verarbeitungsworkflow aufzubauen.

Die in Artikel 4 durchgeführte quantitative Analyse diente der Überprüfung der bestehenden Theorie. Der ausreichend große Datensatz wurde verwendet, um die Thesen über die Notverkäufe und die prozyklischen Auswirkungen von CCP-Margen und Sicherheitsabschlägen zu testen.

5.2 Beitrag zur Praxis

Die vorliegende Arbeit liefert Erkenntnisse, die für verschiedene Gruppen – wie etwa die Marktinfrastrukturbetreiber und Regulatoren – von Interesse sind. Die Artikel helfen dabei, die Besonderheiten von Nachhandelsprozessen für OTC-Derivate zu verstehen.

Die Arbeit liefert ein Argument für die Neuordnung der Struktur der OTC-Derivatemärkte und unterstützt die aktuelle regulatorische Debatte (ESMA 2018a; ESRB 2016, 2017a, 2017b; Raykov 2018). Der Artikel 2 untersucht die Auswirkungen der EMIR- und Dodd-Frank-Regulierung auf die OTC-Derivatemärkte und formuliert klare Handlungsempfehlungen für die Regulierungsbehörden, wie das systemische Risiko durch die konkrete Umsetzung der jüngsten Reformen zu minimieren ist. Darüber hinaus wurden im Rahmen der Untersuchung der prozyklischen Auswirkungen der CCP-Risikomanagementpraktiken (Artikel 4) Empfehlungen für aktuelle und zukünftige Regulierung formuliert.

Die Dissertation unterstützt die weitere Verbesserung des Clearingservices für die OTC-Derivate. Artikel 1 beschreibt die Faktoren, die die Annahme des CCP-Service in den OTC-Derivatemärkten beeinflussen, und gibt den Infrastrukturanbietern, wie bspw. Clearinghäusern, einen klaren Hinweis in Bezug auf die Gestaltung des CCP-Services für OTC-Derivate. Ferner wird im Artikel 3 dieser Arbeit die Empfehlung gemacht, wie man die STP-Rate in der Wertschöpfungskette des Nachhandels der OTC-Derivate verbessern kann. Insbesondere können die Clearinghäuser von den Empfehlungen in Bezug auf die Verbesserung ihres Service-Designs im Hinblick auf eine zu erwartende Marktakzeptanz profitieren.

6 LIMITATIONEN UND WEITERE FORSCHUNG

Dieser Abschnitt geht auf die in dieser Arbeit bestehenden Einschränkungen ein und gibt einen Ausblick auf eine mögliche weitere Forschung.

6.1 Limitationen

Die im Artikel 1 beschriebene Umfrage erlaubte, die Daten zu sammeln, die einen Einblick in die Adoption der CCPs in den OTC-Derivatemärkten ermöglichen. Nichtsdestotrotz weist die Studie eine kleine Stichprobengröße aus. Die in der präsentierten Studie gegebene Stichprobengröße (von 53 ausgefüllten Fragebögen) ist adäquat für eine exploratorische Investigation, für konfirmatorische Studien wäre aber eine größere Stichprobe notwendig. Goodhue, Lewis und Thompson (2006) kommen zur Schlussforderung, dass es keinen Beweis dafür gibt, dass statistisch signifikante Ergebnisse mit einer kleinen Stichprobengröße ungültig sind. Sie behaupten lediglich, dass eine Beziehung, die sich in einer Forschung mit kleiner Stichprobengröße nicht als statistisch signifikant erwiesen hat, nicht als nicht existent interpretiert werden sollte. Das bedeutet lediglich, dass mit einer kleinen Stichprobe schwache Effekte nicht entdeckt und bestätigt werden können.

Das Forschungsmodell, das angewandt wurde, um die Adoption des CCPs zu untersuchen, hat nur eine kleine Aussagekraft bezüglich der Komplexität. Deswegen kann man vermuten, dass außer den von der Innovationsdiffusionstheorie verwendeten noch weitere Faktoren berücksichtigt werden können.

Die Ergebnisse einer numerischen Simulation hängen stark von den spezifischen quantitativen Annahmen über die Parameter des Modells ab. Auch die im Artikel 2 präsentierte Simulationsumgebung basiert auf mehreren Annahmen. Es wurde angenommen, dass die Handelspositionen normalverteilt sind. Dennoch passt diese Annahme nicht gut zu den Positionen, die aus vielen individuellen Derivaten bestehen. Denn bei diesen sind, empirisch betrachtet, große Wertveränderungen wie große Verluste (sogenannte „fat tails") wahrscheinlicher und schiefer verteilt als unter der Normalverteilungsannahme. Das bedeutet, dass die extremen negativen Werte (Verluste) wahrscheinlicher sind als unter der Normalverteilungsannahme. Dennoch, die Aggregation innerhalb einer Anlageklasse von Derivaten kann in eine Netto-Position resultieren, die eine weniger schiefe Verteilung aufweist, da Long- und Short-Positionen aggregiert werden und eine Diversifikation der einzelnen Basiswerte stattfindet. Das gilt vor allem für die Positionen der Derivate-Dealer, die generell beide Seiten des Marktes halten. Die Kunden-Portfolien sind weniger ausgewogen, da sie per Definition entweder aus Kauf- oder Verkaufspositionen bestehen.

Darüber hinaus wurde angenommen, dass Marktrisiko und Kreditrisiko voneinander unabhängig sind. Deswegen wurde die Ausfallwahrscheinlichkeit als eine Variable modelliert, die unabhängig von den

Deutsche Zusammenfassung

Marktpreisänderungen und Positionsveränderungen ist. Eine Verbesserung könnte sein, die Ausfallwahrscheinlichkeit als eine endogene Variable zu betrachten, weil in der Praxis hochkonzentrierte Positionen und eine ungünstige Marktpreisbewegung die Ausfallwahrscheinlichkeit eines Marktteilnehmers signifikant erhöhen könnten.

Die Forschung im Artikel 3 präsentierte eine auf die Anlageklasse der Kreditderivate beschränkte Fallstudie eines Clearinghauses. Die Transferabilität auf andere Anlageklassen ist deshalb teilweise beschränkt. Um zu einem tieferen Verständnis vom Prozessierungsmodell zu gelangen, sollten auch andere Anlageklassen der Derivate untersucht werden. Deswegen wird empfohlen, dass weitere empirische Studien durchgeführt werden, um die Nachhandelsmodelle für andere OTC-Derivate und das Potenzial für die Automatisierung von deren Workflows besser zu erklären.

Die Generalisierbarkeit der Ergebnisse aus Artikel 3 ist ebenfalls begrenzt. Die Daten, die zur Analyse der Auswirkungen der CCP-Risikopraktiken auf die Prozyklikalität der Finanzmärkten verwendet wurden, stammen von einem Clearinghaus. Verschiedene CCPs wenden jedoch möglicherweise unterschiedliche Risikomethoden an, wobei sie die bestehenden regulatorischen Anforderungen weiterhin erfüllen.

Die Parametrisierung und die Auswahl des GARCH-Modells für die Analyse der Zeitreihen beeinflussen die Ergebnisse der quantitativen Analyse (Artikel 4). Einige stilisierte Fakten bezüglich der Finanzdaten steuerten die Auswahl des Modells, die Verteilungsannahmen und die Parameterauswahl. Da die GARCH-Modellierung ständig weiterentwickelt wird, könnten deren neueste Modelle die Anpassungsgüte jedoch vermutlich noch steigern.

Die Forschung zu CCP-Clearing für die OTC-Derivatemärkte ist ein noch immer junges Forschungsgebiet, in dem sich verschiedene Bereiche (Informationssysteme, Finanzen, quantitative Forschung) überschneiden. Diese können mit den verschiedenen Methoden der interdisziplinären Forschung adressiert werden.

6.2 Weitere Forschung

Ein Ziel der letzten Finanzmarktreformen war, die Transparenz in den OTC-Märkten zu erhöhen, weswegen einige Datensätze erst jetzt für die akademische Forschung zugänglich werden. Dies stellt eine Chance für eine weitere Forschung bezüglich der Nachhandelsinfrastruktur für OTC-Derivatemärkte dar. Dazu werden mehrere Bereiche in diesem Abschnitt skizziert.

Einige der der numerischen Simulation (Artikel 2) zugrunde liegenden Annahmen können in zukünftiger Forschung herausgefordert werden. Dies betrifft vor allem die Annahme der Normalverteilung der Handelspositionen und der Unabhängigkeit des Kredit- und Marktrisikos (siehe dazu das Kapitel 6.1). Es ist vorhersehbar, dass unter dem regulatorischen Druck die Transparenz der OTC-Derivatemärkte weiter steigern wird, sodass die simulierten Datensätze teilweise mit realen empirischen Daten ersetzt werden können.

Die Verbindungen zwischen CCPs könnten potenziell die Netting-Effizienz im Nachhandel erhöhen. Deswegen wäre es interessant, den Gesamteinfluss von Interoperabilitätsvereinbarungen zwischen CCPs auf das systemische Risiko zu evaluieren.

Die Untersuchungen in den Artikeln 1 und 3 hatten einen exploratorischen Charakter. Verallgemeinerungen aus diesen Erkenntnissen wären Aufgabe für die zukünftige Forschung. Das Adoptionsmodell des OTC-CCPs könnte um zusätzliche Faktoren erweitert werden, die die Übernahme des CCP-Clearing in den OTC-Derivatemärkten beeinflussen. Die Infrastruktur für die weiteren OTC-Asset-Klassen könnte in Bezug auf ihr STP-Potential untersucht werden.

Abschließend lässt sich feststellen, dass die CCPs, als zentrale Institutionen, selbst das Risiko konzentrieren. Da ihre Bedeutung in der Finanzwirtschaft steigt, wäre es wichtig zu analysieren, welche Mechanismen die CCPs entwickeln, um sich selbst gegen Insolvenz zu schützen. In diesem Zusammenhang könnten in der zukünftigen Forschung die verschiedenen Verlustverteilungsmodelle von CCPs untersucht werden.

Literaturverzeichnis

Abruzzo, N. und Park, Y.-H. (2016). An Empirical Analysis of Futures Margin Changes: Determinants and Policy Implications. *Journal of Financial Services Research*, 49 (1), 65–100.

Acharya, V. V. und Viswanathan, S. (2011). Leverage, Moral Hazard, and Liquidity. *Journal of Finance*, 66, 99–138.

Anderson, S., Dion, J.-P. und Perez Saiz, H. (2013). *To link or not to link? Netting and exposures between central counterparties*. Bank of Canada Working Paper Nr. 6.

Arnsdorf, M. (2012). Quantification of central counterparty risk. *Journal of Risk Management in Financial Institutions*, 5, 273–287.

Ashcraft, A., Gârleanu, N. und Pedersen, L.H. (2010). Two Monetary Tools: Interest Rates and Haircuts. *NBER Macroeconomic Annual*, 25, 143–180.

Avellaneda, M. und Cont, R. (2013). *Close-Out Risk Evaluation (CORE): A New Risk Management Approach for Central Counterparties.* https://ssrn.com/abstract=2247493 (Zugriff 01.02.2019).

Bank for International Settlements (BIS). (1998). *OTC Derivatives: Settlement Procedures and Counterparty Risk Management*. Committee on Payment and Settlement Systems Publications Nr. 27, http://www.bis.org/publ/cpss27.pdf (Zugriff: 05.02.2019).

Bank for International Settlements (BIS). (2003). *A Glossary of Terms Used in Payments and Settlement Systems*. http://www.bis.org/publ/cpss00b.pdf (Zugriff: 05.02.2019).

Bank for International Settlements (BIS). (2007). *New developments in clearing and settlement arrangements for OTC derivatives*. CPSS Publication Nr. 77, http://www.bis.org/publ/cpss77.htm (Zugriff: 05.02.2019).

Bank for International Settlements (BIS). (2015). *Margin requirements for non-centrally cleared derivatives*. https://www.bis.org/bcbs/publ/d317.pdf (Zugriff: 05.02.2019).

Bank for International Settlements (BIS). (2018a). *Derivatives statistics.* www.bis.org/statistics/derstats.htm (Zugriff: 05.02.2019).

Bank for International Settlements (BIS) (2018b). *Incentives to centrally clear over-the-counter (OTC) derivatives. A post-implementation evaluation of the effects of the G20 financial regulatory reforms.* https://www.bis.org/publ/othp29.pdf (Zugriff: 05.02.2019).

Bates, D. und Craine, R. (1999). Valuing the Futures Market Clearinghouse's Default Exposure during the 1987 Crash. *Journal of Money, Credit and Banking*, 31, 248–272.

Bellia, M., Panzica R., Pelizzon, L. und Peltonen T. (2017). *The demand for central clearing: to clear or not to clear, that is the question*. ESRB Working Paper Nr. 62.

Benbasat, I., Goldstein, D. K. und Mead, M. (1987). The Case Research Strategy in Studies of Information Systems. *MIS Quarterly*, 11 (3), 369–385.

Bergman, W. J., Bliss, R. R., Johnson, Ch. A. und Kaufman, G. G. (2004). *Netting, Financial Contracts, and Banks: The Economic Implications*. FRB of Chicago Working Paper Nr. 2.

Best, E. und Weth, M. (2009). *Geschäftsprozesse optimieren. Der Praxisleitfaden für erfolgreiche Reorganisation*, Wiesbaden: Springer, ISBN: 9783834994103.

Biais, B., Hillion, P. und Spatt, Ch. (1995). An Empirical Analysis of the Limit Order Book and the Order Flow in the Paris Bourse. *Journal of Finance*, 50, 1655–1689.

Bliss, R. R. und Kaufman, G. G. (2005). *Derivatives and Systemic Risk: Netting, Collateral, and Closeout*. FRB of Chicago Working Paper Nr. 3.

Bliss, R. R. und Steigerwald, R. (2006). Derivatives Clearing and Settlement: a Comparison of Central Counterparties and Alternative Structures. *Economic Perspectives*, 30 (4), 22–29.

Bollerslev, T. (1986). Generalized Autoregressive Conditional Heteroskedasticity. *Journal of Econometrics*, 31, 307–327.

Brunnermeier, M. K. und Pedersen, L. H. (2009). Market liquidity and funding liquidity, *Review of Financial Studies*, 22 (6), 2201–2238.

Bundesanstalt für Finanzdienstleistungsaufsicht. (2017). *Clearingpflicht bei Derivaten*.
https://www.bafin.de/DE/Aufsicht/BoersenMaerkte/Derivate/EMIR/Clearing/ZentralesClearing/pflichten_zum_zentralen_clearing_node.html (Zugriff: 02.02.2019).

Campbell, J. Y. (2002). Asset Pricing at the Millenium. *Journal of Finance*, 55, 1515–1567.

Cerezetti, F., Sumawong, A., Shreyas, U. und Karimalis, E. (2017). *Market liquidity, closeout procedures and initial margin for CCPs*. Bank of England Staff Working Paper Nr. 643.

Chin, W. W. (1998). The Partial Least Squares Approach to Structural Equation Modeling. In: Marcoulides, G.A. (Hrsg.) *Modern Methods for Business Research*, Mahwah (N.J.): Lawrence Erlbaum Associates.

Cont, R. und Kokholm, T. (2014). Central Clearing of OTC Derivatives: Bilateral vs Multilateral Netting. *Statistics & Risk Modeling*, 31, 1–20.

Cox, N., Garvin, N. und Kelly, G. (2013). *Central Counterparty Links and Clearing System Exposures*. Reserve Bank of Australia Discussion Paper Nr. 12.

Denzin, N. K. (1989). *The research act: A theoretical introduction to sociological methods* (3. Aufl.), Englewood Cliffs (NJ): Prentice Hall, ISBN: 0137743815.

Deutsche Börse. (2014). *How Central Counterparties strengthen the safety and integrity of financial markets.* White Paper. http://deutsche-boerse.com/dbg-en/about-us/public-affairs/publications/white-papers (Zugriff: 05.02.2019).

Duffie D. (2015). Resolution of Failing Central Counterparties. In: Scott, K. E., Jackson, T. H. und Taylor, J. B. (Hrsg.) *Making Failure Feasible*, Stanford: Hoover Institution Press.

Duffie, D., Scheicher, M. und Vuillemey, G. (2015). Central Clearing and Collateral Demand. *Journal of Financial Economics*, 116 (2), 237–256.

Duffie, D. und Zhu, H. (2011). Does a Central Clearing Counterparty Reduce Counterparty Risk? *Review of Asset Pricing Studies*, 1, 74–95.

Dwivedi, Y., Williams, M.D., Lal B., Schwarz, A. (2008). Profiling Adoption, Acceptance and Diffusion Research in the Information Systems Discipline. In: *Proceedings of European Conference on Information Systems (ECIS 2008)*, 1204–1215.

Easley, D. und O'Hara, M. (1987). Price, trade size, and information in securities markets. *Journal of Financial Economics*, 19 (1), 69-90.

Eisenhardt, K. M. (1989). Building Theories From Case Study Research. *Academy of Management Review*, 14, 532-550.

Elliott, D. (2013). *Central counterparty loss-allocation rules.* Bank of England Financial Stability Paper Nr. 20.

Engle, R. (2002). Dynamic conditional correlation: A simple class of multivariate generalized autoregressive conditional heteroskedasticity models. *Journal of Business and Economic Statistics*, 20 (3), 339–350.

ESMA. (2018a). *Guidelines on EMIR Anti-Procyclicality Margin Measures for Central Counterparties.* https://www.esma.europa.eu/sites/default/files/library/esma70-151-1293_final_report_on_guidelines_on_ccp_apc_margin_measures.pdf (Zugriff: 05.02.2019).

Europäisches Parlament. (2012). *Regulation (EU) No 648/2012 of the European Parliament and of the Council of 4 July 2012 on OTC derivatives, central counterparties and trade repositories.* https://eur-lex.europa.eu/homepage.html (Zugriff: 05.02.2019).

European Systemic Risk Board (ESRB). (2016). *Remarks by Vítor Constâncio, Vice-President of the ECB, at the ESRB international conference on the macroprudential use of margins and haircuts*, Frankfurt am Main, 6. Juni 2016, https://www.ecb.europa.eu/press/key/date/2016/html/sp160606.en.html (Zugriff: 05.02.2019).

European Systemic Risk Board (ESRB). (2017a). *The macroprudential use of margins and haircuts.*
https://www.esrb.europa.eu/pub/reports/html/index.en.html (Zugriff: 05.02.2019).

European Systemic Risk Board (ESRB). (2017b). *Revision of the European Market Infrastructure Regulation.*
https://www.esrb.europa.eu/pub/reports/html/index.en.html (Zugriff: 05.02.2019).

Financial Crisis Inquiry Commission. (2011). *The financial crisis inquiry report: final report of the National Commission on the Causes of the Financial and Economic Crisis in the United States,* Washington, DC: Financial Crisis Inquiry Commission. ISBN: 9780160879838.

Financial Stability Board (FSB). (2017). *Review of OTC Derivatives Market Reforms: Effectiveness and Broader Effects of the Reforms.*
http://www.fsb.org/2017/06/review-of-otc-derivatives-market-reform-effectiveness-and-broader-effects-of-the-reforms (Zugriff: 05.02.2019).

Friedrich, J. und Thiemann, M. (2018). *A new governance architecture for European financial markets? Towards a European supervision of CCPs.* SAFE White Paper Nr. 53.

G20. (2009). *G20 Leaders Statement: The Pittsburgh Summit.*
http://www.oecd.org/g20/summits/pittsburgh/G20-Pittsburgh-Leaders-Declaration.pdf (Zugriff: 05.02.2019).

Garratt, R. J. und Zimmerman, P. (2015). *Does Central Clearing Reduce Counterparty Risk in Realistic Financial Networks?* FRB of New York Staff Report 717.

Gibson, R. und Murawski, C. (2006). *Default Risk Mitigation in Derivatives Markets and its Effectiveness.* EFA Zürich Meetings Paper.

Ghamami, S. und Glasserman, P. (2017). Does OTC derivatives reform incentivize central clearing? *Journal of Financial Intermediation,* 32, 76–87.

Goodhue, D., Lewis, L.W. und Thompson, R. (2006). Small sample size and statistical power in MIS research. In: *Proceedings of the 39th Annual Hawaii International Conference on System Sciences.*

Greenspan, A. (2008). *Testimony of Dr. Alan Greenspan. Committee of Government Oversight and Reform,* 23. Oktober 2008,
http://www.studymode.com/essays/Testimony-Of-Dr-Alan-Greenspan-Committee-596739.html (Zugriff: 05.02.2019).

Grunenberg, M., Kunzelmann, M. und Weinhardt, Ch. (2004). *Benefits of Computer based Simulations for Financial Markets.* Workshop Epistemological Perspectives on Simulation, Koblenz, Germany.

Harris, L. (2003). *Trading and Exchanges: Market Microstructure for Practitioners*, New York: Oxford University Press, ISBN: 0195144708.

Heath, A., Kelly, G. und Manning, M. (2013). OTC Derivatives Reform: Netting and Networks. In: *Proceedings of the Conference Liquidity and Funding Markets*, Reserve Bank of Australia, Sydney, 33–73.

Heath, A., Kelly G. und Manning, M. (2015). *Central Counterparty Loss Allocation and Transmission of Financial Stress*. Reserve Bank of Australia Research Discussion Paper.

Hee, J., Chen, Y., und Huang W. (2003). Straight Through Processing Technology in Global Financial Market: Readiness Assessment and Implementation. *Journal of Global Information Management*, 11 (2), 56–66.

Heller, D. und Vause, N. (2012). *Collateral Requirements for Mandatory Clearing of Over-the-counter Derivatives*. BIS Working Paper Nr. 373.

Hull, J. C. (2014). *Options, Futures and Other Derivatives* (9. Aufl.), Pearson, ISBN: 9780133456318.

International Swaps and Derivatives Association (ISDA). (2012). *Interest Rate Swaps Compression: A Progress Report*. https://www.isda.org/a/BeiDE/irs-compression-progress-report-feb-2012.pdf (Zugriff: 05.02.2019).

International Swaps and Derivatives Association (ISDA). (2013). *OTC Derivatives Market Analysis Year-End 2012*. https://www.isda.org/a/FeiDE/isda-year-end-2012-market-analysis-final.pdf (Zugriff: 05.02.2019).

International Swaps and Derivatives Association (ISDA). (2014). *Size and Uses of the Non-Cleared Derivatives Market*. https://www.isda.org (Zugriff: 05.02.2019).

International Swaps and Derivatives Association (ISDA). (2016). *ISDA Research Note: Derivatives Market Analysis: Interest Rate Derivatives*. https://www.isda.org/a/4SiDE/otc-derivatives-market-analysis-dec-2016-v3.pdf (Zugriff: 05.02.2019).

Jackson, J. und Mark, J. M. (2007). *Comparing the Pre-settlement Risk Implications of Alternative Clearing Arrangements*. Bank of England Working Paper Nr. 321.

Krahnen, J. P. und Pelizzon, L. (2016). *Predatory Margins and the Regulation and Supervision of Central Counterparty Clearing Houses (CCPs)*. SAFE White Paper Nr. 41.

Kroszner, R. (1999). Can the Financial Markets Privately Regulate Risk? The Development of Derivatives Clearinghouses and Recent Over-the-Counter Innovations, *Journal of Money, Credit and Banking*, 31, 596–618.

Kroszner, R. (2006). Central Counterparty Clearing: History, Innovation, and Regulation. *Economic Perspectives*, 30 (4), 37-41.

Kubitza, Ch., Pelizzon, L. und Getmansky, M. (2018). *The pitfalls of central clearing in the presence of systematic risk.* ICIR Working Paper Nr. 31.

LeBaron, B. (2006). Agent-based Computational Finance, In: *Handbook of Computational Economics*, Judd, K. L. und Tesfatsion, L. (Hrsg.), 1187−1233, Elsevier.

Li, D. und Schürhoff, N. (2014). *Dealer Networks.* Swiss Finance Institute Research Paper Nr. 50, https://www.federalreserve.gov/econresdata/feds/2014/files/201495pap.pdf (Zugriff: 05.02.2019).

Madhaven, A. (2000). Market microstructure: A survey. *Journal of Financial Markets*, 3, 205−258.

Madhavan, A., Richardson, M. und Roomans, M. (1997). Why Do Security Prices Change? A Transaction-Level Analysis of NYSE Stocks. *The Review of Financial Studies*, 10 (4), 1035–1064.

Mahnke, V., Overby, M. L. und Özcan S. (2006). Outsourcing Innovative Capabilities for IT- Enabled Services. *Industry and Innovation*, 13, 189–207.

Moser, J. T. (1998). *Contracting Innovations and the Evolution of Clearing and Settlement Methods at Futures Exchanges.* Federal Reserve Bank of Chicago, Working Paper Nr. 26.

Murphy, D., Vasios, M. und Vause, N. (2014). *An investigation into the procyclicality of risk-based initial margin models.* Bank of England, Financial Stability Paper Nr. 29.

New York Fed. (2005). *Foreign Exchange Prime Brokerage, Product Overview and Best Practice Recommendations.* Foreign Exchange Committee Annual Report. https://www.newyorkfed.org (Zugriff: 05.02.2019).

Orlikowski, W.J. und Baroudi, J.J. (1991). Studying Information Technology in Organizations: Research Approaches and Assumptions. *Information Systems Research*, 2, 1–28.

Pirrong, C. (2009). *The Economics of Clearing in Derivatives Markets: Netting, Asymmetric Information, and the Sharing of Default Risks Through a Central Counterparty.* University of Houston Working Paper.

Pirrong, C. (2011). *The Economics of Central Clearing: Theory and Practice.* ISDA Research Paper, https://www.isda.org (Zugriff: 05.02.2019).

Pirrong, C. (2012). Clearing and Collateral Mandates: A New Liquidity Trap? *Journal of Applied Corporate Finance*, 24, 67–73.

Raykov, R. (2018). Reducing margin procyclicality at central counterparties. *Journal of Financial Market Infrastructures*, 7 (2), 43–59.

Rehlo, A. und Nixon, D. (2013). Central Counterparties: What are They, Why Do They Matter, and How Does the Bank Supervise Them? *Bank of England Quarterly Bulletin*, 53 (2), 147-156.

Remenyi, D., Williams, B., Money, A. and Swartz, E. (1998). *Doing Research in Business and Management: An Introduction to Process and Method*, London: Sage, ISBN: 9780761959502.

Ripatti, K. (2004). *Central Counterparty Clearing: Constructing a Framework for Evaluation of Risks and Benefits*. Bank of Finland Discussion Paper.

Rogers, E. M. (1995). *Diffusion of Innovations* (4te Aufl.), New York: Free Press, ISBN: 9780029266717.

Sauerbier, T. (1999). *Theorie und Praxis von Simulationssystemen: Eine Einführung Für Ingenieure Und Informatiker (Studium Technik)*, Braunschweig/Wiesbaden: Vieweg Verlagsgesellschaft, ISBN: 9783528038663.

Schloderer, M. P., Ringle Ch. M. und Sarstedt, M. (2009). Einführung in die varianzbasierte Strukturgleichungsmodellierung: Grundlagen, Modellevaluation und Interaktionseffekte am Beispiel von SmartPLS. In: *Theorien und Methoden der Betriebswirtschaft: Handbuch für Wissenschaftler und Studierende*. München: Vahlen, ISBN: 9783800636136.

Sidanius Ch. und Zikes, F. (2012). *OTC derivatives reform and collateral demand impact*. Bank of England Financial Stability Paper Nr. 18.

Singh, M. (2010). *Collateral, netting and systemic risk in the OTC derivatives market*. IMF Working Paper Nr. 99.

Stoll, H. R. (2003). Market Microstructure. In: *Handbook of Economics of Finance*, Constantinides, G. M., Harris, M. und Stulz R. (Hrsg.) 553–604, Amsterdam: Elsevier Science.

Stulz, R. M. (2009). *Credit Default Swaps and the credit crisis*. NBER Working Paper Nr. 15384.

Tornatzky, L. G. und Klein, K. J. (1982). Innovation Characteristics and Innovation Adoption-Implementation: A Meta-Analysis of Findings. *IEEE Transactions on Engineering Management*, 29, 28–45.

US Senate (2010). *Dodd-Frank Wall Street Reform and Consumer Protection Act*, http://www.gpo.gov/fdsys/pkg/PLAW-111publ203/pdf/PLAW-111publ203.pdf (Zugriff: 05.02.2019).

Vicente, L. A., Cerezetti, F.V. De Faria, S. R., Iwashita, T. und Pereira, O. R. (2015). Managing risk in multi-asset class, multimarket central counterparties: The CORE approach. *Journal of Banking & Finance*, 51, 119–130.

Vuillemey, G. und Breton, R. (2014). *Endogenous Derivative Networks*. Banque de France Working Paper Nr. 483.

Yin, R. K. (2003a). *Case Study Research, Design and Methods* (3. Aufl.). Newbury Park: Sage, ISBN: 9780761925538.

Yin, R. K. (2003b). *Application of Case Study Research*. Thousand Oaks (CA): Sage, ISBN: 9780761925514.

Zeigler, B. (1976). *Theory of modelling and simulation*. New York: John Wiley and Sons, ISBN: 9780471981527.

Further Publications

Lewandowska, O. and Mai, E. (2018). The distribution of clearing members' risk exposure and how it matters. *Journal of Financial Market Infrastructures*, 7 (2), 29–42.

Lewandowska, O. (2010). Adoption of a Centralized Post-Trade Processing Market Infrastructure After the Credit Crisis. In: M. L. Nelson, M. J. Shaw and T. J. Strader (eds.), *Sustainable e-Business Management. AMCIS 2010. Lecture Notes in Business Information Processing*, Berlin, Heidelberg: Springer.

Lewandowska, O. and Mack, B. (2010). Squaring the Circle: Clearing Arrangements in Over-The-Counter Derivatives Markets. Paper presented at the *Industrial Organization of Securities Markets* Conference, Germany, Frankfurt.

Curriculum Vitae

Personal Data

Date of birth   November 25, 1982

Place of birth   Warsaw, Poland

Nationality   Polish

Academic Education

2010 – 2019   Doctoral studies at the Goethe University in Frankfurt, Chair of eFinance

2001 – 2006   The Warsaw School of Economics. Master degree in Banking and Finance - Investment Banking. Master's thesis "Mezzanine Finance in Germany"

2004 – 2005   Economics study at Johannes Gutenberg University Mainz, Scholarship of Erasmus Program

ibidem.eu